READING
LOST

READING CONTEMPORARY TELEVISION

Series Editors: Kim Akass and Janet McCabe

janetandkim@hotmail.com

The **Reading Contemporary Television** series offers a varied, intellectually groundbreaking and often polemical response to what is happening in television today. This series is distinct in that it sets out to immediately comment upon the TV *zeitgeist* while providing an intellectual and creative platform for thinking differently and ingeniously writing about contemporary television culture. The books in the series seek to establish a critical space where new voices are heard and fresh perspectives offered. Innovation is encouraged and intellectual curiosity demanded.

Published and forthcoming:

READING

PERSPECTIVES ON A
HIT TELEVISION SHOW

edited by
ROBERTA PEARSON

LONDON · NEW YORK

Published in 2009 by I.B.Tauris & Co Ltd
6 Salem Road, London W2 4BU
175 Fifth Avenue, New York NY 10010
www.ibtauris.com

In the United States of America and Canada distributed by
Palgrave Macmillan, a division of St Martin's Press,
175 Fifth Avenue, New York NY 10010

ISBN: 978 1 84511 836 5

A full CIP record for this book is available from the British Library
A full CIP record is available from the Library of Congress

Library of Congress Catalog Card Number: available

Typeset in Chaparral Pro by Sara Millington, Editorial and
    Design Services
Printed and bound in India by Rakesh Press

Contents

I. Introduction: Why Lost?

Roberta Pearson

A book published in a series called 'Reading Contemporary Television' should require no justification for its focus on a single programme. But *Lost* deserves its own volume perhaps more than any other series currently in production, epitomizing as it does what television scholars now dub 'TV3', which emerged roughly from the late 1990s and is characterized by fragmented, not to say splintered, audiences, distribution through digital technologies and industry panic over audience measurement and advertising strategies.

As I have argued previously, *Lost* seems perfectly designed to meet the requirements of the new multichannel, multi-platform, international mediascape into which it emerged in 2004.[1] It came branded with the name of wunderkind J.J. Abrams, whose previous form persuaded the ABC network to break with industry conventions in its rapid approval of the concept and its vast expenditure on the pilot. Its cinematic visuals and complex narrative warranted the increasingly prized quality label that distinguishes a show from the competition and attracts an upmarket audience. Its international cast, together with its ostensibly international locations, suited it to the international distribution that has become increasingly central to network profits.

Although not technically a runaway production, its location of Hawaii sets it apart from programmes made in Hollywood or New York. Its cult aspects appealed to a technologically savvy audience ready to watch via video streaming, to download it to their iPods, to screen 'mobisodes' on their cell phones or to revel in the complexities of 'The *Lost* Experience', as the producers fully embraced the transmedia storytelling ever more vital to revenue streams.

While broadly representative of TV3, *Lost* is also unique in two respects. First, its initial breakout success proved the continued viability of the drama format, which was under threat from the cost-cutting efficiencies and new financing model of the reality format. *Lost*, together with its ABC stablemate *Desperate Housewives* (Cherry Alley Productions, 2004) showed the continued importance of high-profile dramas to network branding strategies. The other networks took note, producing a succession of *Lost* clones, although only one of these, NBC's *Heroes* (NBC Universal Television, 2006), achieved similar breakaway hit status. Second, ABC has permitted *Lost*'s producers to contravene the most standard practice of an industry that usually keeps the golden goose laying until it produces rotten eggs (see for example *The X-Files*, 20th Century Fox Television, 1993–2002). Not only will *Lost* end after its sixth season in 2010, only 16 (as opposed to the customary 20 or more) episodes will be produced per season. The producers claim that this definitive end point will enable them to carefully plan the rest of the story and provide answers to the myriad questions raised so far. If they achieve this feat, *Lost* will become unique in a third respect, since to date programmes predicated upon central narrative enigmas, most famously *The X-Files* and *Twin Peaks* (Lynch/Frost Productions, 1990–1), have spectacularly failed to provide their audiences with satisfactory resolution.

The contributors to this volume address many of the above points as well as numerous others. Together, the individual chapters document the many determinants of the production, meaning and reception of a television programme, offering a rich understanding of the multimedia phenomenon that is *Lost*. Since *Lost* is emblematic of TV3's conditions of production and reception, this full analysis of one programme tells us much about the contemporary US television industry. The chapters are organized into sections on production and audiences, text and representation.

PRODUCTION AND AUDIENCES

The chapters in this section illuminate the ways in which the pressures of a rapidly transforming industry have shaped *Lost*'s production and distribution. Should producers settle for the steady profits generated by a cult show targeted at a loyal niche audience, or should they aim for the top of the Nielsen Ratings? Stacey Abbott shows how *Lost*, designed by producers with a track record in cult programmes to appeal to cult fans, achieved mainstream success and quality status. This was accomplished in part by mimicking the strategies of the film blockbuster to create 'event television' to appeal to a large and diverse audience. Uniquely, *Lost* has attained both cult and blockbuster status.

How should producers diversify revenue streams at a time when digital technologies (DVDs, DVRs, downloading) enable viewers to avoid advertisements? Derek Johnson argues that *Lost*'s producers rejected the obvious solution, product placement, in favour of a more ingenious one. 'The *Lost* Experience', the alternate reality game (ARG) staged between the show's first and second seasons, spun out *Lost*'s fictional institutions into the real world via a multimedia mix, which blurred reality and fiction and intersected with real-life sponsors such as Jeep and Sprite. How do the new digital technologies affect distribution and viewing? Will Brooker examines the interpretive practices of fans who chose to download *Lost* in addition to, or sometimes rather than, watching the originally broadcast episodes. He argues that downloading and watching on a computer permits juxtaposing windows of extra-textual material with the programme in order to conduct the 'forensic fandom' that *Lost* encourages.

How has globalization shaped production and distribution? Julian Stringer documents how *Lost*'s real location, the Hawaiian island of Oahu, lured *Lost*'s producers to a Pacific paradise, using its landscape and other resources to compete with rival US cities and states to become a global media centre. Once there, the producers took full advantage of the setting, as the narrative progressed across the island's lush and diverse locations, providing the audience with spectacular beauty and visual pleasure in the tradition of such predecessors as *Hawaii Five-O* (CBS Television, 1968–80) and *Magnum, PI* (Belisarius Productions, 1980–8). Paul Grainge addresses the issue of international distribution, showing how the UK Channel 4 shaped *Lost* to its previously established brand through promos and idents aimed at its upmarket audience. The chapter shows that US television programmes have become an essential weapon in the competition among UK broadcasters and media industries for the fragmented audience.

TEXT

The text, as well as the production process, distinguishes *Lost* from the competition, past and present. The producers have taken the recent trend to narrative complexity to new extremes by creating a tightly serialized programme centred upon narrative enigmas. Jason Mittell argues that this feat should be acknowledged, that *Lost* should be considered a 'great' text. Knowing that such a statement verges on the heretical in the culturally relativist and Bourdieu-esque field of television studies, he makes a persuasive case that television scholars should forgo their usual reticence to evaluate texts. Roberta Pearson takes up this challenge, using a formalist approach to demonstrate that *Lost*'s producers have come up with an entirely new construction of the televisual character, one in which every element of character is tied to the central narrative enigmas. Whether the producers do or do not eventually provide solutions to all the island's many mysteries, their narrative innovation should be seen as a significant marker in the history of the television drama.

Ivan Askwith also addresses issues of evaluation, this time from the viewer's perspective, asking why so many fans, believing that the producers do not have a pre-determined narrative arc, have lost faith in the show and abandoned it in droves. What factors cause these fans to place such a high value upon successful narrative resolution? Angela Ndalianis addresses issues of genre rather than narrative. She argues that while the programme itself keeps viewers guessing as to its generic category, incorporating melodrama, romance, horror, science fiction and reality television, its transmedia extensions, particularly 'The *Lost* Experience', foreground science fiction.

REPRESENTATION

The chapters in the final section all deal with the representation, or not, of identity. Michael Newbury's and Jonathan Gray's chapters stage an implicit debate about *Lost* as globalized text, particularly with regard to its orientalist imaginings. Newbury asserts that *Lost*'s flashbacks reify national, racial, and class-based distinctions, undermining the construction of a seemingly transnational subject suited to the age of globalization. *Lost*, he says, is a narrative of American assimilation rather than of multinationalism or transnational affiliation. Gray acknowledges the text's orientalist tendencies, but argues that the narrative reverses its initial orientalist depiction of non-white characters. This reversal causes viewers to question their previous stereotypical understandings of the characters' identity and, in the process, their own subject formations, making *Lost* well suited to globalized television. Celeste-Marie Bernier uses Toni Morrison's concept of the white fabrication of an Africanist persona to interrogate *Lost*'s representation of an African character, as well as its invocation of African and African–American history. Davies and Needham ask why *Lost*, broadcast by the most 'gay-friendly' of the American networks, significantly lacks an out queer character. This striking absence leads them to look for queerness elsewhere in the text, seeking liminal traces of non-heterosexual normativity in the current characters and identifying the particularly queer pleasures that may result from the show's textual strategies.

Taken together, the book's chapters answer many questions about *Lost*. However, this book was completed just as the third season began broadcasting in the USA and, a week later (another striking innovation in globalized television), in the UK. Many questions remain. How will the screen writers' strike, current at the time of writing, affect the already curtailed fourth season? Will the producers ever explain the polar bear, the four-toed statue, Desmond's temporal shifts and all the show's other mysteries? And what about those flashforwards? Given *Lost*'s significance in US and global television history, this book should be one of the initial entries in the field of *Lost* studies rather than the final word on the subject.

Notes

1   Roberta Pearson, '*Lost* in transition: from post-network to post-television', in Kim Akass and Janet McCabe (eds) *Quality: Contemporary American Television and Beyond* (London: I.B.Tauris, 2007), pp.239–56.

Part I
Production and Audiences

II. How Lost Found Its Audience:
The Making of a Cult Blockbuster

Stacey Abbott

Rashomon meets *Gilligan's Island...*
Gilligan's Island meets *The X-Files*[1]

Despite numerous structural and programming strategies to find and maintain a larger audience, J.J. Abrams' spy series *Alias* (Bad Robot, 2001–6) remained a cult show from beginning to end, capturing the attention of a small but loyal audience.[2] With its often fantastic narrative of riddles, polar bears, hidden hatches, cursed numbers, murderous black smoke, visions of the future and the mysterious Others, Abrams' subsequent show *Lost* (co-created with Damon Lindelof) had the makings of yet another cult series, existing, like *Alias* before it, as a hybrid of melodrama and science fiction/fantasy. While these genres have become in recent years the mainstay of the Hollywood blockbuster, with film franchises such as *The Lord of the Rings* (Peter Jackson, 2001/2002/2003) and *The Matrix* trilogies (Andy and Larry Wachowski, 1999/2003/2003) drawing in large audiences and multimillion dollar revenues, such genres on television, as exemplified by *Buffy the Vampire Slayer* (Mutant Enemy, 1997–2003) and *Battlestar Galactica* (various, 2004–8), generally cater to a more marginal, niche audience and as such are often perceived as 'cult'.

Roberta Pearson and Sara Gwenllian-Jones have argued that one of the defining features of cult TV is:

[a narrative structured around] interconnected storylines, both realized and implied, [that] extend far beyond any single episode to

become a metatext that structures production, diegesis, and reception. Cult television's imaginary universes support an inexhaustible
range of narrative possibilities, inviting, supporting, and rewarding close textual analysis, interpretation, and inventive reformula-
tion.[3]

This definition applies to *Lost* in terms of its narrative, fragmented by
flashbacks (and in later episodes 'flash-forwards') that lead the audience through a labyrinth of potential storylines, character connections, enigmas and puzzles. Like a true labyrinth, the path to narrative resolution is marked by twists, turns, dead ends and misleading
clues and the audience is invited to negotiate its way through the
maze along with the series' protagonists. The series' extreme serial
rather than episodic narrative requires a level of commitment from
the audience that is usually discouraged by mainstream television
executives as it is seen to be alienating for the casual viewer. For instance, cult series *Angel* (Mutant Enemy, 1999–2004) and *Alias,* both
noted for their extensive narrative arcs, were, in their final seasons,
put under pressure by the networks to become more episodic in order to draw in larger audiences. *Lost* was therefore ripe for the type
of attentive viewing and reviewing practices that are typical of the
cult TV audience, as well as providing ample narrative scope for the
fans to extend their own interpretation of the narrative beyond the
televisual text through online discussion, fan fiction and fan video
production.

Despite this seemingly clear cult pedigree, the show has been a
phenomenal success with audiences, critics and the industry, averaging 16.2 million viewers in its first season on US television as well as
winning six Emmy awards and one Golden Globe for Best Dramatic
Series. It has also been hugely successful internationally, having been
sold to 183 territories in its first year alone. This chapter will therefore
explore how *Lost* can, despite this high profile success, still be seen
as a cult TV series. In so doing, I will address the tension that exists
between the show's position as a mainstream success and its status
as cult, a position that according to definition implies exclusivity and
marginality, particularly in terms of the fans' perception of the series.
In this I hope to explore how *Lost* has served to redefine our understanding of 'cult'.

CULT AND BLOCKBUSTER TV

In this chapter's title I describe *Lost* as a 'Cult Blockbuster', a potentially contradictory and contentious term. The word blockbuster, however, brings with it a set of meanings that are quite instructive in relation to the show. Usually reserved for cinema rather than television, a block-buster is generally a film which, according to Sheldon Hall, 'is extraordinarily successful in financial terms'. Hall points out, however, that the term can be 'extended to refer to those films which *need* to be this successful in order to have a chance of returning a profit on their equally extraordinary production costs'.[4] Julian Stringer further argues that the blockbuster can be identified through a range of textual characteristics that include size, spectacle and excess, but also the film's sense of exceptionality. The blockbuster, according to Stringer, promises to be something you have never seen before.[5] Finally, Richard Maltby points out that the modern blockbuster has evolved into an 'event movie', that is 'a product designed to maximize audience attendance by drawing in not only the regular 14–25-year-old audience, but also that section of the audience who attend the cinema two or three times a year.'[6]

All of this stands in opposition to accepted understandings of cult in both film and television. Mark Jancovich, Antonio Lázaro Reboll, Julian Stringer and Andy Willis argue in their book *Defining Cult Movies* that cult 'is not defined according to some single, unifying feature shared by all cult movies, but rather through a "subcultural ideology" in filmmakers, films or audiences [which is] seen as existing in opposition to the "mainstream"'.[7] Matt Hills points out that the notion of a cult blockbuster in film is often rejected by fans who associate cult with the minority, reinforcing this notion that cult, particularly in the eyes of the fans, often stands in opposition to the mainstream.[8] Similarly in television, Mark Jancovich and Nathan Hunt have argued that cult fandom 'claims that the industry's commercial considerations lead to a lack of originality in the development of shows and a tendency to ruin established shows in the pursuit of the mainstream audience'.[9] All of this suggests that the active pursuit of a large mainstream audience positions a series in opposition to cult and the cult audience.

When applying these terms and their various meanings to *Lost* in conjunction with one another, however, a different picture begins to emerge. In this light, *Lost* can be read as a form of 'event television':

aiming for a large and diverse audience while simultaneously fostering the interactive engagement with the series that is often associated
with cult, and in so doing courting the niche demographics of loyal and
interactive cult TV fans as well as inviting viewers who might not nor-
mally engage in fan practices to commit to the show on a cult level.

So how might we see *Lost* as simultaneously a blockbuster and cult?
The show was originally conceived as high concept, a notion that is
intrinsically linked to the modern blockbuster. In the hopes of drawing the success of reality TV into television drama, then Head of ABC
Entertainment, Lloyd Braun, proposed creating a fictional programme
inspired by the hit reality series *Survivor* (Mark Burnett Productions,
2000–). However, once Abrams and Lindelhof became involved they
recognised that a simple survivor narrative was too limiting for a weekly drama and introduced an element of genre into the mix. As Lindelhof
explains, 'to execute this show, it's going to have to be weird. There's
going to be something moving the trees at the end of the first act. There
are going to be questions about how the plane crashed. And there are
going to be fantastic things that happen to the people.'[10]

The result of this conception for the series is that the show is often
discussed in high concept terms by both the critics and the creators
– the most common descriptor being '*Gilligan's Island* [CBS Television,
1964–7] meets *The X-Files* [Twentieth Century Fox Television, 1993–
2002]' or, as one critic put it, 'an adult *Lord of the Flies* (or an unfunny
Gilligan's Island) mixed with Stephen King's *The Tommyknockers*'.[11]
Nancy Franklin in the *New Yorker*, however, points out that there are
countless other comparison texts:

> The show recalls so many other shows and movies that people can't
> describe it without resorting to formula: *Gilligan's Island* meets *Sur-*
> *vivor* – or *The Island of Dr Moreau* or *Lord of the Flies* or *Cast Away*. You
> can throw *Jurassic Park* in there too, along with a little *X-Files* and
> *Apocalypse Now*.[12]

The choice of combinations here are quite instructive, for by leaning
toward a mixture of quite mainstream material (i.e. *Gilligan's Island,
Survivor, Castaway*) and more fantastical products like *The X-Files* or
The Island of Dr Moreau, the show seems to suggest a high concept
appropriation of cult material.

Recognising that the international cast gave the series an incred-
ibly broad appeal that is unusual within mainstream television, Buena

Vista International TV increased its marketing spend and sent the
cast around the world for press interviews and featured the series at
the Monte Carlo TV festival as a means of promoting the new and innovative show.[13] Furthermore, as Paul Grainge demonstrates in this
volume, the marketing campaign in the UK presented the launch of
Lost as Event Television. Spending £1 million on marketing, Channel
4 produced a series of 'arty' trailers created by photographer David La
Chapelle and creative director Brett Foraker – and described by Lisa
Campbell of *Broadcast* as 'more like an arty and expensive Calvin Klein
ad with the requisite beautiful people carousing on a beach'.[14] In addition to being shown on TV, these trailers were also screened in the
cinema, a space in which American television is rarely promoted, to
emphasise the distinctiveness of the show and the 'event' of its broadcast. The trailers and billboards were enigmatic and eye-catching but
they betrayed little of the series' narrative complexity, game-like structure or supernatural elements. What they do emphasise is the mystery
surrounding the *survivors* of the plane crash. Similarly, an article published in the UK's leading TV listing magazine, the *Radio Times,* the
week the series was due to air specifically emphasised the mystery of
the show and its cast of characters by describing it as 'the most mysterious series on US TV since *The X-Files*. Fans have numerous theories
about *Lost*'s motley crew of plane-crash survivors on a desert island:
just don't ask the cast – they're as much in the dark as the audience.'[15]
While the cultness of the show is suggested by the reference to *The
X-Files*, the report places the focus upon the mysterious characters and
the cast of actors who are an intrinsic element of this unusual show.

ABC, and later Channel 4 in the UK, also sought to court the cult
TV audience, although momentum was already building due to J.J.
Abrams' involvement – *Alias* was in its third season and had a well-
established fan following. The anticipation of his new series within
SF/fantasy fandom was enhanced, however, when the casting of Dominic Monaghan of *Lord of the Rings* fame was announced. According to
Lynnette Porter and David Lavery, further strategic announcements
about the casting of Matthew Fox and Terry O'Quinn and the hiring
of notable cult TV writers such as David Fury (*Buffy the Vampire Slayer*,
Angel), alongside narrative spoilers about the first episode, intensified
the fan interest in the show.[16]

The advance promotion of the series to cult TV fans culminated
in the screening of the pilot at Comic-Con, a leading American fan

convention, in June 2004 – three months before it was due to air. The successful airing of *Lost* – or any new TV show – at fan conventions serves two purposes. It builds a loyal fan following for the series by acknowledging the importance of fans to any new show and privileging their commitment to science fiction and cult television by allowing them advance access to the programme. It also serves to build word of mouth. As David Glanzer, director of marketing and public relations for Comic-Con, points out: 'These people are on their laptops right there in the room – their reactions are conveyed over a million blogs.'[17] In the case of *Lost*, the fans loved the pilot, which fuelled the growth of the *Lost* fan community before the show had even aired.

In the UK, similar alternative marketing methods were employed to target cult audiences who would respond to the show's generic tropes and game-like strategies. Posters were placed in the online game *Anarchy* so that as 'players move through their virtual world, they will see clips of the series', while a dedicated *Lost* website was developed to provide clues and puzzles for unlocking the mysteries of the series.[18] This approach had worked well in the USA with the online game *I-am-lost.com*, in which players were able to scavenge through the wreckage of the plane looking for clues as to the characters' back stories.[19] In this manner the network and the series creators recognised the marketing potential of aiming this show at a broad audience captivated by the enigma of the narrative and its characters while cult audiences were given insight into the show's more supernatural and game-like qualities in order to gain their attention and foster their interest.

The production style and budget for the series definitely highlights the show's blockbuster credentials. Shot in Hawaii only 12 weeks after the outline for the show was given the green light, the two-hour pilot directed by Abrams features a cast of 14 major characters as well as numerous background characters, major chase sequences and elaborate special effects including the staging of the actual plane crash. At a cost of $10 million, it is one of the most expensive pilots ever filmed. In this opening to the series the blockbuster's emphasis upon high production values, spectacle and excess is clearly evident. While the pilot begins in near silence and solitude as the show's main hero Jack (Matthew Fox) wakes up alone and disoriented in the jungle, once he runs out onto the beach the sounds of screams disrupt this tranquil image. As he follows the noise, the audience, along with Jack, is bombarded by an array of images of death, debris and destruction, shot in a long take and accompanied by Shannon's (Maggie Grace's) non-stop screaming that captures the disorientation and horror of the plane crash. The spectacle of the sequence is enhanced by the cinematography, made up of a combination of hand-held camera work, as Jack surveys the damage, and elaborate tracking and crane shots that capture the scale and chaos of the crash site. The scene is punctuated by two key stunt and special-effect sequences; the first is when a passer-by is sucked into the plane's engine and the second is Jack's narrow rescue of Claire (Emilie de Ravine) and Hurley (Jorge Garcia) as the wing snaps off and falls to the ground in a major explosion. By seven minutes into the pilot, when the credits start and the music begins to play, this opening had established that *Lost* would be truly unlike anything else on television. As Lindelof explains, 'ABC wanted something different and it wanted to make noise. It also responded to the potential for this to have mass appeal – it isn't sci-fi, or romance, or action, or procedural, but all of those rolled into one.'[20]

Despite the perceived mass appeal of the series, the pilot also established the show's cult potential. As promised by Lindelof, following the aftermath of the crash, and having introduced all of the key characters and settled them down to await rescue, the first act of the episode ends with some*thing* crashing through the woods and knocking down trees as the survivors look on in horror. This raises the first of two primary questions for the show's narrative: *what* is on the island with them? This sentiment is reiterated later when the bloody body of the pilot (ripped from the cockpit of the plane by the unseen something) is found balanced on the top branches of a tree and Charlie (Dominic Monaghan) asks the question that ends the episode: 'how does something like that happen?', meaning *what* did this to him? Charlie once again voices the second primary question of the series at the end of the second episode ('Pilot Part II', 1.2) when, having escaped attack from a polar bear and then found that a French SOS message has gone unanswered on the island for 16 years, he asks his fellow survivors: 'Guys, where are we?' These two questions, what (or who) is on the island with them and what is the island's secret, fuel the cult mythology of *Lost*.

Another significant cult element featured in the show is the character Locke played by Terry O'Quinn. While Locke barely figures in 'The Pilot Part I' (1.1), he is given one strange and unnerving moment that enhances the mysterious quality to the show when he watches Kate (Evangeline Lilly) as she scavenges shoes from the dead and meets her gaze and smiles, revealing an orange peel covering his teeth. This shot, much discussed on fansites as either a reference to *The Godfather* (Francis Ford Coppola, 1972) or Locke just being scary and weird, establishes the enigma that surrounds the character. The casting of O'Quinn, alongside actors like Monaghan and Harold Perrineau (from Andy and Larry Wachowski, *The Matrix: Reloaded*, 2003), known for blockbuster fare, further represents the cult/blockbuster dynamic of the series. O'Quinn is a cult film and TV actor known for his regular appearances on *Alias*, the short-lived cult series *Harsh Realm* (20th Century Fox Television, 1999–2000) by *The X-Files*' creator Chris Carter, and most significantly of all for his chilling performance as a serial-killing patriarch in *Stepfather I* (Joseph Ruben, 1987) and *II* (Jeff Burr, 1989). These intertextual references position Locke right from the start as a morally ambiguous and enigmatic character and as such he comes to represent the cult mythology of the series.

The association between Locke and the series' core mythology is further established in 'Walkabout' (1.4) when, having unexpectedly revealed a suitcase full of hunting knives as well as tracking and hunting skills, Locke takes charge of the group's survivalist needs and in so doing comes face-to-face with the island monster, a fact he suspiciously withholds from the other survivors. The climactic flashback of the episode, however, reveals the rationale for his secrecy when we learn that before the crash, Locke was confined to a wheelchair, and it was upon waking up on the beach surrounded by the death and carnage witnessed in the pilot episode that he is able to use his legs for the first time in four years. His destiny, the episode suggests, is indelibly linked with the mysteries of the island, a fact that is reiterated throughout the show. Locke's quest to understand his destiny parallels the audience's investigation into the enigma of the show.

MAINTAINING THE BALANCE

Having seemingly hooked the mainstream and cult audience, the series' producers had to maintain both. To do that, the producers and the network felt that they needed to carefully mask the show's overt science-fiction/fantasy credentials while at the same time integrating those elements into the character-driven plot from the start. While acknowledging the show's relationship to genre television, *Lost* creators Abrams and Lindelof clearly demonstrate that for the network it was necessary to downplay the show's SF heritage. Lindelof openly admits to de-emphasising the series' generic underpinnings when pitching the show to the network because 'network television shies away from that label for a variety of reasons ... They believe its not mainstream, that there's no successful science-fiction show with mass appeal other than *The X-Files*.' He further points out that while the show's DNA is 'firmly rooted in the genre itself ... *Lost* lives in a fairly ambiguous space in terms of declaring such lineage.'[21] This position is supported by fellow showrunner Carlton Cuse who adds, 'we call the show a character-driven drama, but we don't think that and science fiction are mutually exclusive'.[22] The creators, however, clearly see an allegiance between the show's mainstream appeal and its character-driven narrative, while the generic underpinnings are subsumed within the text so as to satisfy the cult TV audiences prepared to unlock those mysteries. Cuse makes this clear when he states:

> We try to keep the emphasis on the character side of the storytelling ... All the questions that we get asked about the show tend to be on the mythological axis. That's the frosting on the cake, and it creates a lot of intrigue. But if we were just focused on the mythology, we would have a small, genre cult audience of 5 million or 6 million viewers. The reason we have 16 million to 18 million viewers is because the emphasis for us is always on the character, and what is the character drama of any given episode.[23]

Many would argue, however, that the focus upon character is not solely the purview of mainstream television, for character is often a key element of a cult series. For instance, Henrik Örnebring has demonstrated that Abrams' decidedly cult series *Alias*, often discussed in terms of its fantastical mythology and complex narrative arcs, is *as* focused upon character as mainstream television. As he points out, 'the seasonal narratives and seriality of the show serve the purpose of what I call *character showcasing*, i.e. providing discursive opportunities not to develop and change the character but to let the character do "what he/ she does best"'.[24] This emphasis upon character in *Alias* is supported by Hillary Robson's discussion of the breakdown of the show's fandom, blamed by many fans upon the increasingly implausible mythology of the series and the *lack* of adequate character development.[25]

Further to this argument, a popular subgroup of cult fandom are 'shippers', what Porter and Lavery characterise as 'fans who believe certain characters belong together romantically', and the expression of this fandom can take the form of discussion groups or fanfiction in which fans write the fiction that brings their chosen characters together.[26] This expression of fandom is completely character driven, and notable pairings in cult TV history have included Kirk/Spock, Mulder/Scully and Buffy/Spike. While *Lost*'s character-driven narrative structure may be credited with the show's mainstream success, it also plays directly into such cult fan preferences. By placing a large group of people onto a deserted island for an indefinite period of time, it is natural for audiences to begin to consider what relationships might emerge. The emphasis upon romantic and/or sexual pairings is a key element of most mainstream television, as for example with the long-running Ross/Rachel relationship on the hit sitcom *Friends* (Warner Bros. Television, 1994–2004). *Lost* equally provides a diverse range of likely and unlikely pairings such as Charlie/Claire, Hurley/ Libby (Cynthia Watros), and Sayid (Naveen Andrews)/Shannon. The major love triangle of Jack, Sawyer (Josh Holloway) and Kate, however, plays into the mainstream focus upon sex and romance, while also providing the shippers with potential pairings to discuss, write and/or create fan videos about. The show invites the audience to declare an allegiance for Kate/Jack, Kate/Sawyer – or even Jack/Sawyer, a possibility that has circulated among the fan community in fanfiction and a number of 'Brokeback Island' fanvideos, alongside numerous other romantic and sexual pairings, and was finally articulated in the season three finale 'Through the Looking Glass' (3.21). When Juliet (Elizabeth Mitchell), one of the 'Others' who has developed a relationship with Jack, is asked by Sawyer if she's 'screwing Jack yet', she replies 'No – are you?'[27] In this manner the strategic focus upon character, seen to be the reason for the series' success, also knowingly contributes to the series' appeal to cult audiences.

While the various statements from showrunners Lindelof and Cuse imply that they carefully structure the show in order to balance its cult and mainstream appeal, writer/producer David Fury, who wrote such noteworthy episodes as 'Walkabout' (1.4) and 'Numbers'

(1.18) both of which are entirely grounded in the series' supernatural and mythological underpinning, argued that the network put pressure on the team to downplay the series' generic associations:

> 'The network and the studio hate the supernatural elements of the show' Fury says. 'They won't admit to that but that's the thing that scared them the most and what they thought would alienate the audience most. They don't understand that that is what is intriguing to people.' According to Fury, the network mandated rational explanations for every potential fantasy element of the show as a fallback position. 'As the show became a success the network was even more protective of the notion that we don't want to alienate anyone.'[28]

Lindelof and Cuse, however, maintain that the rational explanation approach to fantasy and science fiction is, while supported by the network, their own. This assertion is reinforced by their comparison of *Lost* to the science fiction work of Michael Crichton, a writer they view as more grounded in science fact than fiction.[29] They also seem to accept that as 'a network show' *Lost* must 'be accessible to the broadest possible audience' and as such 'in some cases that means they want to push the genre element, in other cases they want to scale it back'.[30] In order to maintain the show's blockbuster/event appeal, the showrunners have to carefully manage the generic elements and the series' mythology so as not to overshadow the character development seen as the show's main draw among some audience segments. Satisfying and maintaining both audiences is the biggest challenge that *Lost* has faced – and it is one that has been faced by others before it, to varying degrees of success.

LEARNING FROM TWIN PEAKS AND THE X-FILES: THE CULT OF LOST

When *Twin Peaks* (Lynch/Frost Productions, 1990–1) came on the air in the spring of 1990, it made a spectacular splash into popular consciousness; the two-hour pilot 'was the highest rated TV movie of the season'.[31] Modelled upon the serialised narrative structure of a soap opera, it was the murder of high school homecoming queen Laura Palmer that gave the show its primary focus and it was the web of

eccentric characters, unexplainable events and quirky small-town be-
haviour surrounding the murder that captured public consciousness.
The large ensemble cast of the series was regularly featured on the cov-
ers of magazines as diverse as *TV Guide*, *Rolling Stone* and *Playboy*, as
well as being interviewed on daytime talk shows like *The Phil Donahue
Show* (WNBC New York, 1970–96) and *The Oprah Winfrey Show* (HBO
Films, 1986–). The series was parodied on *Saturday Night Live* (NBC
Studios, 1975–) and a plethora of merchandising appeared, including
The Secret Diary of Laura Palmer, *The Autobiography of Agent Dale Cooper*
and *Diane: The Twin Peaks Tapes of Agent Cooper*. Furthermore, news
of fans hosting *Twin Peaks* parties, well stocked with black coffee and
cherry pie, began to emerge.

Here we see an early appearance of a hugely successful series actively
encouraging cult-like behaviour in its mainstream audiences. As David
Bianculli pointed out, 'never before, in the history of television, had a
program inspired so many millions of people to debate and analyze it
so deeply and so excitedly for so prolonged a period'.[32] The quirkiness
and the narrative enigma at the centre of *Twin Peaks*, while intriguing
to many, could not sustain the series indefinitely, however, and audience numbers began to drop as the mystery around Laura's murder
was left unresolved at the end of the first season. *Twin Peaks* illustrates
the problem of basing a show on a narrative enigma, for solving the
murder could not be indefinitely deferred. After the revelation of the
murderer and his capture in the episodes 'Lonely Souls' (2.7) and 'Arbitrary Law' (2.9), the show lacked a narrative focus. As a result only the
die-hard fans stayed with the series until its very end, with the season
finale directed by David Lynch 'rank[ing] third in its time slot, losing to
reruns of *Designing Women* (Bloodworth-Thomason, 1986–93), *Mur-
phy Brown* (Shukovsky English Entertainment, 1988–98), and *North-
ern Exposure* (Universal Television, 1990–5) on CBS and to a rerun of a
TV movie on NBC'.[33] Here was an example of a cult blockbuster series
that could not hold on to its mainstream audience.

Lost's second key forerunner is, of course, the monstrously successful *The X-Files*, which ran for a total of nine seasons. *Twin Peaks*
clearly influenced Chris Carter's series, bequeathing it an FBI agent
protagonist in touch with the unexplainable and irrational, and, from
its second season, a narrative of government conspiracy and supernatural abduction. Yet *The X-Files* seemed to have learned from *Twin*

Peaks' failings as it created a balance between episodic and serial narratives that enabled the audience to satisfactorily engage with the series on various levels. As Chris Carter explains, 'There are two approaches to television storytelling right now ... One is where, literally every episode connects to the next. And the other is a sort of "mythology" approach, where you weave the serial element in and out of your series.'[34] The latter was his approach for *The X-Files* and, as Roberta Pearson and Sara Gwenllian-Jones have argued, this enabled the show to 'offer the pleasures of both story line resolutions within single episodes and an endlessly deferred resolution to the overarching puzzle constructed through the series as a whole'.[35] In this manner, it was able to regularly defer its conspiracy and alien invasion narrative by simply providing clues along the way as Agents Mulder and Scully investigated a wide range of supernatural mysteries every week.

The X-Files, however, went on well past its natural shelf life. Frank Spotnitz, one of the writers for the show, has commented that Chris Carter 'did not think that the series would go past five years and planned accordingly' by sustaining the mythology narrative over five seasons and then culminating in the feature film *The X-Files: The Movie* (Rob Bowman, 1998).[36] The success of the series, however, meant that it was renewed for four more seasons in which the writers had to revisit and reinvent the mythology narrative, at times at the expense of premises established in the earlier years. This served to alienate the show's loyal viewers for, as Spotnitz points out, 'the longer you tease people along, the more hooked they become on the mythology of the show and the more disappointed they'll be by however it's resolved'.[37]

In planning and writing *Lost* the creators were very aware of the pitfalls of these earlier cult series. Carlton Cuse cites *Twin Peaks* as a 'cautionary tale' against allowing the mythology to 'overwhelm everything else, principally the construction of believable, plausible characters', while both producers recognise that the curse of success is the network's desire to keep the show on the air. As Cuse explains:

> If we knew this series was 88 episodes, we could plot out exactly where all the pieces of mythology were going to land, and we could build very constructively to an endgame ... But we don't know and we can't know. For ABC, this is a very financially successful enterprise, and rightfully their goal is to have it go along as long as they can have it go along.[38]

Since making this statement, the series' creators have addressed this major hurdle with the announcement that ABC has committed to a total of six seasons for the series and that *Lost* will definitely come to an end in 2010, stating that as a result 'the audience will now have the security of knowing that the story will play out as we've intended'.[39]

The rationale for this strategic move on the parts of the showrunners and the network is the hope that the audience for *Lost*, which has seen a slight decrease each year since the show started, will decide to stay with the show now that an end is in sight. This strategy is reinforced by the third season finale, which reveals, in a series of flashforwards, that at the very least Jack and Kate do eventually get off the island – an end is most definitely in sight. In keeping with each of the previous season finales and season openers, however, this revelation raises more questions than it answers; Jack, for some reason now a broken man, regrets their escape and desperately wants to go back. In fact, this approach to the season finale is a hugely significant strategy used by the show's creators to avoid the pitfall of endlessly deferring narrative resolution to the audience's dissatisfaction. The *Lost* creators simply reboot the series with each season, raising a series of new questions and mysteries to be explored and resolved.

Joyce Millman has rather comically suggested that one way of explaining the mysteries of *Lost* is to read it as a video game, in which 'hapless protagonists [are] endlessly beset by random, inexplicable events and torments'.[40] While her argument is intended as a whimsical take on the series, the narrative is indeed structured along videogame lines in which each season operates as a level of the game. Having successfully completed level/season one, we move onto level/season two with a whole new set of conflicts and dangers. For instance, season one ends with the opening of the hatch and the kidnapping of Walt (Malcolm David Kelley) by the Others, setting up the two key elements that will define the second season: the introduction of Desmond (Henry Ian Cusick), the Dharma computer and the inputting of Hurley's numbers, and the open hostility and opposition between the survivors of Oceanic Flight 815 and the Others. Season two ends with the destruction of the hatch, following Locke's refusal to faithfully enter 'the numbers' into the Dharma computer (bringing an end to that narrative strand of the series), and the capture of Jack, Kate and Sawyer by the Others, who became the narrative focus of season three.

This game-like structure gives the impression that questions are being answered. For instance, the introduction of Desmond and the Dharma computer finally provides the answer as to why the plane crashed in the first place, while the Others transform from a truly enigmatic and ghost-like presence to a very real group of people with their own agenda for the island. Yet these revelations provide information without actually resolving the key mysteries of the show: what is the real secret of the island and why have the survivors of Oceanic Flight 815 been brought together in this manner? It is these questions that fuel the series' dynamic online following of devoted fans committed to unravelling the mystery of *Lost* for, as Porter and Lavery have argued, 'what makes *Lost* fans different is that they have formed a discourse community or knowledge network – a group of individuals devoting time and effort into discussing, analyzing, and investigating their favourite series'.[41] This very strategic structure simultaneously provides narrative progression and deferred resolution and as a result the show has for the most part managed to keep both mainstream and cult fans engaged.

This discussion of *Lost* as an example of blockbuster cult demonstrates that in the changing landscape of contemporary television the notion of a 'cult' no longer exclusively applies to small, fantasy series discovered by a loyal and exclusive group of fans who recognise the show to be high quality, while being neglected by the networks. *Lost* is a series that is cult to the core in terms of its content and narrative structure and yet it has been carefully marketed and strategically structured so as to appeal to as wide an audience as possible while also encouraging a level of engagement with the show previously associated with cult audiences. *Lost* demonstrates that with the changes to programming strategies, viewing habits and broadcast/playback technologies that characterise contemporary television, the cult programme is no longer simply the purview of the discerning viewer distinguishing one show from the mass of mainstream material. Rather, cult has been appropriated for the mainstream.

Does this mean that the cult programme no longer belongs to the cult audience, that there is no place for a genuine cult engagement with *Lost* beyond the corporate machinations of the network? The episode 'Exposé' (3.14) suggests otherwise. In season three, the series creators' introduced two new characters – Nikki and Paulo – played by Kiele Sanchez and well-known Brazilian actor Rodrigo Santoro, described as the 'Brazilian Tom Cruise'.[42] Santoro's casting made strategic sense. While primarily unknown in the USA, as a major movie star in Brazil he has an international appeal that seemed well suited to such an internationally successful series. This move was received with vitriolic criticism from many of the fans of the series, however, who were annoyed by the sudden introduction of two new characters seemingly out of nowhere. 'Exposé' rectifies this misjudging of the fans' willingness to accept the rewriting of the story to include these new characters by staging an elaborate stand-alone episode in which Nikki and Paulo are killed. This very knowing nod to the fans opens with the seeming death of Nikki, right after a flashback to Nikki's career as a TV actress who, when told that she could come back again for the next season despite her character's death responds, 'I'm just a guest star and we all know what happens to guest stars.' This episode both recognises and plays with the fans' intensive scrutiny of the series by revisiting key moments from the show, including the aftermath of the crash, with Nikki and Paulo inserted within the mix. It also acknowledges the fans' extreme dislike of these characters by killing them in the cruellest way – they are buried alive by the series' regulars, who mistake their paralysis for death. Here we are reminded that even a series like *Lost*, which has been manufactured as blockbuster cult, still maintains a cult sensibility at its core, in which the audience and the series' producers recognise the fans' claim to the text. It's their little show that has hit the big time.

Notes

1   Alessandra Stanley, '*Rashomon* meets *Gilligan's Island*', *New York Times (Sunday)* Section 2, 12 September 2004, p.8.

2   For a discussion of *Alias* as cult, see Stacey Abbott and Simon Brown (eds), *Investigating Alias: Secrets and Spies* (London: I.B.Tauris, 2007).

3   Roberta E. Pearson and Sara Gwenllian-Jones, 'Introduction', in Roberta E. Pearson and Sara Gwenllian-Jones (eds), *Cult Television* (Minneapolis and London: University of Minnesota Press, 2004), p.xii.

4   Sheldon Hall, 'Tall revenue features: the genealogy of the modern blockbuster', in Steve Neale (ed.), *Genre and Contemporary Hollywood* (London: BFI Publishing, 2002), p.11.

5   Julian Stringer, 'Introduction', in Julian Stringer (ed.), *Movie Blockbusters* (London and New York: Routledge, 2003), pp.1–14.

6   Richard Maltby, *Hollywood Cinema*, 2nd edn (Oxford: Blackwell Publishing, 2003), p.184.

7   Mark Jancovich, Antonio Lázaro Reboll, Julian Stringer and Andy Willis (eds), 'Introduction' in *Defining Cult Movies: The Cultural Politics of Oppositional Taste* (Manchester and New York: Manchester University Press, 2003), p.1.

8   Matt Hills, '*Star Wars* in fandom, film theory, and the museum: the cultural status of the cult blockbuster', in Stringer: *Movie Blockbusters*, p.179.

9   Mark Jancovich and Nathan Hunt, 'The mainstream, distinction, and cult TV', in Pearson and Gwenllian-Jones: *Cult Television*, p.30.

10   Damon Lindelhof, quoted by Paula Hendrickson in 'Getting *Lost*', *Emmy* xxviii/2 (2006), p.35.

11   Andrew O'Hehir, 'Desert island mix', *Sight and Sound* xv/4 (April 2005), p.5.

12   Nancy Franklin, 'Magical mystery tour: forty-eight castaways win the prime-time challenge', *New Yorker*, 23 May 2005, p.92.

13   Lisa Campbell, 'Brace yourself', *Broadcast*, 5 August 2005, p.21.

14   Ibid.

15   Benji Wilson, 'The lost tribe', *Radio Times*, 6 August 2005, p.23.

16   Lynnette Porter and David Lavery, *Unlocking the Meaning of* Lost: *an Unauthorized Guide* (Naperville: Sourcebooks, 2006), p.159.

17   Quoted in Paula Hendrickson, 'Takin' the show on the road', *Emmy* xxviii/2 (2006), p.37.

18   Campbell: 'Brace yourself', p.21.

19   Porter and Lavery: *Unlocking the Meaning of* Lost, p.163.

20   Quoted in Campbell: 'Brace yourself', p.21.

21   Quoted in Paula Hendrickson, 'Getting *Lost*', *Emmy* xxviii/2 (2006), p. 35.

22   Quoted in Janice Rhoshalle Littlejohn, 'Full esteem ahead', *Emmy* xxviii/2 (2006), p.50.

23   Quoted in Matt Hoey, 'All who wander are not *Lost*', *Written By* x/6 (September 2006), p.23.

24   Henrik Örnebring, 'The show must go on ... and on: narrative and seriality in *Alias*', in Stacey Abbott and Simon Brown (eds), *Investigating Alias: Secrets and Spies* (London: I.B.Tauris, 2007), p.25.

25   Hillary Robson, 'Accusatory glances: the evolution and dissolution of the *Alias* fandom in narrative history', in Abbott and Brown: *Investigating Alias*, p.161.

26   Porter and Lavery: *Unlocking the Meaning of* Lost, p.167.

27 Thank you to David Lavery for reminding me of this quote.

28 David Fury quoted in Jeff Bond, 'Finding *Lost*: co-creator Damon Linde-lof and season one scribe David Fury sound off on the once and future ABC hit', *Cinefantastique* xxxvii/6/7 (Sep/Oct 2005), p.40.

29 Lorne Manly, 'The laws of the jungle', *New York Times (Sunday)*, Section 2, 18 September 2005, p.21.

30 Damon Lindelof quoted in Bond: 'Finding *Lost*', p.40.

31 Richard Thompson, *Television's Second Golden Age: From* Hill Street Blues *to* ER (Syracuse: Syracuse University Press, 1996), p.156.

32 David Bianculli quoted in Thompson: *Television's Second Golden Age*, p.156.

33 Thompson: *Television's Second Golden Age*, p.157.

34 Quoted in Matt Hurwitz, 'Hooked: crafting the serialized storylines that keep audiences begging and new viewers caught up', *Written By* xix/6 (September 2006), p.31.

35 Pearson and Gwenllian-Jones, 'Introduction', in Pearson and Gwenllian-Jones (eds): *Cult Television*, p.xv.

36 Frank Spotnitz quoted in Manly: 'The laws of the jungle', p.21.

37 Ibid.

38 Carlton Cuse quoted in Manly: 'The laws of the jungle', p.21.

39 Edward Wyatt, 'ABC sets spring 2010 as the end for "*Lost*"', *New York Times*, 8 May 2007, available at *www.nytimes.com/2007/05/08/arts/television/08lost.html*.

40 Joyce Millman, 'Game theory', in Orson Scott Card (ed.), *Getting Lost: Survival, Baggage and Starting Over in J.J. Abrams'* Lost (Dallas, TX: Benbella Books, 2006), p.23.

41 Porter and Lavery: *Unlocking the Meaning of* Lost, p.171. For a discussion of the many ways in which online fandom has used new technologies to enhance their analytical engagement with the series, see Chapter IV in this volume.

42 Michael Ausiello, 'Ausiello report: Exclusive! *Lost* Snages "Brazillian Tom Cruise"', TVGuide.com, 25 July 2006, available at *http://community.tvguidecom/blog-entry/TVGuide-Editors-Blog/Ausiello-Report/Exclusive-Lost-Snags/800003996*.

III. The Fictional Institutions of Lost:

World Building, Reality and the Economic Possibilities of Narrative Divergence

Derek Johnson

I n 'Tricia Tanaka is Dead' (3.10), castaway Hurley (Jorge Garcia) happens upon a mysterious, run-down van in the jungle and endeavours to coax it back to life. While Hurley lacks appropriate tools – much less replacement parts – to complete this task, the decades-old case of beer that he finds in the back of the van provides him the perfect enticement with which to enlist the help of fellow castaways Jin (Daniel Dae Kim) and Sawyer (Josh Holloway). Like many television programmes of the past, *Lost* chooses to disguise the corporate origins and brand identity of the beer-filled van that Hurley happens across. Though its unique shape betrays the van as a classic VW Bus, the iconic Volkswagen logo is replaced by the stark, black and white octagonal imprint of the fictional Dharma Initiative, the mysterious research group whose presence on the island has yet to be fully explained. Similarly, the Dharma logo marks the beer in the van as an off-brand – just as unrecognizable, unidentifiable and un-consumable by the viewer at home as the generic bottles of 'cola' and 'breakfast flakes' that might have sat on the kitchen tables of previous television families like the Bradys or Huxtables.

And yet, in the real world, removed from *Lost*'s monsters, mysteries and magnetic fields, these fictional imprints have taken on a cultural and economic significance that transcends similar generic status. Real people walk down the street wearing Dharma baseball caps, headed to work where they might drink coffee out of a Dharma-emblazoned mug and procrastinate by exploring the web space of the fictional Hanso Foundation that supposedly funds Dharma. Meanwhile, other fictional brands of consumables established on the series have bled into the real world; like Hurley, *Lost* viewers can now buy and eat Apollo candy bars.

Of course, only a very few allow the fictional institutions of *Lost* to so permeate their experience of the real world – those devoted fans willing to spend time and money on *Lost* merchandise. These special-ized nodes for experiencing the *Lost* world undoubtedly capture added merchandising revenues for its producer-distributor ABC, but as a niche market (not even inclusive of all hardcore *Lost* fans), products marked with fictional imprints like Dharma, Hanso and Apollo seem inadequate and counterintuitive in the current broadcast television economy. As the bread-and-butter advertising revenues paid to US networks like ABC by *real* corporations became increasingly hard to come by (due to increasing competition between media outlets), com-mercial comedies and dramas have, by and large, moved to foreground those real corporations within the story itself. On other contemporary US prime-time serials, a beer-filled van would surely have presented not just impetus for character action, but also lucrative opportunities for product placement. The producers of *24* (Imagine Entertainment, 2001–), for example, repeatedly enter into contractual relations with automakers like Ford and Toyota, agreeing to outfit heroes like Jack Bauer (Kiefer Sutherland) exclusively with their products each season. *Heroes* (NBC Universal Television, 2006–) made a similar arrangement with Nissan, allowing Hiro's (Masi Oka's) preference for the Versa to become a plot point in an early first-season episode. Programmes like *The 4400* (Renegade 83, 2004–) and *Entourage* (HBO, 2004) strike like deals with alcohol distributors such as Budweiser and Skyy Vodka re-spectively. Automobiles and alcohol, therefore, comprise only two of the innumerable markets that might seem to be product placement no-brainers.

So while Hurley takes full economic advantage of the van and the booze, the producers of *Lost* miss a similar opportunity. Would not Budweiser or Miller Genuine Draft have been thrilled to cough up some cash to be presented as the beer with the everlasting flavour to make such a satisfying reward for Sawyer? What automaker would not have loved to see a popular character like Hurley take so much interest in their van and ultimately use it to stage a heroic rescue in the subsequent season finale? Nevertheless, instead of building content around sponsors' brands, *Lost* emphasizes the assumedly less lucrative project of showcasing the fictional Dharma logo. Despite its non-existence in the 'real' world of global capital, Dharma has been emphasized diegetically as a brand of its own, with its imprint appearing throughout the second and third seasons of the series on consumable goods like wine, macaroni and cheese, cornflakes and composition notebooks. Apparently, Dharma makes and packages its own brands of durable and consumable goods, shutting out corporate suppliers from the real world. In the world of *Lost* the Dharma brand, not those of sponsors, takes priority.

Viewed with rose-tinted glasses, this failure to cater to real-world corporate sponsors could be ascribed to the producers' greater artistic commitment to establishing the enigmatic Dharma Initiative's prior presence and continuing impact on the island. Supposedly founded in 1970 by University of Michigan graduate students and the similarly fictional Hanso Foundation to conduct interdisciplinary scientific and social research across the globe, Dharma studied the castaways' island until the early 1990s, when a group of as-yet-unidentified hostiles violently drove them off. The series has used its trademark flashbacks to introduce a few characters that worked under the Dharma banner (like the mysterious name-changing doctor in the orientation films and Roger, the workman Hurley later finds dead in the van). Yet the castaways' interactions with the Initiative occur primarily at the institutional level: not through characters, but through the Dharma-constructed infrastructure of mysterious hatches, communication towers that promise contact with civilization, and food and supply provisions (that, as the episode 'Lockdown' (2.17) suggests, Dharma may continue to deliver, if only by automation).

Because Dharma manifests itself primarily as an institution, Dharma-brand products as shown in 'Tricia Tanaka is Dead' prove integral to the producers' plotting and world-building efforts. Marked goods like automobiles and alcohol render the faceless Dharma visually tangible as a narrative agent; the integration of real-world products instead would superficially trade story-world depth for a quick buck. Nor could producers easily have their cake and eat it too by stocking those Dharma hatches with name-brand products for the castaways to consume; while producers may have indeed recognized the potential for product placement inherent in the second season introduction of the hatches, the contingent, indefinite nature of the Dharma Initiative would mitigate its attractiveness to potential sponsors. The institution might seem a benevolent, utopian research group one day, but later plot developments could make it a villainous cabal bent on world domination – and few corporations want to be recognized as the official sponsor and supplier of evil. Dedication to deep transmedia storytelling and world-building ambitions, therefore, could rationalize *Lost*'s dismissal of product placement strategies embraced by other television series.

That explanation, however, ignores the economic realities of contemporary television, and the increasing extension of television and displacement of advertiser interest into the digital realm of the Internet and viral video. If so many other narrative series have taken on product placement as a means of funding production, how could *Lost* afford such dedication to the story alone? How were economic needs in a depressed advertising market alternatively met if, given the story the producers wanted to tell, product placement could not be relied upon as it has been in other narrative series? Could the generation of fictional, branded institutions like Dharma actually serve to satisfy those economic exigencies in another way?

To explore these possibilities, this chapter first investigates the economic factors driving *Lost* to experiment with new forms and strategies of promotion, storytelling and extension of fictional brands. What kind of revenue models prove necessary in a weakened broadcasting market in the USA? How do different television genres and modes of storytelling collaborate or confound those economic needs? Second, this chapter examines how branded fictional institutions on *Lost* like Dharma and Hanso have been constructed by producers and engaged with by audiences, both on television and across media platforms. How has the narrative divergence of *Lost* across a range of media introduced fictional brands within the spaces and experiences of everyday life? How do these fictional entities become truly *institutionalized* as structures with which audiences, not just characters, interact? Lastly, this paper explores how *Lost*'s institutional focus on fictional corporations could serve a counterintuitive economic end in an industrial moment where programmes must increasingly foreground real brands within their stories. How might institutionalized fictional brands be developed into alternative revenue models? Why would fictional corporations prove advantageous in making narrative series like *Lost* attractive to real corporate interests?

Ultimately, *Lost* strikes a unique relationship between fictional storytelling and 'reality' – both in the lived realm of everyday life, and the television genre in which non-traditional revenue models have thrived. By refusing to use real corporations in lieu of fictional institutions within the story, *Lost* erects a diegetic boundary that prevents it from following reality TV's lead in designing content around sponsors. In extending those fictional institutions across media and into the real world, however, everyday life overlaps the narrative of *Lost*, allowing real corporate institutions like Sprite and Jeep to become both producers of content and content themselves. *Lost* eschews the product placement of reality TV, but it has proven attractive to advertisers for offering fictional institutions with which real corporations can interface in the mediation of everyday life.

THE ECONOMIC CHALLENGES OF BROADCAST TELEVISION

The US television industry has undergone considerable transition in the last decade, with the networks increasingly reliant on the reality genre and, as a result, decreasingly investing in narrative properties like *Lost*. As Chad Raphael argues, reality television emerged in the 1990s as 'a cost-cutting solution' at a moment when media conglomeration changed the economics of production. Although the debt incurred by corporate expansion made conglomerates leery of heavy investment and deficit financing, the relaxation and eventual 1995 repeal of the Financial Interest and Syndication Rules (which had previously prohibited networks from owning the series they distributed in prime time and sharing in subsequent off-network syndication revenues) incentivized increased in-house production. Cheaper reality programming thus fulfilled both needs.[1]

Similarly, Ted Magder suggests that the reality genre has introduced entirely new economic models to the television industry.

Concerns about viewers skipping commercials via digital video record-ers (DVRs) have required networks to respond to the changing needs of skittish advertisers: 'what reality TV and formats reveal most of all is that the traditional revenue model used to produce commercial tele-vision is becoming anachronistic. We are entering a new era of product placement and integration, merchandising, pay-per-view, and multi-platform content.'[2]

As feminist media critic Jennifer Pozner argues, product place-ment, or brand integration, 'is largely responsible for the reality-TV genre as we know it today, and not vice versa'. The networks followed the course set by programmes like *Survivor* (Mark Burnett Produc-tions, 2000–), in which castaway contestants compete for products like Mountain Dew in immunity challenges, when they realized that instead of 'the network paying actors, advertisers would pay the net-work for a starring role'.[3] Though spot advertising persists for real-ity television in the USA, these programmes recall the days of single sponsorship prior to the quiz show scandals in the late 1950s; spon-sors, their products and their iconic logos have literally became a part of reality TV programmes. On the ratings behemoth *American Idol* (Fremantle Media North America, 2002–), for example, judges drink from Coca-Cola glasses and sets feature Coke iconography. Simulta-neously, finalists produce weekly music videos promoting Ford auto-mobiles that appear during the episode. In exchange for this product visibility, Coke, Ford, and third major sponsor AT&T have paid the Fox network over $20 million each per year.[4]

In the wake of this reality wave and its new economic models, *Lost* must have seemed like a disadvantaged relic – it had all the castaways and tropical trimmings of something like *Survivor*, but with a diegetic boundary to keep sponsors' products out of the story and confined to traditional ad spots. When Matt Roush praises *Lost* in his review for *Broadcasting and Cable*, he singles out the programme for its lack of a franchise brand, lack of a formula, lack of big stars in a huge ensemble cast, and its very existence outside of the reality genre – all qualities that made *Lost* a *less* attractive product in the changing in-dustrial climate.[5] The critical enthusiasm mustered by Roush followed in large part from *Lost*'s rejection of the strategies currently being ex-perimented with to appeal to advertisers. However, in a new world where the resources needed to support traditional, more expensive fictional television had become increasingly scarce, *Lost* seemed like a dinosaur, albeit a narratively compelling one. Consequently, advertisers looked at *Lost* in its initial, single-platform configuration with disdain. As late as September 2004, just prior to the series' premiere, the trade journal *Adweek* lumped *Lost* among several scripted series described by media buyers as 'clunkers', including such short-lived examples as *Father of the Pride* (Dreamworks Television, 2004–5), *Listen Up* (Regency Television, 2004–5) and *Center of the Universe* (CBS Television, 2004–5).[6]

While the report does not explicitly state how *Lost* earned this dubious distinction, shifting industrial attitudes and discourses over the past few years might account for the lack of advertiser interest. As one *Advertising Age* editorial puts it,

> Video is Killing TV ... the ad industry is undergoing a semantic shift that's ousting broadcast TV as its central organizing principle. In its place, a more flexible notion of video is emerging ... every ad agency is trying to structure itself to produce more digital content and escape the box of the 30-second-spot.[7]

Analysts predict heavy revenue losses in television's future as advertisers increasingly turn to media forms that enable them to connect with viewers outside the broadcasting context of the spot advertisement.[8] To stem this tide, broadcasting would have to adapt its operations to the new economic reality by sweetening the opportunities available to advertisers on television. The flood of reality shows that dominated network television development and scheduling prior to the scripted revival that arguably followed in *Lost*'s wake, therefore, can be seen as part of an industrial attempt to provide more flexible options to media buyers during this time of change. To advertisers in 2004, however, *Lost* offered not more flexibility, but more of the same.

WORLD BUILDING AS INSTITUTION BUILDING

Given the networks' increased doubts about the economic viability of scripted programming, *Lost*'s rejection of brand integration in favour of developing in-world fictional institutions like Dharma appears all the more bold – even counterintuitive – in the face of marketplace demands. Contextualizing *Lost* within larger creative and economic trends as well as in a longer history of world building, however, puts into historical perspective the series' attempts to create fictional institutions and then install them within the everyday realms of the real world.

Lost is certainly not the first television series to expend a great deal of energy extending elements of its narrative not just across media platforms, but also into the spaces and experiences of everyday life. Christopher Anderson argues, for example, that the *Disneyland* television series (Walt Disney Productions, 1954–90) worked to enhance Disney's theme park operations by blurring the line between programme and place to create an inhabitable textual space coterminous with consumers' everyday lives:

> Whereas traditional notions of textuality assume that a text is singular, unified, and autonomous, with a structure that draws the viewer inward, Disney's television texts were, from the outset, fragmented, propelled by a centrifugal force that guided the viewer away from the immediate textual experience toward a more pervasive sense of textuality, one that encouraged the consumption of further Disney texts, further Disney products, further Disney experiences.[9]

Disney characters and stories were not confined to closed texts, but began to seep into the lived spaces of consumption and tourism. Rather than draw the consumer into the Disney world, the Disney world was propelled outward into the real world of the consumer. More recently, Jeffrey Sconce has identified in the television industry of the 1980s and 1990s an increased attention to what he calls 'world building', the construction of complex narrative universes that use the relative diegetic depth of episodic television to cultivate new forms of audience engagement in an increasingly fragmented and competitive media marketplace.[10]

Examining similar trends in the 1990s, Kurt Lancaster examines how the series *Babylon 5* (Babylonian Productions, 1994–8) manifested itself as a concrete universe, or 'imaginary entertainment environment', where television textuality spilled not only into ancillary markets, but also into the spaces of everyday life. The diegetic depth of the series lent itself to deployment across media platforms via licensed card games, for example, which in turn gave a physical tangibility to the diegesis as a real place in which viewers could perform roles and take actions through play.[11] Similar arguments have been made by Janet Murray, who predicts that the increasing marriage of television and new media forms will lead not only to more complex narrative worlds, but simultaneously to a greater opportunity to occupy 'a contiguous virtual space and experience events, in persona, that are also happening to the characters in the series'.[12] *Lost*'s attempts to spill its narrative institutions into the spaces of the everyday might indeed substantiate Murray's predictions, but these textual structures are part of a much larger historical trajectory of dispersing the television world into other texts and experiential contexts.

To understand the serial storytelling of *Lost* – and push further our understanding of its 'narrative complexity' – we need to examine the aggregate interrelationships and narrative structures not just between television episodes, but also across media platforms and spaces of consumption.[13] The experiences of narratives and the fictional institutions contained within them will change as serial television content moves out of the box sitting in the living room and across a range of media platforms and spaces. These exchanges and extensions between television and digital platforms have been discussed variably by media scholars as 'overflow',[14] 'hyperseriality'[15] and perhaps most prominently by Henry Jenkins and others as 'convergence ... the flow of content across multiple media platforms, the cooperation between multiple media industries, and the migratory behaviour of audiences who will go almost anywhere in search of the kinds of entertainment experiences they want'.[16]

While these perspectives offer useful lenses for conceptualizing contemporary television's presence across a variety of media platforms, the articulation of such 'transmedia storytelling'[17] to the new aesthetics of digital culture potentially limits our comprehension of shows like *Lost* in at least two significant ways. First, we might miss not only the non-digital historical precedents for world building across media, but also the way in which old, analog media maintain a persistent importance in contemporary convergence narratives: as we will see, print media like newspapers and paperback novels play an important role in the transmedia network of a property like *Lost*. Second, the metaphor of convergence threatens to obscure the way in which the serialized, cross-platform structure of *Lost*'s narrative simultaneously constitutes a coordinated narrative *divergence*. Instead of converging into a single, digital medium, the piecemeal narrative of *Lost* must be parsed together from clues dispersed across a series of media. In the same tradition of the Disney textuality of the 1950s, the divergence of the fragmented text across media platforms enables it to pervade everyday space and experience. In its participation in convergence culture, *Lost* is not a singular televisual narrative, but a manifold, multiplatform, divergent narrative often experienced outside television or any single medium. Given that dispersed textuality is an historical phenomenon, are *Lost*'s current experiments with the fictional Dharma's pervading everyday space in a manner similar to real institutions nothing new?

The fictional television world of *Lost*, like the real world, is structured by institutions. The actions that characters take occur in a world in which regular institutional bodies appear and reappear as fixtures of everyday life; from Oceanic Airlines to the Apollo candy bar, there are companies and products with recognizable images and logos that pervade the fictional world of *Lost*. While only introduced at the beginning of the second season, the fictional Dharma Initiative, funded by the philanthropic Hanso Foundation, has become a pillar of *Lost* mythology and a central site of ongoing narrative enigma. In the third season, increasingly important alongside these institutions became corporate entities like the Widmore Corporation, the company run by the father of Desmond's long-lost love, and Mittelos Bioscience, the company that purportedly recruited Juliet to conduct fertility experiments on the island on behalf of the Others. These organizations have their hand in everything that has occurred in the series, either directly or indirectly, and as such provide a consistent backbone to support the entire *Lost* universe.

The mystery of the island is in large part an institutional mystery – what is it that attracted these institutions to the island, what did these entities do with all those hatches once they got there, and what role, if any, might these institutions have played in bringing the castaways to the island? The ubiquitous nature of these institutions in the *Lost* universe is such that they pervade the narrative even in episodes that are not purportedly 'about' them, often buried in the visuals of the *mise-en-scène*. If we look closely enough, we see that it is Widmore Labs, for example, that not only built or sponsored Henry Gale's hot air balloon, but also manufactured the pregnancy tests taken in several different episodes by Sun (Yunjin Kim), Kate (Evangeline Lilly) and Juliet's sister Rachel (Robin Weigert). *Lost* has become famous for the interconnections between its characters (we learn, for instance, that the fathers of both Jack (Matthew Fox) and Kate have played crucial roles in the lives of other castaways) yet less noticed is that these character relations all occur within a similar network of institutions. The series acquires depth and coherency as a narrative universe – what Matt Hills calls 'hyperdiegesis' – in large part because of the omnipresent nature of these reappearing and very visible institutions. These structural entities glue *Lost* together as 'a vast, detailed narrative space, only a fraction of which is ever directly seen or encountered within the text, but which nevertheless appears to operate according to principles of internal logic and extension'.[18] Much of the *Lost* universe remains unseen, but the institutional nexus of Oceanic, Dharma, Hanso, Mittelos, Widmore, Apollo, *et al.* suggests its extensive expanse. The world-building project of *Lost* is very much an institution-building project.

This alone does not distinguish *Lost* from other 'cult' television series that could also be described as hyperdiegetic. Institution building has played a large role in the *Star Trek* franchise, for example, in which it is the specific, recognizable institutionalism of Starfleet – its command structures, Prime Directive, uniforms, and insignia – that allows different sets of characters operating in different time frames and parts of the galaxy to be understood as part of the same narrative universe (rather than the same genre writ large). The mythology of *Buffy the Vampire Slayer* (Mutant Enemy, 1997–2003) is similarly dependent on the institution of the Watcher's Council that has trained female slayers since the beginning of recorded history. More recently, *24* (Imagine Entertainment, 2001–) has pushed the creation of fictional institutions in more civic-minded, almost mundane, directions, generating a narrative playground for itself by constructing new law enforcement agencies like the Counter Terrorist Unit (CTU) that can interact with recognizable, real-world institutions like Homeland Security and the Office of the President.

Unlike *Star Trek*, the hyperdiegetic space *24* constructs overlaps and intersects with the real-world institutions that structure the everyday lives of audiences. This is a significant development in world building, blurring the boundaries between hyperdiegetic and everyday space. *Lost*'s institutions may be fictional, but like those of *24*, they prove more compatible with mundane, everyday institutions. Yet if *24* offers a civic-minded hyperdiegesis, *Lost* provides a more corporate-minded set of fictional institutions, joining series like *Angel* (Mutant Enemy, 1999–2004), *Arrested Development* (Imagine Entertainment, 2003–6) and *The Office* (BBC, 2001–3), which have created fictional companies like Wolfram and Hart, the Bluth Company and Wernham-Hogg, respectively, to support narrative worlds fundamentally structured by corporate culture. *Lost*'s significance lies in its development of a set of fictional institutions that can interact with the non-fantastic, mundane, corporate institutions of everyday life, a capacity that gives the fictional institution-building project of *Lost* greater economic viability in the current television market. While the fictional institutions of *Star Trek* have certainly contributed to the generation of countless billions of dollars for that franchise, the institutions of *Lost* establish that fictional universe as one coterminous with our own, in which real corporations too can become key institutional players.

BRINGING SPONSORS INTO PRODUCTION AND INTO THE WORLD

Lost continues a historical trajectory of pervasive, divergent, hyperdi-egetic textuality that allows narrative spaces to spill into the spaces of the everyday, but it does so in a way specifically adapted to a shifting television economy in which the economic viability of lavish narrative programming has come into question and opportunities for sponsor participation in the story world have become increasingly advantageous. While producers and executives certainly did not transform *Lost* from a single-platform television series into a multiplatform, divergent narrative *solely* for economic reasons, this development, regardless of its creative motivation, helped to make this 'clunker' into a cherry more attractive to media buyers.

Prior to the 2004 premiere, ABC increased *Lost*'s public visibility by experimenting with new promotional strategies: as one trade article put it, the decline of broadcast viewership meant that networks could 'no longer depend solely on promoting their new shows with their own on-air promotions, as they need to reach people who aren't watching TV'.[19] Lagging behind in the ratings, a desperate ABC hired a number of specialized marketing firms to help it find creative ways to connect content with viewers. One of the resultant campaigns designed for *Lost* targeted vacationers by leaving messages in bottles on sandy beaches. This campaign first moved *Lost* into the realm of the everyday, taking its promotions off air and into the spaces in which vacationers – indeed a valuable market to tap – relaxed away from the television set. By moving the series' castaway theme to physical spaces, these bottles created exposure and additional media coverage in the press. Simultaneously, *Lost* promoters experimented with websites positioned as non-fictional, including an official site for Oceanic Air and a fan page for the diegetic band Drive Shaft. Due to the overall effectiveness of this summer campaign and *Lost*'s unexpected ratings success in the fall, executives expected to see similar non-traditional marketing campaigns follow, hoping to get audiences to 'stumble' upon programmes when away from the television.[20]

Thanks to that surprising performance, media buyers immediately began to re-evaluate the cool reception they had given *Lost*. That success enabled ABC to use *Lost* as a pathfinder for developing new kinds of revenue models around fictional programming. In 2005, *Lost* was among the first fee-based television content available on iTunes and, by 2006, ABC was using the series as a draw for its experimental distribution of free, ad-supported content online.[21] Based in part on the strength of *Lost*, ABC was able to attract ten sponsors to the trial, in which viewers would be given the choice of viewing a traditional spot, or playing an advertiser-sponsored game in exchange for viewing an episode.

Despite this success, *Lost* itself remained the sugar that made the bad medicine of advertisements tolerable. While advertiser-sponsored games may indeed have been fun, the pleasures of *Lost* itself remained cordoned off from sponsors' products by the diegetic boundary between its narrative world and the advertising and promotional apparatus – unlike the attractive integration offered by reality TV. *Survivor*'s castaways competed for Mountain Dew, while *Lost*'s castaways remained removed from the extra-diegetic world of sponsoring products like Sprite. In spot advertisements, sponsoring products remained external to the content desired by audiences. Though the network could force advertisement viewing in these experimental online venues, the popularity of *Lost* with DVR users sustained the economic disadvantage of spot advertisements.

DVR viewing exacerbated the need to develop alternatives to traditional broadcasting revenue models: though *Lost*'s status as the fourth-most DVR-ed programme in 2005 signalled its popularity with technologically elite audiences, it also suggested that advertising time purchased during *Lost* was among the most at risk of being skipped by viewers. As Jim Edwards points out in *Brandweek*, though product placement appears most ubiquitously in reality TV (designed to thwart commercial skippers) and is used most ubiquitously in reality series, no reality series ranks among the top ten most DVR-ed programmes, so advertisers would benefit more from placing products in scripted series. However, as Edwards argues, scripted television is too much of a battleground: 'writers, producers, networks, directors, and talent all have to be taken into account before a brand can appear'.[22] In the words of one executive: 'It's not like in reality where any brand or any product will do.'[23] To stand on equal footing with reality TV's attractiveness to media buyers, then, *Lost* needed to find the right brand.

Unfortunately, the literal isolation of *Lost*'s setting and characters from corporate brands and consumer lifestyles made this a tall order. Because the *Lost* narrative lacked any kind of institutional connection to the real world, there was no point of entry for any potential sponsor. So while the introduction of Dharma and Hanso may have emerged in response to storytelling needs, it had the pleasing side effect of allowing the series to support a brand of its own – a fictional institution that could serve as an intermediary, an interface, between the story world of the show and the corporate world of sponsors and consumers. As early as November 2004, the producers were promising a revamped, 'considerably different' season two.[24] When those changes arrived the next October, the series' focus shifted away from life on the beach to the castaways' discovery and operation of a series of underground installations left behind by the mysterious Hanso Foundation and Dharma Initiative. Ultimately, along with 'a whole new set of questions to ponder',[25] these institutions gave *Lost* a connectivity to the realm of global institutions that, however fictional, enabled the series to bring down the diegetic boundaries between narrative and marketing.

The capability to bring down those boundaries, however, did not automatically generate sponsor interest. With little creative control over the long-term development of Dharma and Hanso on television, direct interface with those fictional institutions remained a dicey proposition for potential sponsors. Yet if the institutional umbrella of Hanso and Dharma widened to encompass experiences in media spaces outside television that sponsors *could* more handily control, creative and economic relationships between the fictional institutions of *Lost* and the corporate institutions of sponsors would become more tenable. If their institutional imprint exceeded the bounds of television, Hanso and Dharma could interact and have business relations with other real-world institutions in the spaces *outside* television less centrally controlled by television writers. So following the start of the second season in fall 2005, Coca-Cola and three other sponsoring partners joined ABC to develop a viral marketing campaign that would transform *Lost* from a single-platform television narrative into a divergent set of media experiences. The idea was to make brands like Coca-Cola's Sprite into key players in a mystery strewn across media platforms, integrating those brands into the expanded *Lost* narrative.[26] This is not to suggest that *Lost* found a means of generating more revenue streams than through product placement. Instead, through the expansion of the hyperdiegetic into the realm of the everyday, *Lost* discovered a means of maintaining sponsor interest in expensive, expansive narrative television by setting a place for corporate marketers both within the sphere of production and within the story itself.

The resultant, coordinated transformation of *Lost* from a television text to a divergent, multiplatform launched as the alternate reality game (ARG) 'The *Lost* Experience' in the summer of 2006. The primary narrative function of the game was to explore enigmas that had accrued over the course of two seasons – what did the mysterious 4-8-15-16-23-42 number sequence mean, and, most importantly, how was it connected to the institutional presence of Dharma and Hanso on the island? But rather than answering these questions in a direct, narratively linear manner, the ARG buried the extended *Lost* narrative amid a range of consumption experiences through the careful coordination of content deployed successively through television and newspaper advertisements, public appearances, corporate websites, published novels, podcasts, guerilla video, and even candy distribution. To piece the narrative together over the course of the summer, viewers would have to pool their collective intelligence and talents.[27] This coordinated multi-platform deployment of content positioned the viewer not as an external spectator looking in on the story, but as a resident situated within the diegetic universe in which that story unfolded. The game hailed the viewer-player as an investigator of the mysterious Hanso Foundation and Dharma Initiative, inviting them to look for clues amid advertisements and promotions that they experienced as a quotidian part of everyday life, not as part of a televisual narrative diegetically bound off from it.

Experiencing *Lost* outside television, therefore, simultaneously meant moving *inside* its narrative world. The fictional institutions Hanso and Dharma, not fictional characters or narrative threads, enabled viewers to experience everyday life as part of the *Lost* hyperdiegesis – not just in the digital realm, but across a range of mediated experience. Advertisements supposedly paid for by the Hanso Foundation aired during ABC programmes, pointing viewers to the Hanso website where they could search for clues on a site that hailed them not as *Lost* viewers, but as web surfers sharing the Foundation's philanthropic interests. Print advertisements begged newspaper readers to discount claims made about Hanso by the tie-in novel *Bad Twin*. As the game continued, digital podcasts and guerilla videos emerged, purporting to reveal to the public the truth about the real Hanso Foundation – but they did so in concert with analog content deployed throughout everyday mediated spaces.

Staged public appearances on *Jimmy Kimmel Live* (Jackhole Industries, 2003–) and at the San Diego Comic Con even went so far as to purport that while *Lost* was fictional, the Hanso Foundation had a real history worthy of both cover-up and investigation. At Comic Con, 'Rachel Blake' (the anti-Hanso guerilla blogger), interrupted the producers' discussion of the show and attacked the writers for their complicity with a real-life Dharma–Hanso agenda. The producers played along with the fantasy, not denying the real-life existence of such fictional institutions, but quashing her conspiracy theory by claiming that they took dramatic licence in their portrayal of them – a response met tersely by Blake: 'you're liars. You're promoting them as some kind of force for good. But they're not.' If Comic Con brought these institutions into the spaces of reality by attacking them, Jimmy Kimmel did so by defending them, giving airtime to 'Hugh McIntyre', the communications director for Hanso. Framed as a public relations intervention, McIntyre claimed that 'the writers and producers of *Lost* have decided to attach themselves to our foundation'. Promoting Hanso's major projects around the globe, McIntryre admitted that Dharma 'was a real project', but that 'it's just not true, the way [*Lost*'s producers are] colouring the project'. Both the Comic Con and *Jimmy Kimmel Live* incidents contrasted *Lost*'s fictional status with the purported real-life existence of Dharma–Hanso, constructing them as bigger and more real than the television programme from which they originated.

Without a doubt, the fact that these new web portals, printed products and promotional appearances could network across distribution outlets owned by Disney, the parent company of ABC, presented an opportunity for classically synergistic revenue multiplication. The appeal of a single property like *Lost* could be used to generate sales of other Disney-owned books, ratings for other Disney-owned television programmes, and hits for other Disney-owned web spaces. But it was the institutionalization of *Lost* across the spaces of everyday life that presented further economic possibilities.

As Marie-Laure Ryan claims, the careful construction required of narrative becomes all too fragile and chaotic when too many interactors have the ability to impact an interactive story.[28] It would be nearly impossible for an ARG like 'The *Lost* Experience' to construct any kind of meaningful interactive narrative in which all participants could be friends with Jack, Sawyer and Kate without sacrificing the agency of those participants in the story world. But by shifting the focus away from characters and towards institutions, the ARG sidestepped these obstacles, generating larger infrastructures that could be effectively shared by a wider range of participants. Players need not encounter familiar *Lost* characters to know they inhabit the *Lost* world, because they interact with it through their shared institutional experiences. Just as Jack, Kate and Sawyer live in a world structured by Dharma and Hanso, so too do the players of the *Lost* ARG. Television characters and ARG players have separate experiences and encounters, but they all occur within the same institutional superstructure. However, perhaps most importantly for the argument forwarded here, the manner in which the institutions of *Lost* decentralize the narrative world (no longer dependent on the central stories represented by Jack, Kate and Sawyer on the island) simultaneously decentralizes the creative power of constructing that world. Not only do these fictional institutions allow viewers to operative narratively within the *Lost* universe, they also provide an interface with which other cultural institutions might enter the story as both content and producers of that content.

Over the course of the second season, the development of 'The *Lost* Experience' moved beyond synergistic Disney tie-ins, reaching out to other corporate interests that could partner with ABC to take advantage of the blurred line between *Lost*'s institutions and the institutionalized spaces of everyday life. In interacting with the Hanso Foundation and Dharma Initiative as if they were real, viewer-players easily entered into a narrative space that would accept the sponsors affiliated with those institutions as legitimate players and sources of narrative detail. Instead of asking viewers to play as compensation for being granted access to the *Lost* universe, Sprite-based games could now be played from *within* the *Lost* universe by consumers play-acting as corporate-investigating, culture-jamming hackers. Similarly, Sprite's 'Sub-lymonal' television commercials ceased to be advertisement, and became potential sources of narrative revelation to be mined for clues to *Lost*'s enigmas. *Monster.com*, a website that allows users to browse job listings and post their own resumes, also participated in this institutionalization of the Hanso Foundation, listing Hanso job openings throughout 'The *Lost* Experience'. In doing so, the corporate operations of *Monster.com* became narratively operative as a source of information about Hanso's hiring practices.

Even more adeptly, the web of clues and narrative threads offered that summer by 'The *Lost* Experience' directed viewer-players to an official Jeep website, where nosy visitors could exploit a convenient security lapse and pry through corporate documents that detailed the relationship between Hanso, Dharma and Daimler Chrysler. Daimler Chrysler literally became a player in the narrative as the unwitting supplier of the Jeep Compass vehicles used by Hanso to illegally transport human organs in South Africa. Examining the evidence exposes us to the new Compass schematics, but also gives the corporation a chance to distance itself from the nefarious schemes of Hanso. The fake memos hidden on the site could take the time to make it clear that while Chrysler did supply Hanso with top-quality merchandise, the automaker would never knowingly aid and abet human organ trafficking. As a partner in ABC's institutional deployment of *Lost* across media platforms, Jeep marketers enjoyed a decentralized creative control unavailable on traditional narrative television written under the aegis of a writing staff. Able to frame its own operations in interaction with Hanso, Jeep could shape its association with this fictional corporation as much or even to a greater degree than it could with product placement. When narrative encompasses the corporate realm of everyday life, the economic exchanges between viewer and advertiser can take place in the context of the narrative. As a report in *Advertising Age* explains, 'The *Lost* Experience' provided the 'must-see, bite-sized content ... [that] ... advertisers have been seeking as the world of multi-platform programming explodes'.[29] By tying its fictional institutions to those of reality, *Lost* was able to refit narrative television for integrated marketing in the age of reality TV, moving brand integration outside of the fictional and into a space sponsors could control.

In institutionalizing the Hanso Foundation and Dharma Initiative, however, *Lost* not only created a space for the integration of sponsors' brands, it also created a brand for itself that it could begin to leverage on its own. As with many series, ABC markets products stamped with the *Lost* logo that acknowledge the fictional status of the series itself; but alongside these more traditional merchandising efforts have arisen a supplementary line of products that, like the *Jimmy Kimmel* and Comic Con appearances, position fictional institutions as bigger and more real than the fiction from which they came. Yet while those appearances might be best described as promotion, these product lines generate revenue in their own right. Although currently limited in scope, a line of Dharma-branded merchandise has emerged that perpetuates the illusion of the institution's reality and maintains its presence in the spaces of everyday life. On *ABC.com*, one can buy not just Dharma-branded T-shirts and hats that increase the institution's presence in quotidian life when the user wears them, but also Dharma-brand composition books (just like those used in the Pearl station!). The fact that these composition books come in a set of three suggests that while severely overpriced – $14.95 for the set, plus shipping – they are packaged for eventual consumption, designed to be used and replaced. Although a relatively obscure tie-in product, these notebooks constitute a significant step in tie-in marketing: these are not just *Lost* collectibles, but a line of consumable goods sold on the brand name of Dharma.

While it may seem far-fetched to imagine the actual distribution and marketing of Dharma beer, macaroni and automobiles, the potential for further mobilization and capitalization on the Dharma brand seems conceivable – especially as other series such as *The Office* (Reveille Productions, 2005–) continue this trajectory by selling Dunder Mifflin T-shirts and paper products. Indeed, in 2007 industry analysts increasingly began to consider the merits of this kind of 'reverse product placement', in which marketers 'create a fictional brand in a fictional environment and then release it into the real world'.[30] Analysts are still unsure of the mass-market potential for reverse product placement, but consider the possibility that it could be more cost effective to launch a product through fiction than typical advertising and marketing channels. The Dharma brand may only be used to sell T-shirts and notebooks at the moment, but the possibility remains that it, and other fictional brands like it, might yet become greater sources of institutionalized revenue in their own right.

CONCLUSION

Ultimately, *Lost* represents the dissolution of boundaries between diegetic space and the space of consumption, allowing narrative, promotion and advertising to overlap. Mike Benson, ABC's senior marketing vice president, suggests that the industry look at marketing

> more like content ... If we can take the program, explore the stories and perpetuate the mystery ... and people can share this stuff, it furthers the relationship with the audience. We're crafting content, and we work with the sales departments and integrate them with the original marketing materials.[31]

While *Lost* heralded a narrative resurgence on US network television to counter the trend toward reality, it simultaneously succeeded in integrating the spaces of narrative, marketing and everyday reality. On television, fictional institutions like Dharma, Hanso, Widmore and so many others serve as the diegetic glue binding together networks of interrelated characters and actions. But when *Lost* diverges as a narrative, moving away from television and into other media and spaces of everyday life, those institutions begin to structure more than just the lives of television characters.

When fictional institutions like Dharma or Hanso become part of quotidian existence, quotidian activities can be subsumed underneath their institutional umbrellas: the actions of audiences and their movements between different platforms of media experience can now take place within the hyperdiegetic world. This is not, however, just a curious evolution in televisual form, but it is also a significant economic development, as the blurred boundaries between narrative consumption and the institutionally positioned experiences of everyday life make sponsors a part of the story world. Real-life corporations that enter into economic relations with fictional institutions can become a creative part of the everyday *Lost* experience. The Dharma–Hanso complex may not be as real as Jeep, *Monster.com* or Sprite, but its institutional relationships with them and to consumer life have increasingly become quite real.

Notes

1   Chad Raphael, 'The political economic origins of Reali-TV', in Susan Murray and Laurie Ouellette (eds), *Reality TV: Remaking Television Culture* (New York: New York University Press, 2004), p.122.

2   Ted Magder, 'The end of TV 101: reality programmes, formats, and the new business of television', in Murray and Ouellette (eds): *Reality TV*, p.152.

3   Jennifer L. Pozner, 'Triumph of the shill: reality TV lets marketers write the script', *Bitch: Feminist Response to Pop Culture* (spring 2004), pp.51–9.

4   Steve McClellan, 'Idol moments ahead for advertisers: Fox's third rendition is an orgy of integrated marketing', *Broadcasting and Cable* cxxxiv/1 (5 January 2004), p.20.

5   Matt Roush, 'Lost and found! An original idea', *Broadcasting and Cable* cxxxiv/41 (11 October 2004), p.44.

6   John Consoli, 'Nets to reduce repeats', *Mediaweek* xiv/21 (24 May 2004), pp.7–8.

7   Matthew Creamer, 'Don't call it TV: rebuilding for the video age', *Advertising Age* lxxvii/14 (3 April 2006), p.1.

8   Diane Mermigas, 'Television biz needs interactive foresight', *Hollywood Reporter* 390 (13 September 2005), pp.8, 53.

9   Christopher Anderson, *Hollywood TV: The Studio System in the Fifties* (Austin: University of Texas Press, 1994), p.155.

10   Jeffrey Sconce, 'What if? Charting television's new textual boundaries', in Lynn Spigel and Jan Olsson (eds), *Television After TV: Essays on a Medium in Transition* (Durham: Duke University Press, 2004), pp.94–5.

11   Kurt Lancaster, *Interacting with Babylon 5: Fan Performances in a Media Universe* (Austin: University of Texas Press, 2001), p.30.

12   Janet H. Murray, *Hamlet on the Holodeck: The Future of Narrative in Cyberspace* (New York: The Free Press, 1997), p.264. By suggesting viewers can experience events in person, she suggests that viewers can themselves be represented by some kind of avatar in the narrative world.

13   Jason Mittell, 'Narrative complexity in contemporary American television', *The Velvet Light Trap* lviii/1 (2006), pp.29–40.

14   Will Brooker, 'Living on Dawson's Creek: teen viewers, cultural convergence, and television overflow', *International Journal of Cultural Studies* iv/4 (2001), pp.448–55.

15   Murray: *Hamlet on the Holodeck*, p.254.

16   Henry Jenkins, *Convergence Culture: When Old and New Media Collide* (New York: New York University Press, 2006), p.2. See also John Caldwell, 'Convergence TV: aggregating form and repurposing content in the culture of conglomeration', in Spigel and Olsson (eds): *Television After TV*, pp.41–74.

17   Jenkins: *Convergence Culture*, pp.20–1.

18   Matt Hills, *Fan Cultures* (London: Routledge, 2002), p.137.

19   Claire Atkinson, 'Networks add alternatives to traditional on-air promos', *Advertising Age* lxxv/25 (21 June 2004), p.6.

20   See John Consoli, 'Nets boost nontraditional efforts despite higher cost', *Adweek* xlvi/35 (12 September 2005), p.7; Jim Finkle, 'New shows, new marketing', *Broadcasting and Cable* cxxxv/8 (21 February 2005), p.8.

21   A.J. Frutkin, 'Big networks differ on best use of "third screen"', *Adweek* 47.19 (8 May 2006), p. 8; Anne Becker, 'ABC's digital evangelists', *Broadcasting & Cable* 136/13 (27 March 2006), p. 13.

22   Jim Edwards, 'Time-shifted viewing figures offer dramatic reality check', *Brandweek* xlvii/45 (11 December 2006), p.9.

23   Ibid.

24   Marc Berman, 'Dy-no-mite!', *Mediaweek* xiv/41 (15 November 2004), p.34.

25 Jennifer Armstrong, 'Love, labor, *Lost*', *Entertainment Weekly* 838/839 (9 September 2005), pp.28–33.

26 Kate MacArthur, 'Bea Perez', *Advertising Age* lxxvii/38 (18 September 2006), p.S4.

27 For more on the concept of 'collective intelligence' see Pierre Levy, *Collective Intelligence: Mankind's Emerging World in Cyberspace* (Cambridge: Perseus Books, 1997). For direct application of Levy's work to media consumption, see Henry Jenkins, 'Interactive audiences?', in Virginia Nightingale and Karen Ross (eds), *Critical Readings: Media and Audiences* (Maidenhead: Open University Press, 2003), pp.279–95. See also Chapter IV in this volume.

28 Marie-Laure Ryan, *Narrative as Virtual Reality: Immersion and Interactivity in Literature and Electronic Media* (Baltimore: The Johns Hopkins University Press, 2001), p.304.

29 Claire Atkinson, 'Getting creative with web games', *Advertising Age* lxxvii/37 (11 September 2006), p.S4.

30 Todd Wasserman, 'Forward thinkers push reverse product placement', *Brandweek.com* (29 January 2007), available at *www.brandweek.com/bw/news/recent_display.jsp?vnu_content_id=1003538681*.

31 Quote in Atkinson: 'Getting creative with web games', p.S4.

IV. Television Out of Time:
Watching Cult Shows on Download

Will Brooker

O n 4 November 2005, Keith, a fan of the TV show *Lost*, visited a gallery in Cleveland. He found a set of business cards lying innocently in small stacks, and picked one up to examine it. It looked like a lottery ticket, with a tropical resort vacation as the prize. Against a background of an Oceanic Airlines logo and a beach scene, the card read 'Match your numbers at *theislandiswaiting.com*.' and 'The Island is waiting.' He scratched the foil off with a fingertip and found a set of digits: 4, 8, 15, 16, 23, 42.

He recognised the numbers. To him, they weren't just numbers but 'The Numbers', the recurring sequence from the first two seasons of *Lost*. He recognised the brand name, too. It was an Oceanic flight that had crashed in the first episode, leaving the survivors stranded. Of course, he knew what the Island was. Keith went straight to his computer, scanned the cards and uploaded them to his favourite discussion board, sharing them with a community of fellow fans he'd never met. The next episode of *Lost* wasn't scheduled to be broadcast for another six days, but for Keith and his online friends, the story and its fictional world could occupy their whole week, seeping into their everyday lives both on and off the computer. Following cult television is now a lifestyle experience.

This chapter focuses on the practice of watching cult series as video files on a personal computer. It suggests key ways in which this experience differs from the conventional viewing of broadcast television at the time scheduled by the network, usually in a shared living area, on a television set some distance from the viewer. My chapter is based on the premise that watching a television show as a digital file on a PC screen, with text and extra-textual materials adjacent to each other as equivalent windows, is quite distinct from watching the show on one screen, as live TV, and having the Internet on another. Downloaded TV gives the viewer the ability to freeze the fiction and click just a millimetre to the left to travel down 'rabbit-holes' into ARG spin-offs and simulation sites (sim-sites), or to minimise the show to check the current frame against an online reference, then grab the image, paste it into a discussion board and wait for the replies.

And while the forensic analysis permitted by downloads is also integral to DVD viewing, by the time a show like *Lost* reaches DVD, the season is complete, a finished text. The case is closed, the detection is over. Watching on download, by contrast, combines the ability to study each shot in close detail with the intensity and immediacy of live TV – there is an urgency for study, for the sharing of new information, for the solving of puzzles and the opportunity for community kudos, before the next episode comes online for download in a week's time.

My key case study is the cult US TV series *Lost*, with contextual reference to the BBC TV series *Life on Mars* (2006–7), the three most recent seasons of *Doctor Who* (BBC, 2005–7) and the first season of NBC's *Heroes* (NBC Universal Television, 2006–7). For examples of audience response, I draw mainly on the discussion board Barbelith (*www.barbelith.com*), whose 'Film, TV and Theatre' forum represents one subsection of a broad online community.

OVERFLOW

When watching a show on a PC, using a device like Windows Media Player, the TV 'screen' is just one window among others. The larger collage can comprise Internet sites both fan-based and commercial; music libraries and podcasts, chat programmes like MSN, webcams, ITunes, MySpace and YouTube. Though the show's borders are protected from and isolated from other television, they are threatened by – even invaded by – these other distractions. Some of these surrounding windows may have the same effect as the interruptions on television as the viewer zaps channels or loses attention during a commercial break, creating what we might call an *interflow* – where the TV 'screen', a media player, is in competition with various other equally demanding 'screens' within a larger screen, and the viewer's attention shifts from one window to the other within the broader frame, perhaps when they pause the TV text to answer a chat request or listen to a specific track, then return to the narrative. The viewer is creating his or her own audio-visual montage, and the television text becomes, potentially, even more choppy and fragmented than it would during a conventional broadcast.

However, this collage of smaller screens within the PC frame can also intensify the viewer's involvement in the fiction and enable a more active engagement with the text. This is the cross-platform convergence I called *overflow*,[1] whereby dedicated Internet sites (usually officially produced) extend the fictional world through simulation – as with, for instance, a tourist site for the imaginary school, church and restaurants from *Dawson's Creek* (Outerbank Entertainment, 1998–2003) – and invite the viewer's deeper involvement through interaction with the text's location and characters – for instance, on a forum where participants could talk to the fictional website developers of BBC2's *Attachments* (World Productions, 2000).[2]

Henry Jenkins dubs the phenomenon 'transmedia storytelling', taking *The Matrix* (Andy and Larry Wachowski, 1999) as a case study that

> unfolds across multiple media platforms, with each new text making a distinctive and valuable contribution to the whole ... a story might be introduced in a film, expanded through television, novels, and comic; its world might be explored through game play or experienced as an amusement park attraction.[3]

He dates the first transmedia story of this type back to *The Blair Witch Project* (Daniel Myrick/Eduardo Sanchez) in 1999, and presents as another example the complex network of Internet-based puzzles that launched as a cross-promotion for Steven Spielberg's film *A.I.* (2001) – but to the code-cracking community involved in it, this became far more immersive and important than the movie itself.[4] *Donnie Darko*, directed by Richard Kelly in the same year, was backed up by a similar, albeit smaller, online labyrinth of cryptic challenges.

The overflow phenomenon has increased since I first wrote about it in 2001, and almost every mainstream TV show will now at least pay lip-service to Internet immersion, offering some official online reference to its fictional world, while a few develop into hugely complex

cross-platform universes. For example, *Doctor Who*'s web presence offers downloadable trailers, and behind-the-scenes footage and games
(on a system of scrolling menus that creates further windows within
the window and thus invites an internal wander around the website's
information and distractions, a microcosm of the broader pattern I
suggested above). However, many of the weekly episodes were backed
up with what we might call sim-sites: web pages that, rather than being 'about' *Doctor Who* as a television programme, treated its mythos
as fact and allow an exploration of the corporation that created the
Cybermen, the stately home Torchwood House, or the school that was
overrun by Krillitane aliens, for example. These sites went online as
the relevant episode was broadcast, without fanfare or announcement,
and could only be discovered by diligent viewers who typed names or
locations from that week's show into a search engine.[5] James Goss,
who produces the BBC's cult television tie-in sites, described this complex network as 'the most ambitious online fictional world ever'.[6]

Lost went even further, however, pushing the boundaries to create not just a world, but an alternate universe that overlapped and
merged with our own. In April 2006, ABC announced 'The *Lost* Experience', a broadly cross-platform interactive extension of the show's
narrative world, described by its producers as a 'hybrid between content and marketing'[7] and by its players as an ARG, or alternate reality game. Alternate reality gaming is also known as 'beasting', after
the pioneering *A.I.* project (dubbed 'The Beast' by its creators), and
'unfiction'. This latter term lends its name to an online community
that serves as a central hub for ongoing puzzle-solving. *Unfiction.com*
defines ARGs as

> an interactive fusion of creative writing, puzzle-solving, and team-
> building, with a dose of role playing thrown in. It utilizes several
> forms of media in order to pass clues to the players, who solve puz-
> zles in order to win pieces of the story being played out. Many times,
> the puzzles that must be solved cannot be solved alone. This genre
> of game almost requires participation in a group or community that
> works together to win past the more difficult hurdles.[8]

'The *Lost* Experience' was unusual, even within ARG culture. It widened the scope of media overflow from Internet puzzles (such as *www.
thehansofoundation.org* another sim-site for a fictional organisation)

to an astonishing range of cross-platform texts: TV advertisements sponsored by Sprite, Jeep and Verizon that linked to Hanso/*Lost*-themed websites and integrated the show's mythos and mysteries with the product's branding; telephone numbers with pre-recorded voicemail messages; advertisements in real-world newspapers advertising a novel (*Bad Twin*) by a fictional character (Gary Troup) within the show; fictional interviews with this author on the Amazon and Barnes & Noble websites; the novel itself, which became a bestseller; online memos from Hugh MacIntyre, the fictional head of the Hanso Foundation, to the real-life president of Hyperion books, calling for the pulping of *Bad Twin*; an appearance from the fictional character Hugh MacIntyre, Hanso's Communications Director, on the real-life talk show *Jimmy Kimmel Live*; messages hidden in the source code of the Hanso Foundation site; and a stunt at the 22 July ComicCon convention in San Diego, where an actress interrupted a session with challenges about the Hanso Foundation and gave a website address before being escorted out. The website was *Hansoexposed.com*, and the actress was playing Rachel Blake, a fictional hacker and blogger who, within the alternate reality of 'The *Lost* Experience', was attempting to take down the Hanso Foundation and its president, Thomas Mittelwerk. Visitors to *Hansoexposed.com* were led into the final stage of the game, which involved finding 70 'glyphs' – enigmatic, iconic images with accompanying codes – and entering them into the website to release 70 sections of video footage, out of its proper sequence.[9] (For more on this see Chapter III in this volume.) Perhaps the most remarkable aspect of the puzzle is the way the glyphs were hidden; and, in turn, that they were found at all. The completed video has been uploaded by fans to YouTube: *www.youtube.com/timdorr*.

Rachel claims on *Hansoexposed.com* that she 'CAN'T TRUST THE MAINSTREAM MEDIA – CAN'T TRUST THE HANSO FOUNDATION DOESN'T HAVE ITS HOOKS IN EVERY LAST ONE OF THEM. SO I'M HIDING IT – EVERYWHERE ON THE WEB', but in fact the glyphs were scattered not just on dedicated websites and specially created blogs, but in various media locations – the armbands worn by the show's producers at ComicCon, a mug on the *Jimmy Kimmel Live* show, a Channel 4 broadcast of *Lost* – and even in real life. Glyphs were discovered in Sydney shop and hotel windows, in London's Greenwich Park, and in Times Square, New York. A final website address was provided on the wrappers of

'Apollo' chocolate bars – a brand created for and featured in the show – which were given out at key locations and specified times in the UK, USA and Australia.

This overflow of television fiction into geographical reality – to use the now-quaint 1990s terms, from 'cyberspace' into 'meatspace' – is still rare at the time of writing. The business cards Keith discovered, like the glyphs scattered in Sydney and Greenwich, are intriguing evidence of this more recent tendency for fiction to spill over into physical reality. Watching *Lost* on download, with the 'TV screen' adjacent to other Internet windows (YouTube, Lostpedia, Unfiction, and so on) clearly assists this process of deep involvement and sustained detection over months at a time. The viewer – or perhaps we should use another word, such as player or participant – can delve like a hacker into the levels of the show's intrigue, then return with a single click to the neighbouring window where the primary text, whether fan video, *Lost* episode, chat show or advertisement, is freeze-framed for analysis. Just as the viewer has become something else, so the show has also transformed, into something that resembles a PC game but goes beyond those boundaries too, as it crosses over into real life and erodes the boundaries between fact and fiction – a sign, perhaps, of the extreme overflow that will doubtless become increasingly more common with cult television in future.

However, while *Lost* remains remarkable even now for its ambitious use of media other than the Internet (newspapers, books, conventions, broadcast television), much of the detection involved could have been carried out online, with patient investigation of various websites – crucially, though some clues lay outside the Internet, they were immediately filmed or photographed and uploaded to online discussion communities where they could be shared. Glyphs discovered in real-life were rushed onto the Internet so the finder could gain bragging rights and credit, but the challenge also required global, group engagement rather than solitary effort. Seventy clues hidden across multiple websites in London, New York and Sydney could not feasibly be tracked down by one person alone: 'The *Lost* Experience' overflowed offline, but solving the puzzle depended on the Internet.

After the event, *Lostpedia.com* recorded all the resources and abilities needed to solve the ARG: among the diverse qualifications were 'working knowledge of trigonometry', 'Korean language fluency', 'subscriptions to *People Magazine*' and 'Vigenère decoder', but an on-line connection headed the list. It came with an important postscript: 'These are the tools used by the "The *Lost* Experience" community to solve the puzzles. The expectation was not that one individual working alone could or would solve all the clues by themselves.'[10] This is the phenomenon described by Jenkins (after Pierre Lévy) as 'collective intelligence' – 'the ability of virtual communities to leverage the combined expertise of their members'.[11] This is the Internet community as *hive mind*, pooling the abilities, knowledge and global resources of its members into a formidable problem-solving unit. Jenkins' case study is the group of 'spoilers' who draw on their contacts with travel agents, government officials and satellite companies to work out what will happen on the CBS reality show *Survivor* (Mark Burnett Productions, 2000–) before broadcast, pitting their wits against producer Mark Burnett.[12]

The notion of a group mind, a pooling of resources, a sense of many-heads-better-than-one, permeates the Internet – from review websites like Rotten Tomatoes (*www.rottentomatoes.com*) and Metacritic (*www.metacritic.com*), which offer a score for films and novels based on an average of all the available opinions, to Wikipedia (*www.wikipedia.org*) the free, open-source authority written and edited by thousands of volunteers.[13] Barbelith itself runs through an 'adhocracy'[14] of 'distributed moderation', whereby no decision can be made without a general agreement from volunteer-administrators: a strategy aimed to 'alleviate the possibilities of abuse and balance workloads between [the community's] citizenry'.[15] As television narratives become increasingly transmedia, evolving into immersive worlds and challenges beyond the screen's boundary, they increasingly become a matter for collective viewing and discussion, rather than individual engagement; but they also, as I will explore further below, start to blur the boundary between viewer and participant.

ONLINE COMMUNITY

The TV 'screen', as media player, sits alongside many other windows. One of those windows is often a community discussion board. A significant part of the cult television experience involves sharing theories, bouncing ideas off fellow fans, picking apart the last episode and guessing about those to come – and this has been the case since the early, pre-Web days of Usenet newsgroups in the late 1980s.[16] When viewing episodes on the PC, with the TV show playing or freeze-framed on the computer screen, the discussion board is obviously in much closer proximity to the user/viewer than in the conventional set-up, where the TV and computers are in separate rooms; and it holds the same textual status, as a neighbouring window.

Because of the discrepancies between broadcast schedules in different countries and on different channels, however, *Lost*'s online communities become fragmented, broken down into subcategories to avoid spoilers for those viewers who are watching earlier episodes in the same season. Those watching on download have to fit into one or other of these categories, depending on their own self-governed viewing schedule of the available episodes. If a show is being downloaded as it is broadcast, then the fan experiences no such disadvantage – he or she is watching the episode just after others have watched it on TV, or may even watch it conventionally on television, then download the text for more detailed study – but the *Lost* follower who downloads a season in bulk for 'binge' viewing may find him or herself isolated and out of time, with no obvious place within an online community that, perhaps quaintly, remains structured around traditional broadcast schedules and global geography.[17]

Barbelith.com, for instance, features *Lost* discussion threads for US viewers, UK viewers (on Channel 4, and the digital channel E4), Irish viewers, and those 'website viewers', or user/participants, who choose to explore the story through its overflow sites. Watching on download can put the lone viewer in an isolated position – Abercrombie and Longhurst's atomised 'fan' category – and to join the 'cultists' and 'enthusiasts', textually productive within a community network, he or she has to adapt.[18] In other words, to be part of the collective intelligence, you have to pace yourself along with the majority.

The forums are often given to discussing the relative pros and cons of watching drip by drip, following the producers' intended rhythm of weekly episodes – which are, frustratingly, often broken by broadcast TV's idiosyncrasies – or in larger chunks, consuming *Lost* in marathon sessions on the PC. The former retains the intended pattern of suspense and cliffhangers, and gives a sense of 'appointment television', with the traditional excitement of sitting down at a certain time, knowing that millions of others are doing exactly the same – offering a feeling of community even if the TV viewer is sitting alone.[19] Following the scheduled broadcasts also keeps the viewer in sync with the carefully scheduled cross-platform overflow such as Hanso commercials, chat-show appearances and newspaper advertisements. Despite predictions at the turn of the century that 'appointment television' would soon be 'a thing of the past',[20] keeping to the producers' intended timing has its benefits, and its followers. Resisting the producers' scheduling, though, brings its own advantages. One online fan, posting in February 2005, during the early months of *Lost*'s first season, pitied anyone still tied to the traditional practice of weekly viewing. 'E-n: I can't imagine what having to wait weeks for each episode must be like. Watching them in a week-long info burst is a fantastic way to catch all the little mysteries that pass by.'[21] In October 2005, another viewer complained bitterly about being dependent on the scattergun, sporadic broadcast schedule. 'Yotsuba and Benjamin: Only three new episodes between now and January. I fucking hate you sometimes, Television.'[22]

During February 2006, fans debated the relative advantages of both forms, at length:

> *Yawn:* Watched the first ten fuckers o season two t'other day. Excellent. Really excellent. The 'other 48 days' was harrowing man, fucking grim. Once a week never again.
>
> *Boboss:* I like the weekly format because of what the spaces in between episodes make possible: the speculation and the anticipation, coming to communities like this and chatting about last week's cliffhanger, going through frame-by-frame trying to spot Easter eggs. People think they want the answers now, and getting a slew of answers would be very pleasurable, but only momentarily.
>
> *Keith Hypnopompia:* Totally agree, Boboss. It's more like taking leisurely time with a good book, which is the main thing I enjoy about plot/arc driven television these days.
>
> *Boboss:* The book analogy holds, but I was working on a post earlier that compared enjoying *Lost* to delaying orgasm...
>
> *Yawn:* I'm usually with you on this – but gorging on ten episodes in two blocks of five was really fucking enjoyable. I'm thinking it'd be cool to wait till the rest of the series is done and then do another binge.
>
> *Sleazenation:* I'm with Yawn on this one – If I hadn't seen the first 12 episodes back to back I probably wouldn't still be watching this...[23]

By March, some of the contributors who had previously defended the intended structure of weekly broadcasts were starting to change their minds, frustrated by the American television practice of annual 'sweeps':

> *Sleazenation:* Isn't it going to be three weeks till the next episode? Will you even remember that your interest in the show has been rekindled in a month or so time...
>
> *Robert B:* 3 weeks? What's going on with this season? I watched the first on DVD so, was it like this as well? Sporadic...
>
> *Boboss:* American network television is what's going on with this show. I think the problem effectively comes down to the Sweeps (a key feature of the US ratings system), the results of which have a significant knock-on effect for the network's advertising revenue. In order to attract high viewing figures over the Sweeps periods (Feburary, May, July and November) the networks pull out the stops and air their most popular shows – or shows that are predicted to be very popular. Hence the fact that *Lost* gets spread out weirdly across the year. Personally I think this kind of programming does shows no favours whatsoever in that it could well damage them over the long term.[24]

Downloading, then, has the disadvantage of placing the fan outside the scheduled structure and therefore outside an obvious community – obliging him or her to catch up with or slow down to join existing discussions, which are still dominated by weekly episodes. The comments above suggest, though, that this focus on the broadcast text may be undergoing a gradual shift, as viewers realise that loyalty to the network schedule often results in frustrating waits between episodes. If the networks fail to keep to the narrative's intended rhythm, then fans will have to find that rhythm for themselves, opting, according to their own tastes, between immersive 'binge' sessions and more leisurely, weekly doses that respect, and try accurately to reproduce, the producers' intended cliffhangers and paced arcs. In some cases, the fan is even obliged to reorder the episodes to retain the intended narrative. Joss Whedon's *Firefly* (Twentieth Century Fox Television, 2002) was originally broadcast in the wrong order and cancelled before its completion; re-viewing the series on download enabled the show's followers to shape the story in the way Whedon originally planned it.

We should remember though, that this is not a case of having to choose one form or the other, whether download or broadcast. Boboss' stated preference for weekly episodes, with the space between each instalment filled by discussion and 'going through frame-by-frame trying to spot Easter eggs', highlights the fact that the traditional 'appointment' with a television show, as part of a broader community all watching at the same time, can be combined with – indeed, can be the overture and prelude to – a slower and more careful study of the same episode on downloaded video during the week, as part of a more specialised online community group.

FORENSIC DETECTION

I suggested that the nature of the download TV 'screen' as one feature of a broader interface (alongside search windows, sim-sites and the like) encourages, or at least enables, entry through those multiple *windows* – which in this case become portals, or, in ARG terminology, 'rabbit-holes' – into a complex, semi-fictional world that transforms a 'show' (something we sit back and watch) into an experience (something we participate in; something we live with, like a journey or a vacation).

The nature of the downloaded text, with immediate, crystal-clear freeze-frame, and the proximity of the viewer to the screen – a matter of inches, rather than the full space of a domestic living area between the TV set and the sofa – also encourages and invites close analysis and forensic detection. DVD technology has already enabled this frame-by-frame study, complete with rewind and slow motion. Prior to DVD and download culture, dedicated fans managed close analysis of cult texts from video and even from broadcast TV as it was screened, scribbling frantic notes on yellow pads and, as Henry Jenkins' study of *Twin Peaks* followers suggested in 1995, 'making the rest of us feel stupid'.[25] Like overflow, then, the forensic detective analysis of cult TV can be dated back at least to the early 1990s. Jenkins notes that

> *Hill Street Blues* (1981–7) was the first major success story of the videotape era ... *Twin Peaks* (1990–1) was one of the first new cult television series to develop an important Internet following. These series, with their ever-more elaborate use of story

arcs and program history, rewarded a viewer who carefully scrutinized the images using the freeze-frame function, who watched and rewatched the episodes on video tape, and who used the Internet as a vehicle for discussion with a larger interpretive community and the Web as a means of annotation.[26]

Watching the TV text as a downloaded video clip simply facilitates this approach, arguably making forensic analysis a wider practice, not just confined to what Jenkins' *Twin Peaks* study suggests was an obsessive minority even among newsgroup users from 1990.

This close analysis – what Laura Mulvey[27] calls 'interactive spectatorship', reconfiguring the viewer into an editor, is frequently invited, even necessitated by scenes in recent cult television, which involve fast-moving montages of subliminal images and background details that require freeze-frame and enhancement. Viewers, in some cases, have to use this method of textual detection to piece together clues to narrative and character – suggesting in turn that cult television shows may now be shot and edited with an eye to this specific mode of viewing, just as feature films, according to Aaron Barlow, are currently made for the DVD experience (close analysis, rewind, directors' commentaries) rather than for the less profitable market, and very different aesthetic, of conventional cinema viewing.[28]

Jenkins writes along similar lines about 1990s television:

> The character of American television has been fundamentally altered as television producers have begun to incorporate a more sophisticated understanding of the active audience into their production decisions. The result has been the conscious production of cult-friendly programs like *The X-Files*, *The Simpsons*, *Buffy the Vampire Slayer*, *Dawson's Creek*, *Xena*, and *Babylon 5*, among many, many others. These series build in opportunities for audience participation and elaboration, recognizing our pleasure in backstory, in-jokes, foreshadowing, and encrypted information; adding fuel to our Net discussions; providing rationales for rereading; offering raw materials for our cultural production; and using the online world to provide unprecedented access to the behind-the-scenes creative decisions shaping the series' development.[29]

As Jenkins suggests, rereading and decrypting information, the process of close analysis and the investigation of dedicated Internet sites are closely related, bound together in this kind of fan engagement with cult television. Like the surrounding intertexts of 'The *Lost* Experience', and to a lesser extent the *Doctor Who* fictional online world, the sequences that require freeze-framed analysis are built in to the text, part of the puzzle constructed by producers for the viewers to solve, part of the enjoyable game between creator and fan. Frequently the two processes overlap, again suggesting the importance of having Internet and TV screen in adjacent windows – a freeze-frame can be grabbed, pasted into a graphics program, uploaded to a discussion board and analysed by other fans, or decoded with the help of further search windows and websites.

'Live Together, Die Alone' (2.23), for instance, briefly showed hieroglyphics on the countdown timer in an underground bunker. The image was swiftly posted online for analysis,[30] linked to a translation[31] and analysed on several other discussion forums, including Barbelith:

> *Buttergun:* those ARE Egyptian Hieroglyphs. I'm getting my PhD translating them. The true meaning of the message also depends on the placement of the glyphs, and their order. It can only mean 'cause to die' or 'death' if there is a glyph of a man lying down. And since the feather of Maat (justice, truth, balance) was revealed, it could not have any meaning related to death.[32]

The same process of freeze-framing, online research, analysis and discussion, combining individual study and group-sharing of ideas, recurred for many sequences within *Lost* – such as the appearance of the Dharma Initiative logos (Shark, Arrow, Swan) in the background or fleetingly within shots, glimpses of The Others, the CGI smoke, and backwards or distorted speech. The 'Blast Doors' provided particularly rich material: featured for only a few seconds in 'Lockdown' (2.17) when a map was revealed under temporary black light, they were pored over, reworked and cleaned up, with the handwritten scrawl deciphered and the Latin captions translated.[33]

On occasion, some fans complained sardonically about the show's increasing reliance on off-air puzzle-solving:

> All over is squiggly writing and arrows and such. Great. Something else I won't be able to fully appreciate because I won't buy a television that costs more than my first car, and I don't have Adobe Photoshop at home.[34]

At other times, the enthusiasm for spotting 'Easter eggs' or half-hidden visual clues led community members to search, self-parodically, for meaning in continuity errors:

> *Boboss:* Anyone notice a gloved hand poking into frame during the final horse scene? An animal trainer perhaps?
>
> *Keith Hypnopompia:* haha, i didn't notice that. i'll have to check it out again. Unless … OMG! TEH OTHERS SET TEH HORSE LOOSE TO MESS WTIH KATE!!!@@#!!![35]

Lost's third season continued this dynamic, with online communities rapidly spotting every possible clue, however briefly glimpsed. Some viewers were happy to store the knowledge away, trusting it would be relevant later, while others, frustrated by season two's unsolved mysteries, declared that they had been pushed too far – although this didn't seem to stop them watching, or contributing to the discussion:

> *Buttergun:* The big 'clue' this week was the photo of the old lady from the previous Desmond-centered episode. She was seen briefly in a photo on the head monk's desk, standing beside the head monk himself.
>
> I'm sure this is causing much 'holy shit!!!' among *Lost*-freaks, but to me … I think it's yet another example of the producers giving bullshit 'clues' which will ultimately lead nowhere.
>
> The thing is, it would be fine if *Lost* had been around for years and years and had a solid track record, i.e. the *Simpsons* – clever little injokes like this would be fine. But what with its disastrous second season and early third, with its slipping ratings, with its frustrating resistance to answer anything – combined with its easy reliance on spinning new threads – it just hasn't earned the right to be so clever.[36]

Other fans, in other communities, retained their trust in the producers. MelissaAndria, on the Television Without Pity (TWOP) forum, logged the same background detail[37] and assumed without question that even the image's bad quality was intentional, without needing a reason: 'Oh, rest assured. We were supposed to see it and and we were supposed to notice how badly it was Photoshopped. Why? I haven't a clue.'[38]

While the producers had tested some viewers' patience too far, apparently planting clues with no payoff, some of the briefly revealed details repaid close attention – enough to justify this painstaking forensic approach. *Lostpedia.com*'s entry 'Satellite Phone' noted, of the episode 'Catch-22' (3.17): 'They comment that the battery seems to be dead, but a closer examination of the screen shows the alert, "Internal Error"... The phone was receiving a signal strength of "three bars".'[39] The episode 'The Brig' (3.19) confirmed that the phone worked after all: the TWOP posters had proved themselves one step ahead of Desmond, Charlie, Hurley and Jin, able to examine a key prop more carefully than the people on the island itself.

Again, the idea of the TV text as puzzle is not new – *Twin Peaks* is a celebrated example, but Dennis Potter's BBC drama *The Singing Detective* (1986) used very similar techniques of layered dream sequences, fantasies and flashbacks. What distinguishes these more recent cult TV shows, apart from their central position in a broader network of pan-media, cross-platform texts, is the speed of the cutting, which in many cases requires analysis of extremely brief, almost subliminal shots, and the producers' awareness that many of the viewers have access to a discussion forum to pool ideas and engage in the enjoyable process of community puzzle-solving.[40]

The technique of building themes or clues across a wider arc – as with *Lost*'s mysterious 'numbers' and Dharma logos, like *Doctor Who*'s seeding of 'Bad Wolf', 'Torchwood' and 'Mr Saxon' 'arc-words' across the 2006–7 seasons, and the recurring, almost subliminal flashbacks in the 2006 season of *Life On Mars* – was also built, on an even grander scale of five seasons, into *Babylon 5* (Babylonian Productions, 1993–8). Creator Michael Straczynski called this concept 'holographic storytelling':

> Not side-by-side images, but *overlapping* images, like old fashioned photographic plates stacked up one on top of the other. Each has a piece of the whole picture. When you line them all up, one behind the other, and look through them all at once, you realize what the picture is. It's three-dimensional storytelling.[41]

Of course, this concept is not new to twenty-first century television, or even 1990s television. What is notable is that this form of storytelling is becoming far more common. Just as 'overflow' and simulation sites were considered an experimental concept in 2000, and have now developed to the point where all shows extend the show beyond the primary text to some degree (and a few have extended into vastly complex, pan-media phenomena), so techniques that were considered auteurist exceptions in 1986 (Dennis Potter), 1990 (David Lynch) and 1993 (Michael Straczynski) are now becoming integral to the most mainstream, popular, commercially successful and long-running shows on British and US television.

The dedicated website for the commercial and critical hit show *Heroes* (Tailwind Productions, 2006–)[42] includes an online graphic novel that expands on the events of last week's show and a blog by one of its key characters, Hiro Nakamura, encouraging visitors' participation in the fiction. The comments treat Hiro as a real individual, and in turn place the fans at least partly within the world of *Heroes*, positioning them as one of a vast crowd of minor characters within the extended story world.

> Nakamura-san,
>
> I think I am a little bit like you, but opposite. I have an office job and love Japan and Japanese popular culture.
>
> Why do you love Star Trek when Yamato is so much better? ~_^ I am silly. Please forgive me! It is probably because Star Trek is different – in the same way you've always wanted to be different. To like Yamato is to be different here. Only a few people know about it.[43]

Visitors can download desktop images and icons, and can click on hidden points in the site's illustrations to read documents from the fictional universe. The most remarkable aspect of this site is that it is no longer remarkable – this is the bottom level, the expected baseline of online presence for a mainstream television show, especially one with science-fiction trappings and cult potential.

At a further remove, the character Claire Bennet (like Martha Jones from the 2007 season of *Doctor Who*) has a MySpace profile where visitors respond to her as a real friend and contact, again entering into the fiction and casting themselves as secondary characters:

> Oh my gosh your in the hospital! Get well soon.
>
> Hi Claire. I am an associate of your father. Keep up the good work with your grades and cheerleading!

> When you crashed with Brody into that wall I was inside the building
> and the collision knocked my monitor over and into my lap and I was
> electrocuted after my monitor exploded. Thanks jerk.[44]

Barbelith's *Heroes* fans, in the first month of broadcast, were already
cross-referencing the TV text against their shared knowledge of comic
book mythos (explaining the characters' powers through comparison
to the DC and Marvel heroes Wolverine, Rogue and Amazo), screen-
grabbing and enhancing shadowy images of 'Future Hiro' to examine
whether he was carrying a *katana*, and identifying the mysterious,
iconic images – nicknamed the Helix and the Eclipse – that, like The
Numbers and Bad Wolf, recur throughout the show's *mise-en-scène*.
From 19 January 2007 the show was supplemented with its own ARG,
'The *Heroes* 360 Experience', constructed from a new network of simulation sites – a viewer–participant could now jump directly from Mr
Saxon's election propaganda to Nathan Petrelli's congressional campaign webpages.[45]

In the final week of May 2007, when both *Lost* and *Heroes*
wrapped up their season finales, some online fans clearly felt that
their forensic examination of freeze-framed images and digitally enhanced screen-grabs had paid off. The careful study of *Lost*'s satellite
phone was fully rewarded when the working device played a key role
in the season three finale; and by extension, this careful method of
viewing also seemed fully validated: these were puzzles deliberately
planted by the producers, rather than continuity errors or incidental details of prop and set design. However, there were still voices of
dissent, with the forensic study method greeted by some discussion-
board contributors with impatience or contempt. A week after *Lost*
fansites slowed and froze the brief glimpses of a new character, Jacob
('The Man Behind the Curtain', 3.20), running footage at half-speed
and Photoshopping the shadowy images of Jacob's profile with shots
of John Locke (Terry O'Quinn),[46] *Heroes* discussion threads attempted
the same analytic comparison on a blink-and-miss-it shot of George
Takei's eyes.

'There are some odd distortions from the surface of the blade that
could be taken to be clues,' the author of one post offered. 'So here's
something to fuel more speculation.'[47] 'For fuck's sake', another fan
snapped, clearly losing patience with not just this specific compari-

son, but the whole approach. '*Lost* and the Internet have a lot to answer for.'[48]

On a broader note, acknowledging wearily that television has become far more than just the primary 45-minute text, one contributor complained, 'Man, this makes watching a TV show *so much work*.'[49] This 'work', though, for those who chose to undertake it, is driven by the pleasures of detection and community – and is based increasingly around the crossing of the boundaries between fiction and the real world. As ARG clues spill over into physical space, so online visitors to characters' websites now construct themselves as part of the story world, and the primary texts are beginning to play with this dynamic.

Lost's third season introduced teasing nods in dialogue that treated the viewer as a confidante – lines pre-empting or echoing fan discourse, such as an incredulous 'Who are you?' when a previously unseen character suddenly took centre stage, or 'Are you two arguing about your favorite Other?', both delivered with a slight wink by the series' charming con man Sawyer (Josh Holloway). Such lines subtly softened the boundary between the fiction and its viewers, flattering fans with another little in-joke and drawing them a little further into the story world. *Heroes*, similarly, knowingly tipped its hat to discussion-board etiquette by having one of its characters, comic book artist Isaac Mendez, warn a fan not to post up any spoiler threads, and the 'Blink' (3.10) episode of *Doctor Who* offered another playful nod: a video store owner discovers the Doctor in a series of DVD Easter Eggs and obsessively discusses the minutiae of the footage with his Internet community.

Watching television on download plays an important part in allowing us to enter the spaces of cult fiction, inviting us to join the community of characters as well as pooling our information and detective skills with a community of fans. As we click from a 'TV screen' to a fictional blog, at the same time interacting with the show's protagonist and our fellow viewers, participating in the narrative and solving the producers' puzzles, we can all be heroes. A note of caution, though, in conclusion. So far none of the clues so carefully examined by these fan communities, whether selected from primary texts or discovered in secondary sources – whether translated maps, grabbed and enhanced flash-frames, supplementary websites, half-hidden arc-words or online graphic novels – have provided any information *fundamentally necessary* to an understanding of the plot or characters. They enable pleasurable puzzle-solving and community bonding, and allow dedicated fans to work out narrative developments in advance, but the information is invariably offered more directly, albeit some time later, to viewers who choose to watch more conventionally – that is, without recourse to screen-grabs, sim-sites or discussion forums.

The *Doctor Who* arc-words tease an alert observer and lead to online pockets of privileged information, but the series inevitably reveals all these secrets and more in the final two episodes of each season. *Life On Mars*' subliminal images extended the viewing experience by setting fans who chose to freeze-frame each flashback an enjoyable challenge each week, but they proved to be decorative rather than integral to the narrative arc, and this storytelling device was largely abandoned in the second series. 'The *Lost* Experience' filled in some historical gaps about the Hanso Foundation, but while this provided participants with a richer level of background detail and depth to the third season, understanding that the Numbers were also called the Valenzetti Equation was entirely superfluous to the show's primary narrative: as the bunker imploded in the finale of season two, translating the countdown's hieroglyphs also turned out to be an ultimately pointless exercise. *Heroes* offered a teasing recurrence of its own icons, the Helix and the Eclipse, in the final minutes of its last episode ('How to Stop an Exploding Man', 1.23), but its closing voiceover implied, with another knowing nod to fans, that the true reward in this puzzle-solving was community bonding:

> The answer to this quest, this need to solve life's mysteries finally shows itself … so much struggle for meaning, for purpose. And in the end, we find it only in each other. Our shared experience of the fantastic and the mundane.

As watching on PC becomes more commonplace (NBC already offers streaming of *Heroes* to US website visitors, while in the UK Channel 4 began its *4 On Demand* service at the end of 2006, with both the BBC and ITV following suit in 2007) we can predict that a TV show's hidden clues and supplementary material will become more integral to understanding the primary text. We are not yet at that stage, however, and TV's online overflow is still a bonus feature, an Easter Egg that offers the dedicated fan a treat on the side rather than the meat of the

narrative. Keith may have been thrilled to find the Numbers in his local gallery but so far they haven't added up to anything.

Notes

1   Will Brooker, 'Living on *Dawson's Creek*: teen viewers, cultural conver-
    gence and television overflow', *International Journal of Cultural Studies*
    iv/4 (2001), pp.456–72; see also Henry Jenkins, 'The poachers and the
    stormtroopers: cultural convergence in the digital age', available online
    at *http://web.mit.edu/cms/People/henry3/pub/stormtroopers.htm* (1998),
    reprinted in Henry Jenkins, *Fans, Bloggers and Gamers* (New York: New
    York University Press, 2006). For the ways in which DVDs have recon-
    figured television viewing see Matt Hills, 'From the box in the corner to
    the box set on the shelf: "TVIII" and the cultural/textual valorisations of
    DVD', in *New Review of Film and Television Studies* v/1 (2007), pp.41–60,
    and Derek Kompare, 'Publishing flow: DVD box sets and the reception
    of television', *Television and New Media* vii/4 (2006), pp.335–60.

2   See Will Brooker, 'Overflow and audience', in Will Brooker and Deborah
    Jermyn (eds), *The Audience Studies Reader* (London: Routledge, 2003),
    pp.322–34.

3   Henry Jenkins, *Convergence Culture* (New York: New York University
    Press, 2006), pp.96–7.

4   Jenkins: *Convergence Culture*, pp.123–5.

5   This concept had already been trialled through the BBC's 'Jamie Kane'
    online game, which went live in August 2005 and was later linked to
    Doctor Who's Deffry Vale school website. See *www.bbc.co.uk/jamiekane/
    index.shtml.*

6   Quoted in *Doctor Who Magazine* 367, cited at *http://en.wikipedia.org/
    wiki/Doctor_Who_tie-in_websites.*

7   For more information see *http://en.wikipedia.org/wiki/Lost_Experience.*

8   See *www.unfiction.com/history/.*

9   The phenomenon has echoes of William Gibson's 2003 science fiction
    novel *Pattern Recognition* (Northampton: Viking Press), in which a cult
    following has emerged around footage fragments.

10 See *www.lostpedia.com/wiki/The_Lost_Experience#Necessary_tools.*

11 See Pierre Lévy, *Collective Intelligence: Mankind's Emerging World in
    Cyberspace*, trans. Robert Bononno (New York: Plenum Press, 1997),
    pp.13–19; Jenkins: *Convergence Culture*, pp.26–7.

12 See also Jonathan Gray and Jason Mittell, 'Speculation on spoil-
    ers: *Lost* fandom, narrative consumption and rethinking textuality',

Participations iv/1 (2007), available online at *www.participations.org/ Volume%204/Issue%201/4_01_graymittell.htm*.

13 Similarly, the Straight Dope website (*www.straightdope.com*) provides answers to submitted questions, its information supplied by a community nicknamed 'The Teeming Millions'. *Digg.com* bookmarks, highlights and logs other Internet sites of interest, based on a non-hierarchical, democratic voting system, while the slogan for collective Q&A site *Metafilter.org* is 'querying the hive mind'. And when the Beast was finally completed, the creators pulled back the curtain to reveal not a single wizard or gamesmaster but a team, the Puppetmasters: the puzzle-setters, as well as the solvers, were a collective. An ARG that constructs and plays out across a fictional universe requires one hive-mind pitted against another.

14 See Jenkins: *Convergence Culture*, p.251.

15 See *www.barbelith.com/faq/index.php/Main_Page*.

16 See Henry Jenkins, 'Do you enjoy making the rest of us feel stupid? alt. tv.twinpeaks, the trickster author, and viewer mastery', in David Lavery (ed.), *Full of Secrets* (Detroit: Wayne State University Press, 1995), p.51, and Susan J. Clerc, 'DDEB, GATB, MPPB, and Ratboy: *The X-Files*' media fandom, online and off', in David Lavery, Angela Hague and Marla Cartwright (eds), *Deny All Knowledge* (London: Faber and Faber, 1996), p.36.

17 See also Henry Jenkins, *Fans, Bloggers and Gamers: Exploring Participatory Culture* (New York: New York University Press, 2006), p.141.

18 See Nicholas Abercrombie and Brian Longhurst, *Audiences* (London: Sage Publications, 1998).

19 See Roger Aden, *Popular Stories and Promised Lands* (Tuscaloosa: University of Alabama Press, 1999), p.80.

20 See Phillip Swann, *TV.Com: How Television is Shaping Our Future* (New York: TV Books, 2000), quoted in Jenkins: *Convergence Culture*, p.75.

21 *Lost* (US) online thread at *www.barbelith.com/topic/19064/from/ 105*, February 2005.

22 *Lost* (US) online thread at *www.barbelith.com/topic/19064/from/ 385*, October 2005.

23 *Lost* (US) online thread at *www.barbelith.com/topic/19064/from/ 735*, February 2006.

24 *Lost* (US) online thread at *www.barbelith.com/topic/19064/from/ 875*, March 2006.

25 Jenkins: 'Do you enjoy making the rest of us feel stupid?' p.59.

26 Henry Jenkins, 'Foreword', in Kurt Lancaster, *Interacting with Babylon 5* (Austin: University of Texas Press, 2001), p.xvi.

27 Laura Mulvey, *Death 24x A Second* (London: Reaktion Books, 2006), p.26.

28   See Aaron Barlow, *The DVD Revolution* (Westport, CT: Praeger Publishers, 2005), p.9.

29   Jenkins: 'Foreword', p.xvii.

30   See 'Flight 815', at *http://flight815.blogspot.com/2006_02_01_flight815_archive.html*.

31   See *http://815.lemon-red.org/glyphsdie.jpg*.

32   *Lost* (US) online thread at *www.barbelith.com/topic/19064/from/805*, posted 16 February 2006.

33   See *Lostpedia.com*, *www.lostpedia.com/wiki/Blast_Door_Map*.

34   Post by Daniel in recap of the 'Lockdown' episode, at *www.televisionwithoutpity.com/articles/content/a910/index-8.html*.

35   *Lost* (US) online thread at *www.barbelith.com/topic/19064/from/630*.

36   *Lost* (US) online thread at *www.barbelith.com/topic/19064/from/1505*.

37   See *www.lostpedia.com/wiki/Image:3x17_Ms_Hawking_Picture.jpg*.

38   '*Lost* General Gabbery' on the Television without Pity forum, at *http://forums.televisionwithoutpity.com/index.php?s=537c62f33577d827aecc277f2208aa98&showtopic=3153226*.

39   See *www.lostpedia.com/wiki/Satellite_phone*.

40   Jenkins states that producers monitor Television Without Pity's boards to gauge the reaction to plot twists (*Fans, Bloggers and Gamers*, p.2).

41   Cited in Kurt Lancaster, *Interacting with Babylon 5* (Austin: University of Texas Press, 2001), p.15.

42   The show proved a surprise hit within its first month. *Variety* declared that it was 'dominating its broadcast competition…the highest regular-slot score [among 18–49 year-olds] for a first-year drama in the past two seasons' (Rick Kissell, '*Heroes* hot for peacock', 24 October 2006, available online at *www.variety.com/article/VR1117952515.html?categoryid=14&cs=1*). By May 2007 it had won a host of awards and honours, including a place in the American Film Institute's top ten shows of the year, and its cast members were celebrated among *Time* magazine's 'People who mattered' (available online at *www.time.com/time/personoftheyear/2006/people/16.html*, 12 December 2006).

43   Cavin, post on *Heroes* official website, at *www.nbc.com/Heroes/*.

44   Comments at *www.myspace.com/clairebennet*.

45   See *www.votepetrelli.com/*.

46   See *http://losteastereggs.blogspot.com/2007/05/11-frames-of-jacob.html*.

47   See *http://forum.rpg.net/showpost.php?p=7303501&postcount=361*.

48   *Heroes* online thread at *www.barbelith.com/topic/25100/from/735*.

49   *Heroes* online thread at *www.barbelith.com/topic/25100/from/35*.

V.   The Gathering Place:
Lost in Oahu

Julian Stringer

The day-dream of being marooned on a desert island still has enormous appeal, however small our chances of actually finding ourselves stranded on a coral atoll in the pacific. But *Robinson Crusoe* was one of the first books we read as children, and the fantasy endures. There are all the fascinating problems of survival, and the task of setting up, as Crusoe did, a working replica of bourgeois society and its ample comforts. This is the desert island as adventure holiday. With a supplies-filled wreck lying conveniently on the nearest reef like a neighbourhood cash and carry.

More seriously, there is the challenge of returning to our more primitive natures, stripped of the self-respect and the mental support systems with which civilisation has equipped us. Can we overcome fear, hunger and isolation, and find the courage and cunning to defeat anything that the elements can throw at us?

At an even deeper level there is the need to dominate the island, and transform its anonymous terrain into an extension of our minds. The mysterious peak veiled by cloud, the deceptively calm lagoon, the rotting mangroves and the secret spring of pure water together become out-stations of the psyche, as they must have done for our primeval forbears, filled with lures and pitfalls of every kind...

And if we find that we are not alone on the island, the scene is then set for an encounter of an interesting but especially dangerous kind...

J.G. Ballard, *Concrete Island*[1]

*L*ost is merely one of a string of recent US television manifestations of the fantasy of being marooned on a desert island (see for example *Survivor* (Mark Burnett Productions, 2000–) and *Temptation Island* (Fox World, 2001–3)).[2] However, it constitutes by far the most ambitious, imaginative and compelling treatment of the subject to date. While we may still enjoy reading Daniel Defoe's 1719 fantasy novel *Robinson Crusoe*[3] – and these days may find ourselves just as equally fascinated by J.M. Coetzee's 1986 book *Foe*[4] or the Hollywood film *Cast Away* (Robert Zemeckis, 2000) – no version of the 'stranded' fable has ever before been produced on such a grand scale. Ambitious in scope and international in theme, *Lost* takes the twin aesthetic day-dreams of island living and island survival into new and uncharted territory.

In creatively utilising the ongoing serial structure of long-format drama to unravel multiple characters, settings and situations across diverse multimedia platforms, ABC's first three seasons of *Lost* rely heavily upon the dramatic and affective possibilities opened up through use of the show's chosen island location. 'The *Lost* Island' is a multidi-mensional sign. It provides narrative focus as well as a central point of dramatic interest; it maps out the terrain upon which all aspects of 'the *Lost* experience' are generated and to which each will eventually return; it supplies sensuous audio-visual pleasure; and it grounds indi-vidual stories in settings both fantastical yet also believable. *Lost* has managed to retain audience interest and enthusiasm in part through skilled use of an enduring desert island fantasy, illustrating in the pro-cess the fundamental accuracy of Ballard's observations.

What makes the *Lost* island such a 'magical' and fascinating place? There are many islands in the world, each of which possesses its own unique and specific characteristics: a certain geographic ratio, localized climate and topography, distinct life forms, and so on. J.J. Abrams and his collaborators chose neither to have their characters fall to earth over an urban or densely populated island like Manhat-tan or Britain, nor over a vast terrain like Australia. Instead, when the passengers of Oceanic flight 815 are blown out of the sky they drop onto a relatively small piece of land surrounded by water located in the middle of what one of the characters identifies, very pointedly, as 'the South Pacific' ('The 23rd Psalm', 2.10).[5] *Lost*'s key locale therefore conforms to the paradigmatic definition of a 'desert island' provided by the *Oxford English Dictionary* ('remote and presumably uninhab-ited').[6] It presents the intriguing spectacle of an inviting subtropical terrain both strange yet familiar. Moreover, as discussed below, the fact that the particular watery enclave depicted in *Lost* possesses its own precise form and character is of significance both culturally and aesthetically.

In dramatic terms, *Lost*'s key location remains an island very much of uncertain identity. In the series' fictional narrative universe, the island is unknown and unnamed – it is a mysterious atoll situated in the middle of the Pacific Ocean, somewhere amid the thousands of miles triangulated by the coastal regions of Sydney, Los Angeles, and Fiji. On this score, *Lost* conforms in very precise ways to one characteristic of the contemporary international co-produced television mini-series identified by Barbara Selznick: it is set in a 'no man's land', a geographically vague location whose very indistinctness encourages the fantastic imaginations of viewers the world over.[7] *Lost* is thus rooted in an ostensibly de-territorialised space not coterminous with any geographically known or precise topography – if territorialised land is acquired through acts of sovereign jurisdiction, de-territorialised space seemingly lacks organised division. In short, this mystery island is a visionary or utopian space – beautiful, lush, 'virgin territory' waiting to be explored – that appeals to the tourist imagination and forms the basis for pleasurable immersion in a much wider cross-media and globalised phenomenon.

However, even the most casual *Lost* viewers surely know that the series is filmed somewhere very precise and identifiable – namely, the island of Oahu in the state of Hawaii in the USA. Not only does the publicity and inter-textual knowledge circulating around the show consistently point this out, the closing credits of each of the 60 episodes to date at the time of writing mention the Hawaiian location: the end credits for each episode of *Lost* say that the show was 'filmed entirely on location on Oahu, Hawaii' and declare that the producers 'acknowledge the cooperation of the people of Hawaii and their Aloha spirit'.[8] In this way, information provided by and about *Lost* works at key moments to re-territorialise Hawaii, and more specifically Oahu, as the precise location of the show's production. Consider how this kind of push-and-pull over questions of territoriality is signalled very clearly by the show's opening and closing titles. The opening title shot for each episode suggests de-territorialisation by presenting the word *Lost* in white capitals moving in corkscrew fashion towards the camera against an indistinct black background. Conversely, as discussed above, the closing credits re-territorialise *Lost* – or return it to the sovereign jurisdiction of the state of Hawaii – by revealing the information that it was filmed entirely 'on Oahu'.

The cumulative effect of these acts of simultaneous de-territorialisation and re-territorialisation is mesmerising. *Lost*'s fictional universe emphasises the unknown location of the Pacific atoll upon which Oceanic flight 815 crashed, but the spectators' knowledge of its real-world location forms part of a wider cultural experience. Viewer immersion in the pleasurable experience of being stranded on this fantasy island can be enhanced by apprehension of the simple truth that anyone with the necessary time and money can get to Oahu – and hence to 'the *Lost* island'.[9]

Lost conceivably could have been filmed on one or more of any number of other possible alternative production locations around the world – perhaps the Isle of Man, Jeju Island, Vancouver Island, or indeed one of the other Hawaiian islands that welcome visitors (Hawaii or 'The Big Island', Maui, Lanai, Molokai and Kauai). Aside from being visually striking, each of these places can offer film and television production crews the services of a professional 'Film Commission' or 'Film Office' to assist with logistical practicalities as well as financial and other matters.[10] As the wealthiest and most densely populated (900,000 people) of the state of Hawaii's inhabited islands, Oahu is known locally – and aptly as far as *Lost* is concerned – as 'the Gathering Place'. Sensing its cue, this chapter attempts to map out the ways in which Oahu's specific island geography and culture attracts media professionals. In addition, it argues that comprehending the reasons why *Lost* ended up being shot in Oahu enhances our understanding of some of the particular aesthetic pleasure presented over time by this latest major US television series to be 'made in Hawaii'. *Lost* has developed specific narrative forms in part because filming in Oahu generates unique dramatic possibilities and offers highly localised sensory pleasures.

THE MAKING OF A US TELEVISION LANDSCAPE

We must first place the decision to film *Lost* entirely in Oahu in historical and industrial context. As the trade press frequently points out, the desire to attract big-budget film and television productions to individual US states has become a key indicator of a region's

ability to remain vital and fiscally healthy in ever more competitive domestic and global media markets.[11] Most state film commissions (for
example Hawaii's[12]) are 'tied to state economic development offices
or local chambers of commerce and offer similar services' to attract
large-scale media projects – 'governors' airplanes, luxury hotel suites,
free-of-charge location scouting services, an amiable workforce', and
so on. Some states 'also include tax subsidies and incentives for film
productions, and some local film commissioners are willing to bend
over backwards to satisfy the whims of filmmakers, offering to change
river flows, grow crops on barren fields, or remove telephone poles so
they don't distract camera moves and angles.'[13]

Michael Curtin has recently considered the increased importance
of inter-state competition for highly valued film and television resources as one aspect of a contemporary tendency for cities, in the
USA and elsewhere, to seek to establish themselves as 'media capitals'.[14] The ambition of a media capital – for example, Hollywood in
the 1910s, Chicago in the 1940s, or Seoul and Vancouver today – is to
survive as an audio-visual production centre by identifying and then
maximising its assets so as to avoid being left behind in the battle
for new film and television commissions.[15] *Lost* symbolically de-ter-
ritorialises rival media capitals, such as London, Los Angeles, Seoul
and Sydney, by depicting them in individual episodes and thus forcing
them to take on the shape of particular Oahu locations – as a result of
this process, these competing global cities accrue the status of satellites circulating around a powerfully re-territorialised Hawaii.

At the turn of the twenty-first century, what assets do the state
of Hawaii in general and the island of Oahu in particular possess as
a media capital? To begin with, as the production scale and subsequent global multimedia success of *Lost* both demonstrate, the state
possesses the ambition and the ability successfully to go after a major television showcase such as this. In addition, the island provides
enough unique selling points to make the prospect of filming there
attractive as well as realistic.[16]

First and foremost among these key location criteria is Oahu's
sheer physical beauty. Situated in the middle of the chain of Hawaiian islands – distant atolls located at a rough equidistance between
California and mainland Japan – Oahu spans almost 600 square miles
and was forged an estimated 44 million years ago by volcanic activity

that created its characteristic pristine lava beaches and stupendous volcanic mountain ranges. One does not have to be an emissary of the Hawaii Film Office to recognise that few places on earth offer a more vivid sense of the geological wonders this planet has to offer: a sub-tropical climate that creates damp lushness on its north and east (or 'windward') coast and a drier topography in the south and west (the 'leeward' coast); expansive valleys; scores of flora and fauna unique to the islands; dramatic contrasts of colours. In brief, Oahu's most abiding natural assets are perhaps best summed up in celebrated Hawaiian musician Israel Kamakawiwo'ole's pithy description of the island's 'High-ridged mountain/Crystal-clear blue water'.[17] From this perspective, the single most revealing scene in *Lost* occurs during 'Exodus – Part 2' (1.24) – right at the climax of series one – when Michael (Harold Perrineau) and his companions on board the escape raft observe the island's spectacular jagged coastline for the very first time after they put out to sea in the hope of being rescued. 'How's a place this big ever get discovered?' Michael wonders aloud as mountain and ocean are juxtaposed together in one visually striking 'money shot'.

Second, the island is fortuitously located near other media capitals, in particular Tokyo and Los Angeles. Not only can Oahu act as a stepping stone, or bridge, between culturally and geographically distinct parts of the world, it also – unlike Kauai, Maui and the other Hawaiian islands – offers the high-tech comforts and resources of a major urban conurbation, Honolulu, from which to coordinate production and conduct business.[18] The state of Hawaii is sometimes referred to as 'Hollywood's tropical backlot', offering convenience and familiarity to California-based professionals while also seeming distant and remote. Certainly, Honolulu International Airport's distance from and yet simultaneous proximity to Los Angeles' LAX accounts in part for the emergence of Oahu as a 'full service film and television production centre rather than a location backdrop'.[19] Los Angeles and Honolulu exist as both neighbour and rival media capitals interacting, as *Lost* demonstrates, through processes of mutual competition and cooperation. Hollywood may be a global byword for glamour and excess, but Oahu too has aspirations to this status.

Third, Oahu embodies Hawaii's distinct 'Aloha spirit'. In 'White Rabbit' (1.5), John Locke (Terry O'Quinn) calls the island 'different', 'special' and 'beautiful' ('We all know it. We all feel it.'). *Lost*'s producers exploit Oahu's unique characteristics, but which elements have they included and which have they excluded? On the UK DVD supplements for season one, Dominic Monaghan (Charlie) talks about Oahu's status as a world surfing capital attracting him to the role. *Lost* could have capitalised upon this particular signifier of 'Hawaii-ness' by exploiting the dramatic potential of surfing. Just imagine: after Locke and Sayid (Naveen Andrews) construct a makeshift board from Kona wood, various characters practise in the sand, strip off for watching eyes, paddle out with a laugh, mount the thing, pose with arms akimbo, and fall over. *Lost*'s various screenwriters have to date studiously avoided such a scenario, however, choosing to emphasise instead other aspects of Oahu's 'magical' aura.

It has been claimed that *Lost* captures and evokes Hawaii's *mana* or spiritual power.[20] The *mana* of *Lost* aligns culture with nature. The first three series borrow all the trappings of bourgeois consciousness identified by J.G. Ballard – the attempt to replicate capitalist living, the selfish investment in the necessity of one's own island survival – but add a uniquely spiritual twist. Island living is periodically expressed in *Lost* through random acts of kindness, goodness, humanity, and respect for land and people – precisely the kinds of themes that immersion in Oahu's geographically 'special' landscape facilitates.

Regardless of the ultimate significance of 'the Hatch' found by the 'Lostaways', nascent environmentalism remains an important aspect of a show airing in an era when the dire potential consequences of global warming are at the forefront of many peoples' minds. As one author wrote not long after the first moon landing in 1969:

> The Apollo astronauts brought to everyone's notice, very effectively, the fact that Earth is a precious, beautiful planet; it is our home, and we are part of it. I repeat: we are part of the Earth. We do not live *on* the planet; we live *in* it, and we have an important part to play in its functioning. We are not living people on a dead planet. We are dead people without the planet. For after all, the astronauts' space modules could not support human life for long without their radio connections with Earth – and this planet is full of a superhuman form of life...[21]

Lost reiterates this philosophy through articulating an animistic belief in the fundamental interconnectedness of all living matter.

Tellingly, the Lostaways' emotional investment in the possibility of establishing radio connection with others best supports their hopes of survival. Throughout seasons one and two, for example, the use of radio connections first establishes potential contact with the outside world, and then connects the two sides of the island – the 'leeward' and the 'windward' – with each other. Sayid's efforts to triangulate the French broadcast in 'The Moth' (1.7) are paralleled by Ana Lucia's (Michelle Rodriguez) attempt to establish a radio signal while on higher ground in 'The Other 48 Days' (2.7).

Finally, Oahu possesses a successful track record of supporting and enabling large-scale international media productions, which otherwise comparable islands have not been able to match. History provides very good reasons to consider the state of Hawaii a US media capital. While the production of films such as *Hula* (Victor Fleming, 1927), *Honolulu* (Edward Buzzell, 1939) and *Song of the Islands* (Walter Lang, 1942) helped consolidate a fantasy image of Hawaii as an island paradise for generations of tourists, the release of movies such as *South Pacific* (Joshua Logan, 1958) and *Blue Hawaii* (Norman Taurog, 1961) helped boost the state's economy after the achievement of statehood in 1959.

Even though the history of film production in Hawaii has yet to be written, it is just as important to recognise the islands' status as an important producer of US television drama. The most famous and obvious example of this is CBS's long-running police series *Hawaii Five-O* (CBS Television, 1969–80) – which, as Paul Swann points out, has done much to bring tourist revenue into the state through what he terms the '*Hawaii Five-O* Effect'.[22] Shot predominantly in Oahu and set primarily in its capital, this long-running cop drama worked by flaunting its greatest assets, the geography and culture of Honolulu itself. Consider the series' famed title credits. The credit sequence for the 'realistic' pilot episode, 'Cocoon' (first broadcast in the USA on 20 September 1968), features a veritable throng of identifiable Honolulu landmarks (a landmark is literally an 'object that marks the land').[23] These individual images work firmly to territorialise this particular Hawaiian production site through offering up such recognisable sights as: a large, rolling wave that looks just about surf-able by anyone who doesn't mind gliding towards oblivion; city views; images of Honolulu International Airport and of the harbour;

Polynesian faces; the Aloha Tower; Diamond Head; the 'Iolani Palace; and Waikīkī.

The impressive worldwide success of *Hawaii Five-O* does not tell the whole story of the state's achievements as a television production destination. Many more successful dramas have also been shot in and around Honolulu. For example, ABC has habitually supported the shooting in Oahu (in whole or in part) of large-scale series or major one-offs: *Adventures in Paradise* (20th Century Fox Television, 1959–62), *The Islanders* (MGM Television, 1960–1), *Fantasy Island* (Columbia Pictures Television, 1978–84), *The Islander* (Glen A. Larson Productions, 1978), *Pearl* (Silliphant-Konigsberg Productions, 1978–9), *The Mackenzies of Paradise Cove* (Viacom Productions, 1979), *Aloha Paradise* (Aaron Spelling Productions, 1981), *Tales of the Gold Monkey* (Belisarius Productions, 1982), *The Winds of War* (Jadran Film, 1983), *The Thorn Birds* (David Wolper-Stan Margulies Productions, 1983), *Hawaiian Heat* (James Parriott Productions/Universal TV, 1984), *Island Sons* (Universal TV, 1986), *War and Remembrance* (ABC Circle Films, 1988) and *Byrds of Paradise* (20th Century Fox Television, 1994). Other networks and studios have supplemented ABC's pre-*Lost* television depictions of Hawaii: CBS (*Gilligan's Island*, CBS Television, 1964–7; *Magnum P.I.*, Belisarius Productions, 1980–8; *Blood and Orchids*, Lorimar Telepictures, 1985; *Tour of Duty*, Braun Entertainment Group, 1987–8; *Raven*, Columbia Pictures Television, 1992; *One West Waikiki*, Rysher Television,1994); Fox (*North Shore*, 20th Century Fox Television, 2004); NBC (*Big Hawaii*, Filmways Pictures, 1977; *From Here to Eternity*, Bennett/Katleman Productions, 1979; *Hawaii*, NBC Universal Television, 2004); and Warner Bros. (*Hawaiian Eye*, Warner Bros. Television, 1959–63).[24]

In the years immediately prior to the commission of *Lost*, the Hawaii Film Office strove to ensure a bright future for the state's film and television sector by remaining competitive in an ever more unstable global media environment. Oahu's existence as a full-service production centre appeared to be guaranteed with the early 2000s renovation of Honolulu's Diamondhead film studio (now the Hawaii Film Studio: many scenes from *Lost*, such as the cave scenes from season one, have been shot there). But such success generated a concomitant anxiety over whether such high levels of achievement could be sustained or even superseded in the early years of the new millennium.

A March 2001 article in the *Honolulu Star-Bulletin* reported that the Hawaii Film Office's interim manager, Donne Dawson, worried that 2000's 'record revenue of $125 million' would be hard to beat: 'It will not be a record low year, but (Hawaii) will be hard pressed to beat $125 million again,' she said. Author Tim Ryan noted that '[j]ust one motion picture has filmed in Hawaii so far this year – Universal's *Dragonfly*, starring Kevin Costner – and one television show, UPN's *Manhunt*. Both were filmed on Kauai.' He compared this with the previous year, 1999, when 'Hawaii also drew $75 million from the filming of *Baywatch Hawai'i*, *Final Fantasy*, *Pearl Harbor*, *Windtalkers*, and *Jurassic Park III*.'[25]

This boom-and-bust mentality would soon be thrown into sharp relief as 2001 took the Hawaii film and television industry on something of a rollercoaster ride. The summer months delivered a welcome high-water mark of achievement as the three big blockbusting films released at that time – *Pearl Harbor* (Michael Bay, 2001), *Planet of the Apes* (Tim Burton, 2001) and *Jurassic Park III* (Joe Johnston, 2001) – had all been shot, in whole or in part, in the state. By the end of the summer of 2001, however, the situation had changed dramatically as the fallout from 9/11 hit Hawaii hard. 'You did not know what spot would be attacked next,' explained basketball coach Riley Wallace, recalling his reaction on watching the terrorist atrocities live on television. 'That is a scary feeling because you don't know if Hawaii could be attacked again.'[26] Airports in the islands were more or less completely shut down for days following the 11 September attack; over the next two months domestic tourism fell by 39 per cent and international tourism by more than 50 per cent; nearly 7,000 jobs were lost and thousands of workers saw their hours of employment cut.

More fundamentally, the varied responses collected in *Hawai'i Remembers September 11* – a book of interviews collated by students at the University of Hawai'i, Hilo, immediately after the event – testify to a widespread re-evaluation of core values on the part of Hawaii's population as well as a heightened investment in Hawaii's specific and unique identity. Time and again respondents make the same kinds of comments: Hawaii is vulnerable; we in the islands are far too dependent on air travel and tourism; we are isolated; we need to diversify and to 'look at other ways of survival besides tourism' (Sam Choy); we need to reassert expression of the 'true feelings of *ohana*' (Edith 'Kit' Dobelle).[27]

Lost's justly celebrated pilot episode (1.1) opens by explicitly tackling head-on the psychological fallout of a violent plane crash that kills many innocent people going about their daily business – an explicit narrative engagement with an all-too-real spectacular act of mass murder that affected countless television viewers around the world. Consider in this regard the fact that while media reports continue to draw attention to the nearly 3,000 people killed on 9/11, as well as to the hundreds of thousands or more personally affected by its aftermath, far less attention has been paid to the possibility that the events of 9/11 also psychologically traumatised millions who witnessed the events unfurl on television – domestic 'victims' of the mediated violence seen and heard that day. In *Lost*, the twin towers of the World Trade Center are depicted through an office window in 'Adrift' (2.2) in the scene where Michael visits his lawyer in New York City. More importantly, in 'White Rabbit' (1.5) Jack (Matthew Fox) diagnoses his fellow survivors as suffering from 'post-traumatic stress'. In short, *Lost*'s initial few minutes forge resonant emotional connections between the show and the specific location of Hawaii. Not only is Hawaii the state most identified, pre-9/11, with tragedy visited upon America from the skies (in the form of the Pearl Harbor attack), it is also, post 9/11, the far-off US atoll uniquely vulnerable to the disruption of air traffic between Oahu and the mainland. *Lost* announced its appearance in Hawaii by plugging into very real contemporary anxieties.

While the Hawaii Film Office could claim periodic triumphs during the years 2002–3, the securing of the production of *Lost* provided a sorely needed post-9/11 godsend. It was felt that this show might instantly revive flagging fortunes and reassert Hawaii's unique identity as well as its desirability as a full-service production centre.[28] A 'quality' and ground-breaking 'cinematic' multimedia phenomenon, *Lost* broke generically with previous televisual representations of Hawaii. It was neither an island crime show (like *Hawaii Five-O*) nor a sexploitation fest (like *Baywatch Hawaii*), but like these predecessors it still depended upon its Oahu location.[29] The remainder of this chapter delineates *Lost*'s representation of Oahu through its narrative arc and aesthetic style.

MAPPING THE ISLAND

In *Atlas of the European Novel 1800–1900*, Franco Moretti observes that in literary works '...*each space determines, or at least encourages, its own kind of story* ... What happens depends on where it happens.' He further remarks that '[s]pecific stories are the product of specific spaces ... *without a certain kind of space, a certain kind of story is simply impossible.*'[30] Of all major US television productions, *Lost* most clearly illustrates this imbrication of space and narrative. If the show's first three seasons had been filmed anywhere other than Hawaii, they would doubtless have taken significantly different forms.

The crucial decision to situate *Lost*'s production in Oahu created the ability – nay, the necessity – to generate particular narrative situations as well as highly localised sensory pleasures. These possibilities are structured primarily around the omnipresent beauty of the island's landscape, but also, secondary to this, around Oahu's associated cultural and social environment. Numerous websites, complete with frame-grabs, map the landscape of *Lost*'s fictional island onto Oahu's own specific geographical characteristics.[31] I want to concentrate here upon one particular aspect of this relationship: the manner in which island topography, Hawaiian culture and the ongoing narrative demands of US serial drama habitually overlap with one another.

Lost's first three seasons conform to one simple and overarching dramatic principle: as the mysteries deepen and the characters' pasts unfold, the island gradually opens up. The very first scenic views of Oahu's stupendous landscape unravel as 'teaser' shots in the first and second episodes of the 'Pilot' (1.1). The survivors setting off to explore the island's interior (not unlike Ballard's 'adventure holiday'), and climbing to higher ground to obtain a radio signal, provide narrative justification for the further unveiling of more wide open spaces and spectacular scenery.

The episodes 'White Rabbit' (1.5) and 'House of the Rising Sun' (1.6) continue to map the island's terrain. 'White Rabbit', which introduces the discourse of the island as 'magical', opens with point-of-view shots taken from the perspective of someone in the ocean looking at the island from a distance.[32] Shortly afterwards, a new angle of the beach begins to open up the space of the island a little more. Meanwhile, Jack's repeated glimpses of a mystery man motivate him to give chase frantically, allowing the camera to explore the island's grassy terrain in further detail. A pan shot of the beach finally reveals the island's distant coastline in extreme long shot. Such images function as establishing shots, albeit ones that carry the burden of having to establish only very gradually the spaces of a long-format television series set on a relatively small and bounded island location.[33]

In 'House of the Rising Sun', some of the survivors trek through an unfamiliar ravine and the jungle towards the caves where Jack has found water. In 'The Moth' (1.7), Sayid's attempt to place the second antenna on higher ground justifies the presentation of numerous Oahu beauty spots: three synchronised fireworks launched into the Pacific air authorise three different camera angles emphasising different aspects of island topography. The camera then does a 360-degree track around Sayid, affording more dynamic new vistas of the ocean and jagged landscape beyond. In 'Confidence Man' (1.8) Sayid sets out to walk the shore and 'map the island', the narrative development following logically from the previous episode's aesthetic developments.

'Punctuation shots' of the beach and surrounding locale intersperse the narrative arc, varying plot tempo while also advertising Oahu as island paradise by freezing the narrative for viewer contemplation. 'The Greater Good' (1.21) contains one of Lost's many compelling still-lives of palm trees and sandy beaches (familiar tropes from tourist and Hollywood iconography), while a particularly vivid example of a brilliant orange Pacific sunset may be found in 'Born to Run' (1.22). These landscape shots brand Lost as an Oahu product, as does a repeated series trademark – the establishing long shot from the beach that looks out at a cliff coast and then pans to reveal survivors engaged in various activities (see, for example, 'Do No Harm', 1.20). The foregrounding of Oahu's 'High-ridged mountain/Crystal-clear blue water' integrates the landscape into the storytelling. In the openings of two back-to-back scenes from 'The Hunting Party' (2.11), the camera first focuses on a distant cliff-top before panning right to reveal characters talking to one other (Jack, Sawyer (Josh Holloway) and Locke in the first instance, and Michael and Walt (Michael David Kelley) in the second). Similarly, in 'Dave' (2.18), Oahu geography determines the location of Hurley's (Jorge Garcia) potential suicide: a cliff-top high above the ocean. 'Solitary' (1.9) further opens up while simultaneously utilising island geography through Hurley's construction of a primitive golf course (the sport is one of Oahu's major assets and tourist attractions). Beautiful scenery encompasses the golf game, with lush green mountains dominating the background as players take their swings in the foreground.

Such treatment of Oahu landscape and culture as aesthetic trope continues across the remainder of series one as the crash victims inch ever nearer the 'dark territories'.[34] Finally, new locations open up dramatically in 'Exodus – Part One' (1.23) with the sudden appearance of black volcanic rocks on the seashore.

Lost's second season does not deviate from this primary narrative structure. The season brings together the different parts of the island – broadly identifiable as the 'windward' and the 'leeward' – through the introduction of new characters and new meetings. (As Mr Eko (Adewale Akinnuoye-Agbaje) puts it in 'What Kate Did', 2.9: 'On the other side of the island we found a place much like this.') 'One of Them' (2.14) includes a reference to the island's 'North Shore', which presages the gradual revelation of this 'other' location as the season moves inexorably towards its climax.[35] As Jin (Daniel Dae Kim), Sun (Yunjin Kim) and Sayid sail towards unfamiliar land in 'Live Together, Die Alone – Part 1' (2.23), the development of key plot points justifies the presentation of more and more previously unseen topographical features. These include the strange moonscape that Desmond (Henry Ian Cusick) traverses in flashback as well as Oahu's popular Kualoa Point and conical Mokoli'i Island.[36]

In mapping this particular narrative configuration – to repeat, the unfolding of plot mysteries combined with the gradual revelation of new topographical information – *Lost* also establishes a series of important visual contrasts. While season one made distinctions between the green of the land and the blue of the sea, season two emphasises the colour black as the various mysteries deepen. For example, in 'S.O.S.' (2.19), high-angle shots of the beach juxtapose Bernard's (Sam Anderson) black lava stones against the brilliant white sand. In addition, numerous other aspects of Hawaii's cultural, natural and social environment are seamlessly integrated into *Lost*'s story structure: island music (such as the song 'Troubles Wash Away' in 'Tabula Rasa', 1.3, and the ukulele music heard in 'Raised by Another', 1.10); fishing and exotic sea life ('Walkabout', 1.4; '...And Found', 2.5); subtropical flowers ('House of the Rising Sun', 1.6) and fruit ('What Kate Did',

2.9); and unique indigenous life forms such as the wild boar ('Outlaws', 1.16, *et al.*).

Season three proceeds in line with the key dramatic and aesthetic principles outlined above. The unexpected introduction of a previously unseen village community at the start of 'A Tale of Two Cities' (3.1) motivates the mapping of yet more new topographical features, while a visually striking extreme long-shot depicting one entire side of the island is reinforced by the opening up of previously unseen spectacular vistas in 'Further Instructions' (3.3). This process of gradual unfurling is then intensified in 'Not in Portland' (3.7), with revelation of the knowledge of the existence of a second island. Perhaps inspired by the empirical fact that Oahu occupies a place within a wider chain of volcanic islands collectively known as Hawaii, *Lost* draws once more upon the possibilities opened up through use of its specific production locale.

Lost's cast and crew continue to find dramatically resourceful ways of exhibiting Oahu's scenery and culture across the rest of season three. For example, in 'Par Avion' (3.12) Kate and other Lostaways are forced to climb over a large pylon, thus motivating elevated views of the countryside around them. In 'Through the Looking Glass – Part One' (3.22), Hurley, Sawyer and Juliet (Elizabeth Mitchell) are dwarfed by the immensity of the landscape in a strikingly composed extreme long-shot reminiscent of classical Chinese painting. Perfectly befitting Oahu's island location, boats and rafts continue to be firmly integrated into the narrative form of various episodes (starting with 'The Glass Ballerina', 3.2). Finally, as with seasons one and two, season three also ends with a trek to a previously unseen location, in this case the radio tower depicted in the two-part 'Through the Looking Glass' (3.22 and 3.23).

The manner in which *Lost* imbricates space and narrative in season three, however, is also subtly different. If seasons one and two extracted maximum dramatic potential from the *Lost* island's uncertain identity, season three takes a slightly different tack. Secure in the knowledge that by now viewers all around the world cannot help but be familiar with the show's Hawaiian locations, *Lost* provides knowing in-jokes, trading upon its existence as an allegory of Oahu.

For example, in season three Oahu's most popular tourist destination – the Pearl Harbor military installation – is both alluded to through references to 'Pearl Station' and 'Pearl City' in 'Par Avion' (3.12), and is then utilised as a location destination for scenes incorporating a submarine in 'The Man From Tallahassee' (3.13) and 'One Of Us' (3.16). Following Moretti, we may therefore note how at this point *Lost* demonstrates that Oahu encourages stories involving submarines, or that without Pearl Harbor as a location backdrop, stories involving submarines may never have found their way into *Lost* in the first place.[37] The same may also be said of the introduction of *lei* (the Hawaiian garland or necklace of flowers) in 'Catch-22' (3.17) and the close-up of a *Hula* doll in the same episode.[38] In 'The Man Behind the Curtain' (3.20), the island greeting 'Namaste' is invoked as a thinly veiled linguistic substitute for 'Aloha'.

All of these developments are accompanied towards the end of season three by regular commentary from various characters on the beauty of the island (see for example 'The Man Behind the Curtain', 3.20, and 'Greatest Hits', 3.21). Such statements – 'It's beautiful, isn't it? No matter how much time you spend on the island, you just never get tired of this view' ('The Brig', 3.19) – may be thought of as *Lost*'s version of product placement, or as propaganda for the Hawaii Film Office. (After all, *Lost* is the most ambitious, imaginative and compelling audio-visual postcard Oahu has ever dispatched, and it is easy to imagine that the state wishes the show to continue to lure many a tourist.) Equally, however, the last few episodes of season three feel positively valedictory and nostalgic, almost as if the show is saying goodbye to the island for the very last time. This tone of melancholic sadness is underlined at the end of the season by the unexpected plot twist of showing characters leading seemingly 'post-island' lives in flash-forwards. Indeed, the power and shock of these flash-forwards is intensified precisely because characters have already talked of the beauty of the *Lost* island in a way that suggests they may be about to leave it forever.

At the time of writing, as the fourth series of *Lost* draws near, millions of fans around the globe eagerly anticipate the presentation of yet more mysteries and yet more revelations. The eventual discovery of what it all 'means' may or may not prove to be a disappointment. However, for its many admirers, being kept on anxious tenterhooks will continue to provide the sense of pleasurable uncertainty that has driven ABC's success with the show over the past three seasons. One crucial component of that uncertainty involves geographical location. Where will season four be filmed? If it is shot in Oahu, then logic decrees that, for example, we may expect *Lost*'s screenwriters to utilise one of Oahu's greatest natural resources – volcanoes (see 'The Man Behind the Curtain', 3.20) – in its developing story arcs. If filmed elsewhere, then we may expect new production spaces to determine or encourage new and as yet unanticipated kinds of stories.

Regardless of whether or not Oahu continues to act as a full-service production centre for *Lost*, the Hawaii Film Office is doubtless already searching for ways to move on and, if possible, up. For judging by the strength of the synergies *Lost* has forged between its singular production site and its associated multimedia 'experience', this particular show constitutes a vivid and highly successful example of how and why regional 'film commissions' in the USA are so anxious to remain involved in the design and delivery of long-format television drama. Indeed, *Lost* may be thought of as the *locus classicus* of this specific aspect of US commercial media. The show is ambitious in scope and international in theme, and in de-territorialising and then re-territorialising an island's geography *Lost* long ago found its ultimate meaning and purpose. Oahu.[39]

Notes

1   J.G. Ballard, *Concrete Island* (London: Vintage, 1994 [1973]), pp.4–5.

2   Within its individual episodes, *Lost* references numerous other literary, film and television antecedents that have drawn upon the same conceit, such as *Gilligan's Island* (CBS, 1964–7), H.G. Wells, *The Island of Dr Moreau* (London: Heinemann, 1896) and William Golding, *Lord of the Flies* (London: Faber and Faber, 1954) (film directed by Peter Brook, 1963).

3   Daniel Defoe, *Robinson Crusoe* (London: W. Taylor, 1719).

4   J.M. Coetzee, *Foe* (London: Viking, 1986).

5   All quotations from and references to *Lost* episodes in this chapter refer to the UK DVD releases. For more on the Hollywood movie *South Pacific*'s (Joshua Logan, 1958) role in the US cultural imaginary see Rob Wilson, *Reimagining the American Pacific* (Durham: Duke University Press, 2000) and Christina Klein, *Cold War Orientalism: Asia in the Middlebrow Imagination, 1945–1961* (Berkeley: University of California Press, 2003), pp.143–90.

6   J.B. Sykes (ed.), *The Concise Oxford Dictionary of Current English*, 6th edn (Oxford: Clarendon Press, 1976).

7   Barbara Selznick, 'World-class budgets and big-name casts: the miniseries and international coproductions', in Greg Elmer and Mike Gasher (eds), *Contracting Out Hollywood: Runaway Productions and Foreign Location Shooting* (Lanham, MD: Rowman and Littlefield, 2005), pp.157–75.

8   The meaning of the word 'Aloha' is defined by Mary Kawena Pukui and Samuel H. Elbert in their *Hawaiian Dictionary: Hawaiian–English, English–Hawaiian* (Honolulu: University of Hawaii Press, rev. edn 1986), p.21, as 'love, affection, compassion, mercy, sympathy, pity, kindness, sentiment, grace, charity'.

9   See websites such as *www.Hawaiilost.com*.

10   For a useful discussion of the function and contemporary rise to importance of 'film commissions', see Paul Swann, 'From workshop to backlot: the Greater Philadelphia Film Office', in Mark Shiel and Tony Fitzmaurice (eds), *Cinema and the City: Film and Urban Societies in a Global Context* (London: Blackwell, 2001), pp.88–98.

11   This process is different from (but linked to) the phenomenon of 'runaway productions', or the migration of US film and television programmes overseas. Hawaii occupies an interesting position in this regard. On the one hand, it is part of the USA and hence subject to the same legal and financial stipulations as the other 49 states. On the other hand, it is geographically disconnected from the US mainland, and continues to enjoy close ties with Japan, South Korea and other regions of the Pacific Rim.

12   See *www.hawaiifilmoffice.com*.

13   Aida Hozic, *Hollyworld: Space, Power, and Fantasy in the American Economy* (Ithica: Cornell University Press, 2001), pp.87–8.

14   Michael Curtin, 'Media capitals: cultural geographies of global TV', in Lynn Spigel and Jan Olsson (eds), *Television After TV: Essays on a Medium in Transition* (Durham: Duke University Press, 2004), pp.270–302.

15   For Vancouver as a film and television production centre, see Greg Elmer, 'The trouble with the Canadian "body double"', in *Screen* xliii/4 (winter 2002), pp.423–31.

16   It has been estimated that a full 70 per cent of the budget – $45 million – of the first series of *Lost* was spent on location costs.

17   Israel Kamakawiwo'ole (after John Denver and Toots and the Maytals), 'Take Me Home Country Road', on his album *Facing Future* (Big Boy Record Company, 1993).

18   As numerous Internet sites and media reports reveal, the first three seasons of *Lost* were filmed at a range of both public (such as Mokoleia

Beach, Police Beach) and private (Kualoa Ranch) locations no more than between 30 minutes' and two hours' drive from downtown Honolulu and the high-rise apartments, hotels and condominiums of Waikīkī Beach.

19   See *www.hawaiifilmoffice.com*.

20   Pukui and Elbert define *mana* as '[s]upernatural or divine power, mana, miraculous power; a powerful nation, authority' (*Hawaiian Dictionary*, p. 235).

21   E.T. Stringer, *The Secret of the Gods: Exploring Hidden Mysteries of Earth and the Universe* (London: Neville Spearman, 1974), pp.14–15.

22   Swann: 'From workshop to backlot', pp.94–5.

23   Alvin H. Marill, *Movies Made for Television* (New York: Da Capo, 1980), p.17.

24   Sources consulted: Luis I. Reyes, *Made in Paradise: Hollywood's Films of Hawai'i and the South Seas* (Honolulu: Mutual Publishing, 1995); Alex McNeil, *Total Television: A Comprehensive Guide to Programming from 1948 to the Present* (London: Penguin, 1980); and Tim Brooks and Earle Marsh, *The Complete Directory to Prime Time Network TV Shows 1946– present* (New York: Ballantine Books, 1979).

25   Tim Ryan, 'Reel hot seat', *Honolulu Star-Bulletin*, 2 March 2001, pp.D-1, D-7.

26   Riley Wallace, quoted in Thom Curtis (ed.), *Hawai'i Remembers September 11* (Hilo, Hawai'i: Hagorth Publishing Company, 2002), p.153. Wallace is referring to the memory of the attack by the Japanese air force on the Pearl Harbor military installation, located just outside Honolulu, Oahu, on 7 December 1941.

27   Curtis, p.21, 24. *Ohana* is defined by Pukui and Elbert as 'Family, relative, kin group; related' (*Hawaiian Dictionary*, p.276).

28   Indeed, 2004 brought a record revenue of $130 million to the state (see *www.hawaiifilmoffice.com*).

29   This is not to claim that *Lost* does not draw upon crime show and sexploitation elements – it does. However, in scenes such as the one where Kate (Evangeline Lilly) and Sawyer discover a waterfall in 'Whatever the Case May Be' (1.12) – wherein sex and crime are interwoven – these elements are presented in disguised form. Such moments recall the soft 'heteroeroticism' of movies like *The Blue Lagoon* (Frank Launder, 1949) and its remake (Randal Kleiser, 1980) – both of which were filmed on Fijian islands.

30   Franco Moretti, *Atlas of the European Novel 1800-1900* (London: Verso, 1998), pp.70, 100. Italics in original.

31   See, for example, *www.lostvirtualtour.com*.

32   This sequence anticipates the Oahu 'money shot' referred to earlier. It is 'answered' in season two by the ocean point-of-view shots taken from the perspective of crash survivors at the beginning of 'The Other 48 Days' (2.7).

33   Contrasts between film and television are worth bearing in mind at this point. While film needs very quickly to establish primary narrative spaces, television can tease out this process over a longer period, particularly when the space in question is itself relatively small. (Television crews can also shoot from different angles to make one space look like several.)

34   Does *Lost* exploit stereotypes of primitivism or does it explore them? Hawaiian cultural nationalism is a factor complicating tourist understanding of the islands' cultural identity as it very frequently insists upon the need to recognise and preserve indigenous Polynesian traditions. Although not pursued here, the argument that *Lost* 'displaces natives' provides a powerful counterweight to the show's own self-celebration of its much-vaunted 'Aloha spirit'. For discussion of the commodification of Hawaii's cultural history – for example, *Hula* dancing and indigenous music – see Elizabeth Buck, *Paradise Remade: The Politics of Culture and History in Hawai'i* (Philadelphia: Temple University Press, 1993) and Houston Wood, *Displacing Natives: The Rhetorical Production of Hawai'i* (Maryland: Rowman and Littlefield, 1999).

In its first three seasons, *Lost* speaks the word 'native' aloud just once ('The Man Behind the Curtain', 3.20), but it does still allude to such thorny issues as the over-development, through the prioritisation of tourist economics, of the main Hawaiian islands together with associated struggles over land rights and the eradication of Native and Polynesian cultures. *Lost*'s scriptwriters give Sawyer the job of neutralising the relevance of these important and ongoing matters by at least acknowledging their existence. 'I take comfort knowing someday this is all gonna be a real nice shopping complex. Maybe even an auto mall,' he says to Kate in 'Outlaws' (1.16) while out hunting boar; and in 'Exodus – Part 2' (1.24) he answers Michael's question, 'How's a place this big ever get discovered?' with the words, 'Don't know. But you could build yourself one hell of a beach resort right over there.' Fundamental questions of geographical territoriality – for example, 'Who owns the *Lost* island?' or 'Who are or were its first inhabitants?' – are raised most explicitly, and tantalisingly, across the last few episodes of season three.

35   The North Shore of Oahu is famous as a tourist destination, especially for its beaches, sunsets and surfing.

36   These scenes occur at 'Pala Ferry' in 'Live Together, Die Alone – Part 2' (2.24). Mokoli'i Island is otherwise known as 'Chinaman's Hat' – the

unusual and picturesque land mass that Michael and Walt sail past on the start of their journey away from the island at the very end of season two.

37 It is entirely possible that such scenes may have the future effect of generating a curious form of second-order tourism – that is, fans of the show may end up visiting Pearl Harbor not because it is the site of the infamous 1941 attack, but because it is a 'Lost location'.

38 This is also the episode where Lost's scriptwriters have the affrontary literally to parachute a new character – Naomi (Marsha Thomason) – into the narrative.

39 'Name of the most populous of the Hawaiian Islands and the seat of Honolulu. The name has no meaning' (Pukui and Elbert, Hawaiian Dictionary, p.275).

VI. Lost Logos:
Channel 4 and the Branding of American Event Television

Paul Grainge

In March 2007, the UK satellite television provider Sky unveiled a national media campaign carrying two banner statements: 'Don't Lose *Lost*' and 'Get Jack Back'. Appealing directly to the loyal audience of the imported American dramas *Lost* and *24* (Imagine Entertainment, 2001–) – both shown on Sky One having been poached from British terrestrial rivals Channel 4 and BBC 2 – the advertorial campaign was a defensive salvo in a dispute between Sky and Virgin Media over the latter's decision to drop key Sky channels from its digital cable service. While cast in the business press as a struggle of will between corporate owners Rupert Murdoch and Richard Branson, the carriage dispute also revealed two different approaches to media marketing, with Sky seeking leverage in the pay television market by enticing viewers through the acquisition of popular shows, and Virgin Media seeking to emphasize the technological benefits of its cable package.[1] The different priorities given to 'content' and 'technology' were duly emblazoned on the transit vans installing digital pay-television in British towns and cities. In a mobile public relations battle, Sky vehicles were adorned with characters from its flagship programmes (from the hapless face of Homer Simpson to the brooding cast of *Lost*) while Virgin's fleet advertised broadband capacity as part of 'the real deal'. Not for the first time, US television became linked to calculated branding strategies in the British media market, with the whereabouts of the latest 'must-see' viewing becoming, for Sky at least, both promotional tool and bargaining chip.

Of all the recent imported hits to which Sky had acquired the rights, *Lost* had the most valuable combination of brand equity and hype. Not only was the show a global phenomenon, becoming the fastest-ever selling US television series since its launch on ABC in 2004, it also functioned as a multi-purpose franchise. Sold to over 200 countries worldwide, the series was designed to travel across a range of ancillary markets and media platforms. Together with the array of books, toys, trading cards and merchandise commonly associated with high-budget products from the US entertainment industry, *Lost* was made to translate across technological formats. In developments keenly observed by the entertainment and marketing trade press, original content for the series was produced for iPods and mobile phones, extending further the transmedia world developed through websites, alternative reality games (ARGs) and Internet podcasts and blogs. Typifying the new migratory patterns of industrial texts, *Lost* was a signal form of 'convergence television', which John Caldwell associates with the growing impetus to 'calculate, amass, repackage, and transport the entertainment product across the borders of both new technologies and media forms'[2] According to the *Los Angeles Times*:

> What's happening with *Lost* is a harbinger of the changing nature of TV watching itself, dividing its followers into two groups: the loyal audience that tunes in every week and the fans who devour every bit of information made available to them on the Internet, books and magazines.[3]

For Sky, *Lost* was emblematic property. Most immediately, it was a blockbusting TV serial that generated audience loyalty and could motivate Sky subscriptions. At the same time, *Lost* was a media brand that met the best ambitions of 'content streaming' in the digital age.[4] It was perhaps inevitable, in these two respects, that Sky would outbid Channel 4 for the British rights to screen the third series of *Lost*. Paying nearly £1 million an episode, Sky began showing *Lost* in November 2006 after a marketing campaign that reconfirmed the fragile hold that terrestrial channels had on event or 'appointment' television nurtured as such. Against the visual iconography of an impending island storm, the posters for the third series would state triumphantly, '*Lost*: Now Found on Sky One'.

This chapter concerns the UK promotion and branding of *Lost* before its Sky acquisition. For many television scholars, branding has become the defining industrial practice of the multi-channel era, which Catherine Johnson maps along the two lines of development borne out in the relations between corporations like Sky and Channel 4 and media content such as *Lost*. She writes:

> First, the branding of television networks enables them to compete effectively in an increasingly crowded marketplace by creating strong, distinctive and loyal relationships with viewers. Second, television programmes themselves can act as brands that can be profitably exploited across a range of different media platforms in order to increase profits for the owner of the associated trade mark.[5]

Johnson argues that branding should be viewed 'not simply as a logo or set of values, but as a set of relations between producers, writers, networks, texts and viewers, that emerges in the branding of networks and in the branding of programmes'.[6] If, as she suggests, we must begin to examine how network and programme brands function together, this means accounting for the way that programmes can contribute to the brand equity of more than one corporation in the international television marketplace. I wish to develop Johnson's analysis by considering the particular entwining of channel/programme branding that framed the early history of *Lost* in the UK market.

Examining the identity of Channel 4 as the original brand home of *Lost*, I focus in particular on the 'promotional surround' of the series when it was launched on British terrestrial screens, analysing the assorted textual ephemera (such as commissioned trailers, series sponsorships, channel promos and idents) that helped to position and domesticate *Lost* for British audiences before the renewal rights were surrendered to Sky. Concentrating on the promotion of *Lost* for those tuning in to Channel 4 every week, I explore the specific co-creation of channel/programme branding within televisual marketing strategies. While critical attention has been focused on the viral marketing of *Lost* on the Internet, I aim to concentrate on the kinds of promotional work that remain central to everyday viewing, and that are directly aimed at terrestrial viewers who watch in real time.[7]

CHANNEL 4 AND THE LURE OF US ENTERTAINMENT IMPORTS

That Channel 4 should find *Lost* an attractive proposition is hardly surprising given the corporation's historical, and sometimes controversial, relationship with imported US programming. From its inception in 1982, Channel 4 has drawn upon US imports to support its programming schedule. This has included sitcoms such as *Cheers* (Charles/Burrows/Charles Productions, 1982–93), *Roseanne* (Carsey-Werner Company, 1988–97) and *Friends* (Warner Bros. Television, 1992–2004), comedy dramas like *Ally McBeal* (20th Century Fox Television, 1997–2002), *Sex and the City* (Darren Star Productions, 1998–2004) and *Ugly Betty* (Touchstone Television, 2006–), and serials such as *Hill Street Blues* (MTM Enterprises, 1981–7), *ER* (Constant c Productions, 1994–), *The West Wing* (John Wells Productions, 1999–2006), *Six Feet Under* (HBO, 2001–5) and *The Sopranos* (HBO, 1999–2007).

Using US material has proved highly successful in attracting younger, more affluent audiences, but this strategy has been criticized by those who find in it the abdication of Channel 4's public service responsibilities. Established with a parliamentary remit to provide innovative programming not found on other British channels, and expected to commission the majority of its programmes from independent television producers from the UK, Channel 4 has found the use of US imports historically problematic, inviting splenetic attacks from the likes of the departing ITV boss Charles Allen, who excoriated the channel at the Edinburgh Television Festival in 2006 for being dominated by 'reality, lifestyle, US acquisitions and shock docs'.[8]

Such criticism, periodically levelled, has not precluded Channel 4 from using US imports as a scheduling cornerstone. Ever since the 1990 Broadcasting Act, which allowed Channel 4 to sell its own advertising for the first time, emphasis has been placed on popular programming that is able to attract both upmarket and youth audiences. Indeed, a key legacy of Michael Grade, who steered Channel 4 between 1988 and 1997, was the reduction of experimental minority output and the acceleration of soap operas and US entertainment imports able to generate the markets sought after by advertisers. While advertising-funded, Channel 4 is also externally regulated, and this hybrid mode of public service broadcasting has occasionally led bodies such as the Independent Television Commission to force Channel 4 to utilize more domestic productions. However, there is no doubting the importance of US programmes to Channel 4's survival and market success, helping it to achieve 10 per cent of the total audience share by 2001, rivalling its two immediate competitors, BBC 2 (11.1 per cent) and Sky (6 per cent).[9]

By the end of the tenure of Michael Jackson, Grade's successor as Chief Executive (1997–2001), US programming had become central to the brand identity of Channel 4 and was especially significant in helping the corporation position itself for the future of digital television. With the intensified competition of the multichannel environment, Jackson helped instigate a period of rapid commercial expansion at Channel 4, designed, according to Georgina Born, 'to increase and diversify the revenue streams coming into Channel 4 in order to cushion the main public service channel from future budget shortfalls'.[10] Seeking to develop new multi-revenue business models (following the example of Sky with its combination of digital platforms and premium subscription channels) Channel 4 launched the youth-oriented digital channel E4 in 2001.[11] Pursuing the lucrative youth market by screening first-run US imports, E4 helped consolidate the channel's self-declared identity 'as the home of cutting-edge entertainment'. With top US series increasingly sold with free-to-air and pay television rights bundled together, E4 was a calculated brand extension; it became a strategic means of fending off Sky in the competitive market for US imports, and of protecting the main channel from the accusation that US television was being used to define the 'cutting edge' at the expense of British fare.

Although US imports have caused problems with the regulator, they have nevertheless been at the forefront of Channel 4's efforts to clarify what it stands for, playing an important part in giving definition to the channel as somewhere 'for viewers who expect to be challenged, provoked and entertained by new ideas and new talent'.[12] As June Dromgoole, the controller of Channel 4 acquisitions, said in 2004: 'Channel 4 has become known as the home of top US programming. It's a point of distinction that has been carefully nurtured over many years by hand-picking the best shows to suit the Channel audience and brand.'[13] This sense of distinction has been notably developed through the channel's use of comedy and drama series from the

US network HBO. Here, we return to Catherine Johnson's observation that programmes can contribute to the brand equity of more than one corporation. Specifically, Johnson explores how 'quality' dramas such as *The Sopranos* and *Six Feet Under* have helped construct not only the brand identity of HBO but also that of Channel 4 as they have been sold and repackaged abroad. She writes:

> In many ways, the brand values of HBO are shared by Channel 4. As with HBO, Channel 4 has a commitment to screen the kinds of television programming not found elsewhere on British television. As with HBO, Channel 4 has a remit for creativity and innovation in its programming.[14]

There is an undoubted kinship in the brand identity of HBO and Channel 4. This does not mean to say, however, that Channel 4 has limited itself to HBO as a source of programming content. As Paul Rixon points out, broadcasters like Channel 4 are involved in a constant process of acquiring and assimilating US shows into British television schedules, and by the mid-2000s Channel 4 was looking with increasing interest to the output of ABC.[15]

Anticipating the gaps in its schedule left by the end of *Friends*, *Frasier* (Grub Street Productions, 1993–2004) and *Sex and the City*, Channel 4 bet on the success of two prospective ABC hits in 2004: *Lost* and *Desperate Housewives* (Cherry Alley Productions, 2004–). Outbidding terrestrial rival Five, Channel 4 signed a deal at the June trade previews that gave it exclusive UK rights to both programmes, to be screened in the year after their domestic launch. Justifying their considerable hype, and to the relief of ABC executives, both shows would become central to the ratings success of the beleaguered US network, with the first series of *Lost* averaging 16 million viewers in the USA, appealing to the key 18–49-year-old demographic. This gave a much needed boost to ABC's network identity. After a long period of stagnation and a number of limp rebranding initiatives following its takeover by Disney in 1996 – typified by a campaign that associated ABC with the colour yellow – it was original programming that ultimately fired the revival of ABC as a network brand, with its rejuvenation in the mid-2000s driven by the success of the island drama that Disney Chief Executive Michael Eisner had initially, and infamously, dismissed.

In market terms, *Lost* would become an indicative franchise in the changing landscape of US television, designed by its makers as something to watch but also as something to inhabit and explore. Mindful of its digital television strategies, Channel 4 spared no expense in promoting *Lost* as a brand event. Similar to the domestic launch of the series on ABC, Channel 4 ran a major marketing campaign, spending over £1 million on posters, billboards, trailers and new media advertising. As a measure of the programme's significance, the marketing budget for *Lost* was second only to that reserved for the launch of the corporation's new digital channel More4. Compared with the promotion of other acquired serials, including *Desperate Housewives*, the campaign for *Lost* was one of the most expensive of its kind. It was also one of the most experimental. For instance, Channel 4 became the first European television advertiser to purchase billboard space within a virtual Internet game. Describing the appearance of *Lost* clips within the role-playing game *Anarchy Online*, Channel 4's director of network marketing, Polly Cochrane, said: 'It's partly to drive word of mouth – and doing something cool in this space means it's going to be seen by a younger audience.'[16]

In the lexicon of brand marketing, online strategies helped establish 'buzz' over 'hype' among a core target niche, enabling the 'infectious chatter that spreads from consumer to consumer about something of genuine interest to them'.[17] Just as important as the actual effects of this approach, however, was the message sent to others in the television industry about the competence and creativity of Channel 4 as a brand home. With Internet marketing generally seen as 'nice to do but not essential', Cochrane summarized the channel's multimedia approach to *Lost* with a telling rationalization of self-promotion: 'It's good for the show, it's good for the department and it's good for the Channel 4 brand.'[18]

On certain terms, *Lost* enabled Channel 4 to display its marketing prowess. However, the series also came with its own promotional challenges; internally, it was perceived as a harder sell than the glossy, and more openly seductive, *Desperate Housewives*. In a competitive television environment where audiences may only commit to two or three drama series at a time, Channel 4 had to think how best to attract people to a serialized mystery of indeterminate genre, a 'thriller' based on having more questions than answers. Channel 4's broad response, like that of ABC, was to devise a promotional strategy that could foster, and then sustain, depth of curiosity about *Lost*. As programme-maker and trademark owner, ABC developed this approach by expanding the range of ancillary texts exploring the show's mythology, fostering audience loyalty by transforming the series into a content 'experience' freed from the constraints of its own 'network-hosted logic'.[19]

These platform strategies helped redefine the parameters of *Lost* as a television text, including the traditional marketing/merchandising techniques used to transform entertainment commodities into franchise phenomena.[20] Like ABC, Channel 4 would exploit the ancillary and interactive potential of the series, releasing a companion book called *The Lost Chronicles* and developing its own *Lost* website with links to downloadable videos, episodes and radio shows.[21] Experimenting with multimedia content/marketing, Channel 4 sought to position *Lost* in the UK by creating 'a rich environment around the programme [so that] it feels part of a 360 degree space.'[22]

However, not being a rights-owning producer (such as ABC) or a distribution-controlling platform owner (such as Sky), Channel 4 also sought to develop and strengthen its brand value as an 'aggregator of content', developing marketing strategies in relation to *Lost* that made the channel stand out as a television carrier.[23] It is in this particular context of industrial pressure and need that we might analyse how *Lost* was sold to British television audiences, and how it was framed, or rather refracted, through the prism of Channel 4's own promotional imperatives.

THE PROMOTIONAL SURROUND OF LOST

In analysing the role that domestic broadcasters play in helping British audiences to consume, understand and experience US programmes, Paul Rixon looks at the various means by which imported shows are inserted into British schedules, and are potentially changed in their viewing and reception as a result. He suggests that broadcasters such as the BBC, ITV and Channel 4 draw upon their particular understanding of domestic audiences and the British television environment to 'actively mediate' the use and experience of US programmes. This process of mediation can take one of a number of forms: by means of a channel re-editing a programme or reordering a series for

particular scheduling requirements, by changing a programme's relation to the ratio and structure of advertising breaks, by changing the
time at which a programme is broadcast on British television, or by
altering the context or 'narrative image' through which a programme
is formally marketed.[24] It is the last of these that interests me in considering the assimilation of *Lost* on British television screens. Specifically, I want to consider how elements of television's promotional flow
– trailers, sponsorships, idents, and so on – helped frame the series
in relation to the branding strategies of Channel 4, particularly its association with quality popular television.

As I have mentioned, Channel 4 developed awareness of *Lost*
through a range of multimedia strategies, adapting many of the viral
and ancillary marketing approaches used by ABC. Diverting from the
approach of the US network, however, was an elliptical trailer made
by Channel 4 that choreographed the 'pre-image' of *Lost* for British
viewers. Directed jointly by the fashion and advertising photographer
David LaChapelle (known for his music video collaborations with artists such as Moby and for fashion ads for companies like H&M) and
Channel 4's creative director, Brett Foraker, the trailer was a signature
promotional text designed to create a particular understanding of *Lost*
and the channel on which it was to be shown. Shot on location in Hawaii in March 2005, it featured cast members of *Lost* dancing, as if in a
daze, in front of the wreckage of an aircraft. In atmosphere, the trailer
was a cross between a music video and a perfume commercial; set to
ambient dance music, it involved a beach of beautiful people performing a series of apparently meaningful, but wholly unexplained, gestures and gyrations. Certain individuals danced together (Jack and
Kate, Kate and Sawyer, Boone and Claire, Sayid and Shannon, Sun
and Jin), some danced or walked alone (Charlie, Hurley) and others
were shown conducting as if the entire performance were some kind
of symphony (Locke and Walt). Most wore torn or bedraggled evening
wear that would not feature in the series itself, with Locke dressed
in a white dinner jacket, Sawyer in a waistcoat, Kate and Sun in evening gowns. The trailer's high-concept style re-imagined imagistic features of *Lost* in ways that could appeal to Channel 4's core audience
of young, affluent viewers.[25] First shown on E4 in the months leading
up to the terrestrial launch of the programme on 10 August 2005, the
trailer could also be seen on the main channel, on Channel 4's *Lost*

website, and in cinemas before Hollywood blockbusters such as *War of the Worlds*, *Charlie and the Chocolate Factory* and *Wedding Crashers*.

In marketing terms, the trailer was designed as a hybrid cultural text – a promotional object but also a self-standing visual entertainment. Rather than advertise *Lost* through edited sequences of narrative and character action, Channel 4 developed a conceptual mood for its latest US acquisition. This marked a departure from ABC. As a major network promoting what it hoped would become a mainstream hit, ABC was inclined to use 'show and tell' trailer rhetoric to launch the first series. As a publisher broadcaster with a reputation for being, in its own words, 'a place of individual authorship, a consistent source of surprise, invention and brainfood',[26] Channel 4 approached *Lost* somewhat differently, promoting the show through reading protocols attuned to its younger and 'cooler' audience, and in line with the channel's reputation for high-calibre US programming.

In audience terms, while ABC looked to the core 18–49 age demographic, Channel 4 addressed *Lost* to young, urban adults aged between 16 and 34. With its brand identity forged in the early 2000s on the back of US dramas such as *ER*, *The Sopranos* and *Six Feet Under*, Channel 4 framed *Lost* in ways that drew upon its association with quality US imports. It developed a style of advertising that one American fan, discussing Channel 4's trailer on the online forum *www. tvsquad.com*, called 'very HBO-ish, not something I could see shown on American networks'.[27] The reference to HBO here is telling. According to Catherine Johnson, HBO has established itself as a premium brand by distinguishing itself from American network television using the discourse of high popular culture (or 'high pop') to offer 'something more than television, more than mass culture, while providing it paradoxically through television, as television'.[28] This marketing sleight of hand is exemplified in the brand slogan 'It's not TV. It's HBO.' While Channel 4 is a public broadcaster rather than a niche cable operator, it has staked its identity on a similar idea of programming difference and distinction. Consistent with the 'core values' that Channel 4 has routinely ascribed to itself in marketing talk since the Jackson era, it promoted *Lost* as if it were an HBO product, a show that finessed the corporation's brand association with 'innovative', 'contemporary' and 'smart' US programming. This was most apparent in the enigmatic and expressive design of its trailer.

On first viewing, it was not apparent that Channel 4's trailer for *Lost* was a trailer at all; this only became clear when the '4' logo appeared at the end with the words '*Lost* – coming soon'. Two versions of the trailer were cut, both deliberately oblique in advertising *Lost* as a series. The first used the Portishead song 'Numb' as the accompanying music track. This choice was suggestive of the way Channel 4 sought to encode those elements of *Lost* that met its own brand image, reflecting itself in programming that was positioned as trendy, innovative and otherwise 'cinematic' in feel. Describing the propensity for pop songs to be used as stock music within contemporary British television, Kevin Donnelly suggests that instrumental or 'image-friendly music', in particular electronic dance, has become a staple within British trailers, programmes, continuity segments and montage sequences aspiring towards a concept of the cinematic. Such music, he writes, 'is premised upon "atmosphere" and the construction of soundscapes in a similar manner to the way film composers and sound designers construct film soundtracks'.[29] In terms of budget and production value, *Lost* was, from the outset, more cinematic than televisual in style, with the first episode costing upwards of $12 million, the most expensive pilot in television history. Channel 4 sought to accentuate this quality by turning its promotional trailer for *Lost* into a proto-cinematic event, an ancillary video text that would eventually appear as a bonus feature on the UK DVD box-set of *Lost*'s second series.

If this trailer was designed to pique interest among key taste constituencies, a second version would provide more direct and suggestive clues about the character-driven focus of the show. Instead of using 'Numb', the second trailer used a chorus of personal secrets (voiced by the principal *Lost* characters) to accompany the same dance sequence. The so-called 'voice-over version' went as follows: 'All of us have a secret. One of us is a hero; one of us is a fraud; one of us is a junkie; one of us is a cop; one of us is a saint; one of us is a sinner; one of us is a martyr; one of us is a murderer; all of us are guilty; all of us are lost.' This trailer established the show's proposed appeal as a serial mystery, but restrained from giving away anything else about genre or story.

Both trailers were designed to deepen audience curiosity about *Lost*, most immediately for those with no prior familiarity with the programme, but also for those potentially acquainted with the show through spoilers, Internet discussion and residual hype from the USA. Channel 4 took a particular approach in its spot advertising of *Lost*, developing the show's pre-image through trailers that established the meaning of the show (and its promotion) as a talking point. In one sense, this applied strategies used by ABC in helping to establish the programme as a 'water-cooler' event. At the same time, the commissioned trailer bore the promotional hallmarks of Channel 4, using a fashion-inspired piece of commercial art to project the broadcaster's relation to quality US imports. As a promotional text, the trailer was a striking example of the way that Channel 4 made attempts to mediate the identity and experience of *Lost* for a particular subset of British viewers – to make connections between the programme and the Channel 4 brand.

The terrestrial scheduling of *Lost* further developed these connections. Having advertised *Lost* through trailers that accentuated its proto-cinematic quality, the launch episode was scheduled around a midweek *Big Brother* eviction. Unlike much of Channel 4's HBO programming, which often contains graphic language, sex and violence, *Lost* was suitable for a pre-watershed audience.[30] As such, the first episode was aired on a Wednesday night at 8.30pm, just before *Big Brother*. (A similar slot to that scheduled by ABC, which aired *Lost* on Wednesdays at 8pm). A second instalment was then shown at 10pm., directly after *Big Brother*'s surprise eviction. This would become the programme's 'strand' slot in the Channel 4 schedule, a time often reserved for US imports such as, previously, *Desperate Housewives*. As Channel 4's largest single ratings generator, *Big Brother* (Bazal, 2000–) enabled *Lost* to maximize its audience, with schedulers designing a double-bill of event television. This was seen in the trade press as a 'brilliant' execution, and the debut episode of *Lost* drew 6.1 million viewers (an audience share of 26.8 percent), and the second instalment attracted 5.9 million (an audience share of 29.6 per cent).[31] This beat all competitors in both slots, and was a record audience for the launch of a US import, outdoing *Desperate Housewives* (4.6 million) and exceeding the previous record audience held by *ER* (5 million).[32]

Wrapping *Lost* around *Big Brother* became a significant tactic in positioning the show. Unlike Channel 4's sometimes erratic scheduling and promotion of shows like *The Sopranos* and *Six Feet Under*

– often moving them between different time slots late in the evening – *Lost* was offered up as a more dedicated form of 'appointment' television. While the promotional trailer framed the pre-image of the series through high pop aesthetics appealing to the channel's 'cool' and 'quality' demographic, the scheduling of *Lost* was designed with a mind to capturing the loyalty of an audience attuned to the interactive pleasures of reality television, and who may well have memories of the desert island reality show, *Survivor* (Mark Burnett Productions, 2000–), used by ABC chairman Lloyd Braun to pitch the series to senior Disney executives.[33] In a series of ways, Channel 4 sought to aggregate niche taste cultures for its latest brand property, providing different discursive and scheduling frames for *Lost* as quality/popular television.

These frames were refined by the sponsorship credits that accompanied *Lost* as a series, one of a number of US imports on British screens to be sponsored by the telephone enquiry service 118-118. With the relaxation of television sponsorship rules by the regulator Ofcom in 2005, sponsorship messages and their related 'break bumpers' (sponsor-produced texts that signal the movement between programme and ad break) became more elaborate and creative in the mid-to-late 2000s. 118-118 was a notable example of a tailored form of sponsorship designed to integrate itself into the experience, expectation and ritual of watching a show. Rather than append its corporate name to a particular programme or channel – such as Cadbury's sponsorship of *Coronation Street* (Granada Television, 1960–) on ITV or the Channel 4 film sponsorships by Stella Artois – 118-118 associated itself with a genre type: quality television drama. By sponsoring *ER* and *The Sopranos* on Channel 4, *Prison Break* (Rat Entertainment, 2005–) on Channel 5, and *Lost* on Channel 4 and later Sky, 118-118 became a generic badge in the British television landscape. Unlike Stella Artois, however, which sought to equate its brand (a 'reassuringly expensive' beer) with the cultural prestige of quality film (its rhetoric of sponsorship referencing European art cinema), 118-118 developed a retro sensibility attuned to the taste culture of a young and media-savvy target market. Unconcerned with projecting images of cultural distinction, two moustachioed figures from the 1970s performed a range of visual gags and parodies that would differ between ad segments and would often gesture towards programme content. For example,

118-118's sponsorship of the second series of *Prison Break* featured a host of breakout gags, while its sponsorship of the third series of *Lost* on Sky would relate specifically to the island drama, with the two figures performing different jokes on a tropical beach, searching for hotels, cinema listings, train times, spas, and so on. Coding the genre of quality drama, the commercial sponsorship also reinforced the ironic form of address favoured by Channel 4 (and especially E4) in promoting popular television serials.

The 118-118 sponsorships were one of a number of texts that would circulate beyond and below *Lost* as a television event. John Caldwell outlines the growing significance of such texts in the multichannel environment, considering how 'secondary' or 'tertiary' production texts such as channel idents, sponsorships, promotional videos, making-of documentaries and TV–web synergies persistently migrate towards 'primary' textual status. In particular, Caldwell draws attention to those elements of television's promotional flow that have become industry-authored forms of content in their own right. Together with commissioned trailers and series sponsorships, we can point finally in this context to the marketing work that Channel 4 undertook on its own behalf, a significant factor in the analysis of the promotional surround of *Lost* and the entwining of channel/programme branding. Creating texts that address both production and viewer cultures, Channel 4 promos have regularly used actors and images drawn from its popular US imports, with the corporation presenting a range of US shows (formally belonging to the stables of NBC, HBO and ABC) as the key to its own brand value and meaning as a television channel.

According to John Ellis, 'The brand of all generalist channels lies in the schedule and how that schedule is known by their client audiences.'[34] Of all the terrestrial channels, Channel 4 has made its schedule a point of brand articulation. From the mid-2000s, this was borne out in a series of channel promotions featuring stars of its schedule responding to an inferred off-screen question, for example, 'What was your first car?', 'What is your favourite drink?', 'Where were you happiest?' or 'What is the best way to your heart?' Providing a montage of frank and comic answers, these sequences have featured presenters like Davina McCall (*Big Brother*), Jon Snow (*Channel 4 News*) and Jimmy Carr (*8 out of 10 Cats*), protagonists of lifestyle shows and documentaries like Gordon Ramsay (*Ramsay's Kitchen Nightmares*) and

Jamie Oliver (*Jamie's School Dinners*), and actors from US programmes including *ER*, *The West Wing*, *Six Feet Under*, *Desperate Housewives*, *Ugly Betty* and *Lost*. In the case of *Lost*, Mathew Fox, Evangeline Lilly, Josh Holloway, Dominic Monaghan and Naveen Andrews all appeared in Channel 4 branding during the British airing of series one and two. These appearances were unsurprising given the importance of the global television market to US programme-makers and the inclination of Buena Vista International Television (the Disney-owned distributor of *Lost*) to send its stars to Europe to generate free publicity for the show. Interesting in this case, however, is the role that cast members of a US network show assumed in the promotion of a British television company, highlighting the reciprocal marketing relations that take place *between* programme and channel brands.

The purpose of these quirky channel promotions was to cultivate Channel 4's 'brand relationship' with its client audience, to produce, in marketing parlance, 'a memorable sensory experience that ties in with the positioning of the company, product or service'.[35] For Channel 4, this meant defining its identity in and between a diverse range of programmes and people, using a format that developed a fond and cheeky familiarity with the channel 'family'. This was accompanied by the production of distinctive channel idents. Having abandoned what Mark Brownrigg and Peter Meech call the 'fanfare' style of television ident in 1996, Channel 4 moved decisively towards customized 'funfair' idents in the late 1990s and early 2000s.[36] From 2004, this would include a striking ensemble of idents projecting the '4' logo in panoramic and geographically dispersed scenes. Collectively known as 'Atlas', these idents

> recaptured the essence of the original nine piece figure 4 and displayed it in a wide variety of three-dimensional locations including a council estate, bowling green, Tokyo Street, panorama of electricity pylons, Trafalgar Square, diner and a television viewer's living room.[37]

With expanding variety, and accompanied by different ambient music in each case, Atlas idents appeared before scheduled programmes and would sometimes even correspond to their content or genre. For example, the council estate ident would frequently appear before the working class drama *Shameless* (Company Pictures, 2004–) (also sponsored by 118-118), while an ident of flitting alien lightships would come before programmes like the hoax reality show *Space Cadets* (Zeppotron, 2005). Reinforcing the significance of US imports, a number of idents would correspond, atmospherically, with key Channel 4 US comedy and drama series – as with a skyline ident evoking the title sequence of *Sex and the City* and a motel ident summoning the backdrop of *My Name is Earl* (20th Century Fox Television, 2005–).

Reflecting the coastal scenery of its latest US import, it is perhaps no surprise that a 'rock' ident appeared towards the end of Channel 4's airing of the second series of *Lost*. Similar to the other Atlas idents, 'rock' amalgamated live action plates and digital technology to create a playful dimensionality – the camera panned a rugged coastline to reveal the figure 4 as a rock formation jutting into the sea. Although using images of the British coastline, the sapphire colour of the sea and the tree-topped cliff-face suggested other island geographies. In distinguishing itself as a television carrier, the 'rock' ident became a mark of Channel 4's brand relation with *Lost*, part of an ensemble of logos that would denote the landscape of Channel 4's terrestrial identity in the present as well as in the past. Even as *Lost* was spirited away to Sky One, the rock ident would continue to appear on the main channel, becoming a visual reminder of the show's one-time place in the Channel 4 family – a programme introduced to UK audiences and nurtured by Channel 4 before leaving for the moneyed charms of pay television.

In a multichannel environment defined by competition for audience loyalty, and where networks fight for recognition among viewers and the producing communities who sell their shows, idents and channel promos have become a proliferating subgenre within television culture. As John Caldwell suggests, idents have become a form of textual production that, along with trailers and other promotional fare, 'stand simultaneously as corporate strategies, as forms of cultural and economic capital integral to media professional communities, and as the means by which contemporary media industries work to rationalize their operations in an era of great institutional instability'.[38] While Channel 4's idents and promos were fleeting and fun, the corporation's integration of *Lost* within its own marketing efforts was hardly frivolous; it became a means of expressing the channel's 'attitude' as an aggregator of content at a time when other channels and television providers were beginning to encroach on its status as a natural brand home for quality US imports.

Watching the first two seasons of *Lost* in Britain was a brand experience at many levels; it was framed by the logos of the programme itself as a global television franchise but also by the domesticating logos of the channel on which *Lost* was scheduled, screened and sponsored. It has been my argument that the textual ephemera surrounding the British airing of *Lost* – from customized trailers to the weekly use of break bumpers and channel promos and idents – played an important early role shaping the narrative image of the programme in the UK. Specifically, *Lost* was positioned less as a mainstream prime-time serial, as in the USA, than as an example of quality popular television growing out of the intensified competition between Channel 4, Five and Sky to stake market territory via the acquisition/assimilation of the best new US comedy and drama series. With the prohibitive cost of renewing both *Lost* and *Desperate Housewives* in 2006, Channel 4 decided to replace *Lost* with another ABC hit, *Ugly Betty*. This decision was unsurprising given the escalating cost of *Lost* episodes and the ratings slip that Channel 4 experienced during its airing of the second season – with audiences for *Lost* dropping from 4.1 million (a 21 per cent audience share) to 2.8 million (16 per cent). Nevertheless, *Lost* remained a core and sought-after television brand, with Sky One paying £40 million to bring *Lost* to the satellite broadcaster.

This switch did not significantly alter the programme's narrative image in Britain. It did coincide with a dramatic reduction in the time lapse between the US and British airing of the series, however. To combat the pirated downloads that were threatening their global distribution operation, Disney and ABC made increasing efforts to transport their product overseas quickly.[39] In 2007, they began sending digital files of *Lost* to BSkyB the day after its airing in the USA. Like something borne of the Dharma initiative, these files were transmitted through a data line under the Atlantic Ocean, enabling *Lost* to be converted into the European television format and broadcast in the UK just four days later. In key respects, Sky maintained the same marketing and scheduling strategy as Channel 4 in positioning the series, making small adjustments by moving *Lost* to a Sunday 10pm slot, and accentuating the programme's spread across digital media platforms. Different, however, was the near-synchronous transatlantic viewing of the third series for those in Britain who could afford the subscription fee.[40] While audience figures dropped to 1.2 million for *Lost*'s debut on Sky, these were still seen as solid ratings. Vindicating the satellite provider's decision to poach the show from Channel 4, the third series of *Lost* offered, at the same time, a portent of the new global temporalities of event television in the age of digital.

Notes

1   See Nichola Dobson, 'Brand loyalty vs. show loyalty, the strange case of Virgin vs. Sky', *Flow* v/10 (2007), available online at *http://flow tv.org/?p=119*.

2   John Caldwell, 'Convergence television: aggregating form and repurposing content in the culture of conglomeration', in Lynn Spigel and Jan Olsson (eds), *Television After TV: Essays on a Medium on Transition* (Durham: Duke University Press, 2004), p.50.

3   Maria Elena Fernandez, 'ABC's *Lost* is easy to find, and not just on TV', *Los Angeles Times*, 3 January 2006, p.E1.

4   Sky One's programming chief, Michael Woolfe, explained: 'Today's audiences demand more quality and flexibility than ever before, so we are intending to use various digital platforms to make *Lost* available to our customers when and how they want.' See Mimi Turner, 'Sky One: let's get *Lost*', *Hollywood Reporter*, 20 October 2006. On the development of 'content streaming' as a media principle, see Simone Murray, 'Brand loyalties: rethinking content within global corporate media', *Media, Culture & Society*, xxvii/3 (2005), pp.415–35.

5   Catherine Johnson, 'Tele-branding in TVIII: the network as brand and the programme as brand', *New Review of Film and Television Studies* v/1 (2007), p.8.

6   Ibid., p. 20.

7   This resonates with Michael Svennevig's suggestion that 'it is clear that people continue to value TV as medium precisely because it is not the Internet in the sense that it is pre-produced for specific purposes, and designed to deliver ready-made benefits to the audience' (Michael Svennevig, 'Television audience research – UK', in Douglas Gomery and Luke Hockley (eds), *Television Industries* (London: British Film Institute, 2006), p.83.

8   Cited in Stuart Jeffries, 'Where did it all go wrong?', *Review* in the *Guardian*, 22 March 2007, p.7.

9   See John Sedgewick, 'The economics of television – UK', in Gomery and
     Hockley (eds): *Television Industries*, pp.1–5, and Sylvia Harvey, 'Chan-
     nel Four and the redefining of public service broadcasting', in Michele
     Hilmes (ed.), *The Television History Book* (London: British Film Institute,
     2003), pp.50–4.

10   Georgina Born, 'Strategy, positioning and projection in digital television:
     Channel Four and the commercialization of public service broadcasting
     in the UK', *Media, Culture & Society* xxv/6 (2003), p.780.

11   This followed on from the launch of FilmFour in 1998 and paved the
     way for More4 in 2005 and Channel 4 + 1 in 2007.

12   *Channel Four Television Corporation: Report and Financial Statements*
     (London: Channel 4 Television Corporation, 2000), p.8.

13   Cited in Paul Rixon, *American Television on British Screens* (London: Pal-
     grave, 2006) p.97.

14   Johnson: 'Tele-branding in TVIII', p.12.

15   Rixon: *American Television on British Screens*, pp.83–105.

16   Steven Brook, 'Channel 4 launches 1m campaign for *Lost*', Guardian Un-
     limited, 25 January 2005, available online at *www.guardian.co.uk/me-
     dia/2005/jul/25/marketingandpr.advertising*.

17   David Lewis and Darren Bridger, *The Soul of the New Consumer* (London:
     Nicolas Brealey, 2001), p.104. Theorizing a new marketing environment
     defined by consumers who are more active and informed than ever be-
     fore, Lewis and Bridger write: 'cynical New Consumers who pay little
     attention to expensively created hype are strongly influenced by street-
     level gossip or buzz. Once persuaded by buzz, however, New Consumers
     are far more receptive and willing to be persuaded by hype' (p.111).

18   Brook, 'Channel 4 launches 1m campaign for *Lost*'.

19   Caldwell, 'Convergence television', p.49.

20   Describing the way that ancillary texts such as Internet games and 'mo-
     bisodes' (short content pieces for mobile phone viewing) were developed
     in creative partnership between studio marketers and series producers
     (both seeking to extend the promotional-cum-narrative environment
     of *Lost* on new platform technologies), ABC's senior vice president of
     marketing, Mike Benson, commented: 'I actually look at marketing
     more like developing content for the show ... while we can hype and sell,
     I'd rather tell a story than sell a story.' Cited in Fernandez: 'ABC's *Lost* is
     easy to find', p.E1.

21   Mark Cotta Vaz, *The Lost Chronicles* (London: Channel 4 Books, 2005).
     Channel 4's *Lost* website can be found at *www.channel4.com/entertain-
     ment/tv/microsites/L/lost/*.

22   Brook: 'Channel 4 launches 1m campaign for *Lost*'.

23   Georgina Born coins the phrase 'aggregator of content', relating it to Channel 4's 'vulnerable position in the new broadcasting chain'. Born: 'Strategy, positioning and projection', pp.788–9.

24   Rixon, *American Television on British Screens*, p.126.

25   The extra-diegetic display of this high-concept trailer would change aspects of the programme's narrative. While characters were dressed differently – inspired by Jack Vettriano's paintings of butlers dancing on a beach according to Richard Burdett, the head of Channel 4's in-house ad agency 4creative – it was especially noticeable to fans that Claire was not pregnant. In a glossier application of his photographic style, LaChappelle would also shoot the *Desperate Housewives* campaign for Channel 4.

26   *Channel Four Television Corporation: Report and Financial Statements*, p.8

27   See *www.tvsquad.com/2006/09/22/very-weird-lost-promo-video/*.

28   Johnson, 'Tele-branding in TVIII', p.10.

29   K.J. Donnelly, 'Tracking British television: pop music as stock soundtrack to the small screen', *Popular Music* xxi/3 (2002), p.337.

30   The 'watershed' describes the 9pm boundary in the British television schedule before which 'adult' scenes of sex and violence are not shown by the major terrestrial channels.

31   The average viewing figures were less in the 10pm slot than in the peak 8.30pm slot, hence the second instalment attracting greater audience share with fewer viewers.

32   Chris Tryhon, 'Channel 4 equals ratings high', Guardian Unlimited, 15 August 2005, available online at *www.guardian.co.uk/media/2005/aug/15/broadcasting*; Claire Simpson, '*Lost* and BB top ratings', *The Bookseller*, 19 August 2005, p.10; Maggie Brown, 'Channel 4 finds mass audience with American *Lost*', *The Stage*, 18 August 2005, p.13.

33   According to insider accounts, Braun pitched *Lost* to sceptical Disney executives as a cross between *Survivor* and the Tom Hanks movie *Cast Away* (Robert Zemeckis, 2000). See James B. Stewart, *DisneyWar* (New York: Simon and Schuster, 2005), p.485.

34   John Ellis, *Seeing Things: Television In the Age of Uncertainty* (London: I.B.Tauris, 2002), p.166.

35   See Bernd H. Schmitt and Alex Simonson, *Marketing Aesthetics: The Strategic Management of Branding, Identity and Image* (New York: Simon and Schuster, 1997), p.4. On branding and the entertainment industry see Paul Grainge, *Brand Hollywood: Selling Entertainment in a Global Media Age* (London: Routledge, 2008).

36   Mark Brownrigg and Peter Meech, 'From fanfare to funfair: the changing sound world of UK television idents', *Popular Music* xxi/3 (2002), pp.345–55.

37 See Christine Fanthome, 'Creating an iconic brand – an account of the
    history, development, context and significance of Channel 4's idents',
    Journal of Media Practice viii/3 (2007), pp.255–71. Like the UK *Lost*
    trailer, the Atlas idents were designed by Channel 4 creative director
    Brett Foraker in collaboration with, in this case, Russell Appleford of
    the visual digital effects company The Moving Picture Company.

38 John Caldwell, 'Critical industrial practice: branding, repurposing, and
    the migratory patterns of industrial texts', *Television and New Media*
    vii/2 (2006), p.102.

39 Aaron O. Patrick, 'The race to get TV shows overseas', *Wall Street Jour-
    nal*, business section, 28 March 2007.

40 While a four-day lag is still significant, especially for those eager to
    participate in online fan discussion, it compares to the normal lapse
    of 3–12 months between a programme's broadcast in the USA and its
    appearance in the UK.

Part II
Text

VII. Lost in a Great Story:
Evaluation in Narrative Television (and Television Studies)

Jason Mittell

Lost is a great television programme. Such a statement should be almost self-evident given the existence of this book, dedicated to exploring and analysing its significance. *Lost*'s numerous successes, in generating a worldwide fan base, spawning a multimedia franchise, and accumulating awards and critical accolades, should all point toward a consensus opinion about the show's quality and value. If you are a fan of the show then you will almost certainly agree, as perceived greatness is a common, if not essential, rationale for fandom.

However, for the readers and writers within this book's core genre of television studies, such an explicit assertion of evaluation and praise probably seems out of place, as evaluation is generally off-limits for television academics. For a typical instance, the preface to Jeremy Butler's *Television*, probably the most in-depth overview of US television textuality, dismisses questions of evaluation in a few sentences:

> *Television* does not attempt to teach taste or aesthetics. It is less concerned with evaluation than with *interpretation*. It resists asking, 'Is *The O.C.* great art?' Instead, it poses the question, 'What meanings does *The O.C.* signify and how does it do so?'[1]

Such distinctions between evaluating television programming and interpreting the processes of meaning-making frame virtually the entire field – we media scholars are heavily invested in understanding how meaning is made, conveyed and consumed, but we parenthesize questions of evaluation as outside the scope of our expertise. It is not as if we avoid completely the act of *judging* in our scholarship, as we regularly evaluate television programmes on their political merits, their social relevance, their economic motives, their impacts on the television industry, or even their appeals to popular tastes. But while we may judge a show's various merits or flaws on these more sociological grounds, it is seemingly off-limits to reflect on whether we think the programme is ultimately any good.

LOSING VALUE

The evacuation of the evaluative from our field's critical purview is lodged within the intellectual history of television studies. For the earliest decades of television, questions of aesthetics and value were seen as losing battles – justifying the medium's study by asserting its aesthetic merits, an avenue pursued in the early years of film studies, was to engage the debate on hostile terrain. Detractors of television, both within and outside the academy, effectively framed the medium as aesthetically inferior to, or at best a low-resolution imitation of, other media like film, theatre, literature and radio. Instead, television emerged as an object of study on sociological terms, serving an important role in conveying ideologies, defining identities and influencing behaviours. Social scientists in the USA created a paradigm invested in cataloguing the various social ills and 'effects' caused by television, creating a de facto condemnation of the medium's quality based on all of the horrible things that television allegedly did to us. For critics unsympathetic to the pseudo-scientific claims of media effects researchers, an alternative paradigm emerged out of British cultural studies – the idea that audiences were active agents, not passive subjects, and thus studying decoding processes enabled a defence of television through the surrogates of sophisticated viewers who might have less than sophisticated tastes.

Television studies today, as influenced by cultural studies, still cares about issues of quality and value, but locates evaluation on its agenda once removed, placing 'quality' and 'value' within the conceptual safety of scare quotes (or inverted commas, depending upon your side of the Atlantic). Following Pierre Bourdieu's sociological takedown of aesthetics, television scholars look at quality and value as discursive formations practised by the industry, by journalistic critics, by viewers, by activist groups – essentially by everybody except television scholars. While in most other fields Bourdieu's critique of aesthetic judgment emerged after decades or centuries of canon formation and cultural hierarchies, television studies never had an era of evaluative innocence – we never even had a chance to construct a canon to be deconstructed! For the most part, evaluation's place on the agenda of television studies is solely as an external practice to be observed and critiqued, not a potential avenue of scholarship in itself.

A similar firewall has emerged around how we teach television studies. After reading Susan Douglas's *Where the Girls Are*, my students are usually swayed by her claims about the ambivalent gender politics of *Charlie's Angels* (Spelling-Goldberg Productions, 1976–81) – not because she is intrinsically correct, but because she makes a good case.[2] However, after screening an episode, my students always comment about how 'bad' the show is, with simplistic narratives, lack of suspense, wooden acting and bland visual style. As per the unstated boundaries of media scholarship, the acceptable responses are either 'well, we're all entitled to our opinions', or 'what cultural hierarchies are you endorsing by valuing suspense, complex writing, subtle acting, or visual vibrancy?' The boundaries of media studies propriety seem to forbid discussions of our own tastes and evaluations while wearing our expert garb, whether in print or in the classroom, restricting the discussion of evaluation to the casual realms of the water-cooler or barstool, or their online surrogates.

When evaluation does occur by scholars, it comes in disguise. Surveying the field of television studies – or the other volumes in this book series – it becomes apparent that a great deal of scholarship focuses on the programmes that scholars find most 'compelling', 'interesting,' 'engaging' and 'complex' (i.e. the shows we like), such as *The Sopranos* (HBO, 1999–2007), *The West Wing* (John Wells Productions, 1999–2006), *The X-Files* (20th Century Fox Television, 1993–2002) and *The Simpsons* (Gracie Films, 1989–). How else can we account for the fact that *Buffy the Vampire Slayer* (Mutant Enemy, 1997–2003), a cult show with marginal cultural and industrial impact that the vast majority of US television viewers have barely heard of, has more books published about it than the number of scholarly articles published about *Law & Order* (Wolf Films, 1990–), a much more successful, widespread, long-running and influential franchise? It is not because *Buffy* has more sociological relevance or resonance, as *Law & Order* would be just as fertile terrain for exploring the cultural representations and identity politics that constitutes a good deal of Buffy Studies. The only plausible explanation is the one that is almost never explicitly articulated – for most television scholars, *Buffy* is a better show than *Law & Order*.

It is time to let evaluative criticism out of the closet. It is not enough to use coded signifiers of value like 'sophistication' and 'nuance' in referring to television programming worth studying or teaching – let us admit openly when we think a programme is great. Especially in the context of a book dedicated to exploring a single programme in depth, we must be explicit in acknowledging the roles of evaluation and aesthetic judgment that help to frame our research and drive our field. Many of our scholarly efforts are focused on programmes that we enjoy, value and think are better than others, a forbidden admission that is more often assumed in other fields like film or literary studies, where engaging in close study of an author or a text often constitutes an implicit endorsement of its aesthetic merits. We simply cannot pretend that our own taste and evaluation do not matter.

Even if we admit that we write about shows that we like, some might question the purposes of evaluative criticism – why waste ink explaining why we like something? Isn't it just a futile attempt to treat a personal opinion as something to be proven? And aren't there dangers in claiming quality for certain shows over others, with fears of elitism and exclusion – if scholars assert their tastes as 'correct', will marginalized groups be exiled even further and will ideological systems of oppression masquerading as aesthetic value be maintained? Such concerns echo a defensive posture embedded in television studies, as the medium, per Charlotte Brunsdon's reference to 'poor old television', is always bound to end up on the low end of cultural hierarchies below both older and newer media.[3] Especially in the often-caricatured populist turn of television studies of the 1990s, any assertion of taste or value could be seen as hegemonic impositions of bourgeois norms against the popular taste for the vulgar and base. However, even within the realm of the vulgar and base, we must acknowledge that some crap is better than other crap. Might we benefit from understanding why 'the people' discern between choices that might otherwise seem identically awful to outsiders?

Claims that evaluative criticism would disempower marginal tastes seem to misread what is meant by criticism and scholarship, as well as overstate their cultural power – while what I write usually reflects what I believe, my scholarly arguments are not statements of fact, but rather assertions to be discussed and debated. In positing the value of a programme, I am not offering such a judgment as incontrovertible fact but strong belief, starting a debate with a defensible position that matters only in relation to other opposing positions: in stating that *Lost* is a great programme, I am starting a conversation, not ending one. I don't yearn for a day in which television studies publishes a definitive canonical list delineating the best of television once and for all, but I relish the opportunity to debate openly the value of programmes without suggesting that all evaluations are equally justifiable as idiosyncratic personal taste or simple ideological manifestations. Just because aesthetics can be done in a way that disenfranchises some positions does not require the evacuation of evaluative claims altogether in the name of a egalitarian (and, I believe, ultimately dishonest) poetics of inclusion.

Television programmes offer different meanings, different politics and different aesthetics – and we should be able to engage with these differences without worrying that asserting an evaluative claim might offend someone's taste. Our individual tastes are certainly both socially forged and individually idiosyncratic, but they are also shaped by our study of the medium and influenced by the basic fact that television scholars (hopefully) know much more about television than most viewers or critics (that may be an elitist position, but I am pretty sure 'expertise' is part of the job description for teaching and studying something). If our scholarly expertise helps shape our tastes, which I am certain it often does, we should acknowledge and examine how this happens, making arguments as to why a programme might be seen as more valuable by following particular criteria, and examining how those criteria function culturally.

Thankfully there have been signs in recent years that some cultural studies scholars have turned back to some of the field's earliest writings to explore the role of aesthetics and evaluation in popular culture. Before Stuart Hall effectively defined the scope of one strain of television studies with 'Encoding/Decoding', he co-wrote *The Popular Arts* with Paddy Whannel, offering a defence of popular culture via aesthetic analysis and evaluation. For Hall and Whannel, the category of popular art is forged by the type of distinctions made unfashionable by Bourdieu, but still possible even after the recognition that aesthetic judgments are embedded more in cultural power than transcendent essences of beauty. Hall and Whannel, like other early cultural studies work by Raymond Williams and Dick Hebdige, look for the aesthetics of everyday life, attempting to understand popular culture on its own terrain, not measured against alien paradigms of high art.[4] Likewise, a number of newer works of cultural studies,[5] and a few in television studies,[6] return to questions of aesthetics and value to open up the possibilities of evaluative criticism, although this trend has been more common among British and Australian scholars than in US media studies. Following the lead of this return to questions of form and value, we must look closely at popular texts to understand the ways that taste, evaluation and aesthetics matter to both scholars and everyday viewers – by allowing ourselves to evaluate, we can strengthen our understanding of the broader cultural practice and importance of evaluation.

In offering my own evaluative criticism here, I am not trying to convince anyone that *Lost* is the essence of television, or the pinnacle of the medium's artistic possibilities. But it is a great show, and I wish to explore why. I hope to model a mode of evaluative criticism that avoids the universalistic and canonistic tendencies that other fields have been fighting over for decades. I imagine an explicit awareness of the practices of evaluation in all spheres of television creation and consumption, including a discussion and defence of our own taste practices. Such a mode of evaluation would not seek to make taste judgments the final words of a debate, but the openings of a discussion. What makes shows like *Buffy* and *Lost* so appealing to scholars? How do criteria of cultural politics and poetics intersect or conflict? How might we account for our own shifts in taste as tied to changing cultural contexts, textual exposures, formal education and transformed aesthetics? What might a non-foundational aesthetics of television look like, and how might we use such contingent evaluations in our teaching and scholarship? Just because we want to avoid the flaws of traditional aesthetic criticism does not mean we cannot imagine a more sophisticated, historically aware – and, yes, better – way to place evaluation on the agenda of television studies and proudly acknowledge and examine our own tastes.

VALUING LOST

As I have already asserted, *Lost* is a great television programme. To understand why, we need to consider how it works as a television show, how it adopts some core conventions of the medium and innovates others. There is no singular aesthetics of television – great television can aspire to artistic ambition, or revel in lowbrow attractions, or do both at once. However, even if televisual aesthetics are plural rather than universal, we can still explore how a show fits into a particular set of aesthetic possibilities and judge how it fulfils its ambitions. Aesthetic plurality is not the same as aesthetic relativity – greatness might come in a variety of packages and styles, but that does not mean everything is equally great.

In arguing for *Lost*'s greatness, I will consider four aesthetic norms that the show successfully achieves – unity of purpose, forensic fandom, narrative complexity and the aesthetics of surprise – suggesting that these aspects account for much of the show's value. This is not an exclusive list: there are certainly other great elements of the show for which I do not give an account, and there are certainly many other aesthetic norms or qualities that *Lost* fails to achieve. Nevertheless, I believe these qualities provide a compelling argument for the show's value, and at least provide a starting point for a debate over televisual aesthetics.

Unity of purpose

Lost is a unified text, with every episode contributing to a larger whole. Perhaps more than with any other US television series, this 'wholeness' is central to our understanding and appreciation of the programme. The pilot episode (1.2) ends with Charlie (Dominic Monaghan) asking a seemingly simple question, 'Where *are* we?', which seems to define the entirety of the series. Every episode, every flashback and every character's story can be understood as contributing to a larger understanding of the nature (or artifice) of *Lost*'s island locale. Unlike nearly every other television series, *Lost* features no stand-alone episodes, and no 'monsters-of-the-week' that offer reprieves from the serialized mythologies as on ancestral shows like *The X-Files* or *Buffy*. As unity has long been valued aesthetically as an essential component of narrative art, it is not surprising that a television series that can deliver a compelling sense of its whole offers particular pleasures and values.

Unity is particularly complicated, however, within the serialized form of television. As of this writing, *Lost*'s first three seasons have aired, comprising just over half the anticipated entirety of the series. Thus my claims toward aesthetic unity are, ironically enough, inherently partial. However, for serialized narratives in progress, unity is less of an absolute quality than an ideal to be anticipated and perceived – viewers watch *Lost* with a mind toward the totality of the series, working to assemble each segment into a unified narrative that will not be fulfilled for years to come. As the series unfolds, fans judge each episode in large part against their own notions of the show's whole, and frequently rework their assumptions about this whole in light of new narrative twists and storytelling strategies. For instance, the twist of concluding season three with flash-forwards, scenes with characters finally off the island, reset *Lost*'s basic storytelling strategies and norms, changing our focus away from the question of 'Will they get off the island?' to the broader quest of understanding how post-island life fits in with the narrative world that we have already seen.

US television has an additional challenge with unity, as a successful series is typically rewarded with continuation toward infinity, or at least until ratings sag. Before May 2007, it would have been impossible to even gauge what portion of the series had aired, as US broadcast television typically equates a show's conclusion with failure and cancellation, not planned narrative resolutions. The unprecedented announcement of the show's planned date of conclusion three years in advance made an explicit nod toward this ideal of unity – in ABC's press release announcing the end-date of May 2010, producers Damon Lindelof and Carlton Cuse noted:

> We always envisioned *Lost* as a show with a beginning, middle and end. By officially announcing exactly when that ending will be, the audience will now have the security of knowing that the story will play out as we've intended.[7]

Thus the producers' conception of the show's unity eventually triggered ABC to grant the unique gift of a planned conclusion, although as of this writing, that plan is in jeopardy due to the ongoing Writers' Guild of America strike of 2007–8.

More than utilizing the unity of a continual narrative, *Lost*'s aesthetics value a perceived purpose motivating its narrative whole. The story's unified scope and shape follow a design, and much of the aesthetic pleasure offered by *Lost* involves viewers attempting to parse out the rationales behind the show's storytelling. At times this sense of purpose links directly to authorial intention, as typified by some fans' cultish devotion to Lindelof and Cuse's podcasts, Comic Con appearances and media interviews, citing producer commentary as divine proclamations from TPTB (The Powers That Be). However, the show's unity is not always tied to the specificities of authorship, as many fans recognize the collaborative nature of television writing and the shifting involvement of key production figures like J.J. Abrams, David Fury, Drew Goddard and Javier Grillo-Marxuach. Rather, the motivation behind *Lost*'s unity stems more from the assumed sense of purposefulness that seems embedded in the narrative design at the textual level more than in its actual process of creation. When fans lose faith in the show, underlying doubts are often triggered by a sense of disunity stemming from the fear that the show is 'made up as it goes along', rather than having been planned out carefully in advance.[8]

For me, one of *Lost*'s great pleasures is the sense of faith in its narrative design and purpose that the show manages to instil. Some of this faith stems from extra-textual consumption of interviews, podcasts and the like, but more often it is the recognition of thematic and factual continuities that attest to a master plan, or at least more advanced planning than is typical of series television. For instance, Rousseau's (Mira Furlan) maps first seen in 'Solitary' (1.9) briefly show a smaller island next to the main island – and season three reveals the existence of this smaller Hydra Island, a minor internal consistency that proved reassuring to viewers' doubts of coherence and purposefulness. Such instances extend faith that other narrative pieces still dangling after three seasons, such as Adam and Eve from 'House of the Rising Sun' (1.6) or the statue of the giant foot in 'Live Together, Die Alone' (2.23), will eventually receive a narrative pay-off true to *Lost*'s internal unity.

The pleasure of purposeful unity directly contrasts with other serialized programmes that cannot live up to this ideal of internal logic.

Programmes like *24* (Imagine Entertainment, 2001–) and *Heroes* (Jackson Films, 2006–) arguably fall short of this goal, with illogical plot twists, dropped characters, or questionable continuity raising doubts about the show's consistent sense of purpose and design, even for ardent fans. Other programmes, like *Alias* (Bad Robot, 2001–6) and *Veronica Mars* (Silver Pictures Television, 2004–7), experience radical shifts in tone, style or narrative structure as seemingly motivated by network pressure to boost ratings by making the show less complex and easier for new viewers to join. Such shifts fracture a sense of unity, which many fans attribute to the commercial constraints of television narratives rather than a loss of faith in the producers' storytelling abilities. *Lost*'s ability to withstand such commercial pressures, and even to feature moments when creative purpose trumps network norms (as with the announced end-date), attest to the show's purposefulness and appeal to the aesthetic value of unity.

Forensic fandom

If one of the great pleasures and values of *Lost* is its purposeful unity, the show extends this narrative logic to support a particular mode of engagement that might be termed 'forensic fandom'. Since the show's internal logic is motivated around the central mystery of the island and its complex history and powers, *Lost*'s narrative structure encourages viewers to parse the show more than simply consume it. Research in both cultural studies and cognitive theories of comprehension highlights how viewers are actively engaged in the act of consuming programming, being mentally and emotionally involved with media rather than passively accepting meanings. However, most of this research has highlighted either how viewers 'read against the grain' by creating dissonant meanings within the conventional and unchallenging margins of popular culture, or how texts set the terms for their narrative comprehension and emotional reactions in an active but still highly conventionalized manner.

Lost's narrative design discourages casual consumption. While there are certainly moment-to-moment pleasures of humour, suspense, action and romance, the show's most distinguishing attribute is its central mystery, which demands a hyper-attentive mode of spectatorship. To be a *Lost* fan is to embrace a detective mentality, seeking out clues, charting patterns and assembling evidence into narrative hypotheses and theories. This forensic engagement finds a natural home in online forums, where viewers gather to posit theories and debate interpretations, and fan 'wikis' like *LostPedia.com* allow the sharing of fan-produced knowledge and theories. While many fans certainly do watch the show in a more self-contained fashion, *Lost*'s moments of information overflow, as in the blast door map first seen in 'Lockdown' (2.17) or the brainwashing video shown to Karl (Blake Bashoff) in 'Not in Portland' (3.7), seem to demand a mode of forensic engagement to organize and uncover a wealth of narrative data.

The show even reflexively comments on this mode of engagement – Locke (Terry O'Quinn) responds to the Swan orientation film in 'Orientation' (2.3) with a line that has become a motto for forensic fandom: 'We're going to need to watch that again.' For Steven Johnson, this mode of engagement suggests television's power for cognitive exercise and intellectual development; whether such programmes trigger self-improvement or not, we cannot deny the mental pleasures of forensic fandom that shows like *Lost* provide.[9]

Traditionally, texts that demand and encourage a mode of close reading and repeat engagement position themselves in rarefied categories of high art and narrow appeal for connoisseurs, whether for the literary modernism of James Joyce and Thomas Pynchon, or the art film aesthetics of Michelangelo Antonioni and David Lynch. For television aiming toward popular culture rather than modernist art, immersive forensic fandom is often performed on texts for corrective ownership rather than aesthetics – fans of long-running soap operas or science-fiction stalwart *Star Trek* (Desilu Productions/Paramount Television, 1966–9) often command greater mastery of narrative backstory and continuity than the producers themselves, making 'nitpicking' fandom less a case of textual pleasure than one of policing and competitive claims of ownership. While other series have tried to mine the pleasures of forensic fandom aimed at complex mythologies, innovators like *Twin Peaks* (Lynch/Frost Productions, 1990–1) and *X-Files* have typically fallen short of the balance between spinning a satisfyingly complex mystery and achieving sufficient consistency and coherence to meet the expectations of viewers' narrative investigations. Thus far, *Lost* seems to be the first popular show to successfully mobilize fans' forensic impulses toward sustained narrative pleasure over frustration – although its success rate might certainly change over the final three seasons.

Lost's successful fostering of forensic fandom attests to the show's ambitions that extend beyond the televisual text itself. The show has been hailed as one of the primary examples of 'Television 2.0', extending the narrative through transmedia storytelling strategies that serve not just as spun-off ancillaries but core additions to *Lost*'s central narrative design and mythology. The show's aesthetic successes as a television series are highlighted by its comparative failures in other media – the tie-in novel *Bad Twin*[10] was seen by most as a fairly incoherent add-on blurring boundaries between fictional worlds, and as of this writing fans have not seen the other videogame and tie-in ancillaries as essential. The alternate reality game (ARG) 'The *Lost* Experience' extended the forensic model of participation most successfully, but the majority of fans either were dismayed by the overt commercialization of the game, or disappointed that the ARG's narrative revelations did not seem to resonate within the core television series during season three. Despite such ambitious but unsatisfying paratextual extensions, fans have remained invested in parsing the narrative world constructed on the television series, especially after the show's resurgence in the latter part of season three.

Narrative complexity and the operational aesthetic

Both the show's purposeful unity and forensic mode of engagement are grounded in *Lost*'s innovative narrative complexity. As I have examined elsewhere, US television in the 2000s has embraced a mode of narrative complexity marked by heightened seriality, formally innovative techniques of temporal and narrational experimentation, and a toleration for storytelling confusion and delayed gratification.[11] I argue that one of narrative complexity's chief pleasures is an 'operational aesthetic', that is, calling attention to how the machinery of storytelling works as an additional level of engagement beyond the storyworld itself. *Lost* is exemplary of this operational aesthetic at work – we watch the series not just as a window into a compelling fictional universe, but also to watch how the window itself works to distort or direct our line of vision. Watching a series like *Lost* demands dual attention to both the story and the narrative discourse that narrates the story, with particular pleasures offered exclusively at the level of a story's telling.

The third-season finale, 'Through the Looking Glass' (3.22), provides one of the show's most exceptional and lauded storytelling tricks. *Lost*'s season finales have typically offered rewarding cliffhangers in their final moments, such as Walt's (Malcolm David Kelly) abduction in 'Exodus' (1.24) and Penny's (Sonya Walger) discovery of the island in 'Live Together, Die Alone' (2.23) – twists that raise narrative suspense and point future stories in new directions. However, season three concluded less with questions of story suspense than with what we might term 'narrational suspense' – by revealing that Jack's (Matthew Fox) supposed flashbacks were actually flash-forwards to life after escaping the island, the show invites us to marvel at its own storytelling mechanics. The suspense created by this revelation raises questions about how the story will be told in future seasons. Will it focus on life on the mainland with flashbacks to the island? Will there by more flash-forwards to characters post-rescue? Is this one of many alternate futures? For once, the key question isn't 'What will happen?' (as we learn that at least Kate (Evangeline Lilly) and Jack will be rescued), but 'How will they tell us what happens?' To appreciate this moment requires viewers to think about the show's narrative mechanics, embracing the operational aesthetic to enjoy the storytelling spectacle provided by this narrational cliffhanger.

The operational aesthetic can even serve as the focal point of entire episodes. 'Exposé' (3.14), with almost parodic rewriting of island history to include Nikki (Kiele Sanchez) and Paulo (Rodrigo Santoro), divided fans' opinions about the episode's quality and relevance to the series as a whole. To appreciate the episode, it seems necessary to engage it at the level of storytelling discourse, considering how the revisionist history of island life resembles fan fiction rewriting of canonical events, scribbling in the margins of the established story world. For fans who disliked the episode, one chief complaint was the lack of continuity and disruptions of what they felt had already been established – the episode presented new information about already-established events, but did not seem to contribute toward the greater mythology. However, for fans willing to play the storytelling game that 'Exposé' offers, the pleasures stem from the wilful knowledge that the episode is marginal to the point of being almost non-canonical, play-fully tweaking some of the fan's forensic obsessions for continuity and coherence.

Lost's operational aesthetic offers particular expressive possi-bilities that only become available to a serialized form like television narrative. The show develops intrinsic norms over time, establishing conventions and rules that viewers internalize as defining the show's storytelling strategies – for instance, that each episode features a flash-back of a single character intercut with island life. Episodes violating these norms stand out as exceptional, either in violating fan expec-tations or providing unexpected pleasures. 'Maternity Leave' (2.15) and 'Three Minutes' (2.22) feature flashbacks internal to island life, which signals a narrative mode of filling in crucial story gaps during Claire (Emilie de Ravin) and Michael's (Harold Perrineau) respective absences from the main group of protagonists, which thus escalates viewer expectations for crucial plot revelations rather than the char-acter backstory resonances typical of flashbacks. 'Flashes Before Your Eyes' (3.8) offers a more ambiguous temporal rupture, with Desmond (Henry Ian Cusick) reliving and potentially altering moments from his past, rather than presenting such moments as temporally distinct (as in a typical flashback). To understand this episode and its larger narrative importance, viewers must be operationally attuned to the show's intrinsic storytelling norms and consider the significance of such a violation upon its broader formal narrative system, positing questions about the show's treatment of temporality that have yet to be answered.

Most television mimics cinematic narration's goals of invisibility and transparency, presenting the story world in a style that viewers have learned to regard as naturalistic and unmediated. Typically films that embrace self-consciousness and invite viewers to reflect on their storytelling processes use reflexivity for comedic purposes, as in self-aware moments in cartoons, parodies or musicals, or they embrace a formal game along a modernist aesthetic typical of the art film or its popularization in contemporary indie films like *Memento* (Christopher Nolan, 2000) and *Donnie Darko* (Richard Kelly, 2001).[12] Narratively complex television programmes, ranging from *Seinfeld* (Castle Rock Entertainment, 1990–8) to *Veronica Mars*, *Scrubs* (Doozer, 2001–) to *Battlestar Galactica* (various, 2004–9), embrace a model of self-conscious narration and formal play, but they import this art-film aesthetic to the realm of mainstream popular culture and genre fiction. Although *Lost* plays with highbrow themes of fate versus free will, and namedrops philosophers from Rousseau to Bakunin, ultimately the show is clearly lodged within the realm of popular culture, with pulpy genre moments drawn more from science-fiction and adventure tales than art cinema. However, *Lost* tells its stories using formal techniques atypical of mainstream genre programmes, providing its dedicated and forensically minded fans an additional level of pleasure to be explored via the operational aesthetic, simultaneously invested in the story and analyzing how it is being told.

The aesthetics of surprise

Many of the long-term aesthetic values of *Lost* can be understood through the show's investment in narrative complexity, encouraging an analytical mode of viewing and generating a larger sense of unity and purpose. On the moment-to-moment level, much of *Lost*'s pleasure stems from the show's ability to confound expectations and deliver a sense of authentic surprise. Even though US television is nearly defined by its predictability – of schedule, of genre, of narrative form, of character type and of commercial rationalization – *Lost* aims to surprise us at nearly every turn. While many shows offer surprises and thrills, from *Law & Order*'s heavily promoted plot twists to *South Park*'s (Comedy Central, 1997–) daring refusal to respect any taboo, *Lost* is innovative in embedding surprise into every level of the series.

For me, the show's pilot pleasurably confounded expectations. The first surprise was the show's opening depiction of the plane crash – few sequences I have seen in my years of television connoisseurship offer such unflinching intensity and sense of heightened dramatic stakes. My expectations were at once raised and diminished – how might this possibly work as a series? Like many, I approached *Lost* with frames of reference from other deserted-on-an-island narratives, from *Lord of the Flies* to *Survivor* (Mark Burnett Productions, 2000–) or, if it turned out to be a true disaster, *Gilligan's Island* (CBS Television, 1964–7), assuming that the story would focus on the castaways' struggles to survive in and escape from an isolated world. And if this were the sole thrust of the narrative, it would have been disappointing, as nothing could match the intensity of the show's opening moments.

However, as with nearly every element of *Lost*, the first impressions were misleading. The island is not what it seemed at first, just as each character and event turn out to be more than they first appeared. Thus the show's genre is not what it first appeared to be: this is not television's attempt at a disaster show, a genre seemingly unsuited for an ongoing situation and storyline. Ultimately the show's genre still remains uncertain three seasons in – is it a supernatural thriller, a scientific mystery, a soap opera in the wilderness, a religious fantasy, or all of the above? Unlike previously lauded genre mixtures like *Twin Peaks* or *Buffy the Vampire Slayer*, *Lost* refuses to wear its genre references on its sleeve, preferring to allow audiences to speculate on relevant interpretive and aesthetic frameworks, and then to confound our expectations through twists and reversals.

An exemplary episode is 'Walkabout' (1.4), a fan favourite that certainly catapulted the programme into my personal canon. This episode is the first to focus on John Locke, the island's resident shaman/safari guide whose expertise seemingly knows no bounds – a role that is confounded when flashbacks reveal that, before the crash, Locke was a cardboard box salesman with a penchant for phone sex. On the island we learn that Locke travelled with a suitcase full of hunting knives and can hunt wild boar, whereas the flashbacks reveal that Locke was bound to a wheelchair and denied a chance to go on an Australian walkabout, the reason he is on the doomed flight in the South Pacific. The island's first manifestation of seeming paranormality, the sequence revealing Locke's earlier disability and subsequent healing, is breathtaking, visually intricate and heightened by the power of Terry O'Quinn's engrossing performance. While this twist ending might simply have been a *Sixth Sense*-style fake-out, the show's serial form allowed this singular surprise to resonate throughout *Lost*'s narrative architecture, as it raised questions within the backstories of many characters and signalled that life on the island might be markedly different from the passengers' pre-crash existences.[13]

Such surprises and violations of expectation and convention are key reasons why viewers flock to the show. In an online survey of *Lost* fans, conducted to understand why people read spoilers about this twisty and suspenseful show, the pleasures of surprise and the show's uniqueness compared to other television were among the most cited rationales for watching, with over three-quarters of respondents high-lighting these reasons.[14] For me and many other viewers, the ability to be pleasantly surprised by a television series violating conventions and expectations keeps us tuning in and anticipating future twists, of-fering a wealth of pleasures within both the show's story content and storytelling form.

To be clear, these aesthetic qualities of surprise, complexity, foren-sic engagement and unity are not a universal ideal to be elevated for all television to strive toward. Indeed, the rarity of a series meeting or even attempting such goals might account for *Lost*'s unique pleasures, as the element of surprise extends to the ability of a mainstream com-mercial television programme to deliver such uncommon goods. Com-paring *Lost* to another show with entirely different aesthetic goals – for instance, the conventional sitcom *Everybody Loves Raymond* (CBS Tele-vision, 1996–2005) – highlights how television can offer a wide range of pleasures and expectations. *Raymond* neither achieves nor aims for any of *Lost*'s attributes of unity, forensic engagement, complexity or surprise, yet it still offers its own pleasures of comfortable routine and familiarity, consistency in delivering humorous moments and perfor-mances, and a real sense of place and locale that feels tangibly human. I offer this comparison not to demean *Raymond*'s seemingly 'lesser' achievements, but to highlight how no iteration of aesthetic norms should be regarded as universally applicable or ideal for all television. While I ultimately prefer *Lost*'s more ambitious goals and accomplish-ments, there is sufficient room in the range of television's aesthetic possibilities to embrace both innovative genre mixtures and well-ex-ecuted conventional genre pieces, and thus we need to judge any show on its own terms of purpose and design.

Additionally, *Lost*'s aesthetic values are not limited to these four qualities. For many viewers, the show's core pleasures might be found in specific characters portrayed with psychological depth and com-pelling performances, in the relationship dramas and love-triangles celebrated by 'shipping' fandom, in the exceptional production values capturing the island locale and visualizing action sequences in medi-um-transcending 'cinematic' quality, in the melodramatic moments of emotional revelation and transcendence that *Lost* offers amidst the conspiracies and action sequences, or in the broader philosophical themes and issues that often underlie the dramatic action. Any assertion of aesthetic evaluation is inherently subjective and open for debate, but cannot be dismissed as merely opinion without justification or rationale. We should debate the comparative merits of *Lost*'s textual achievements and failures, holding it up to other programmes and measuring relative quality not to arrive at an objective hierarchy of taste, but to engage the processes of taste-making that comprise a central part of our television consumption.

Hopefully it is clear not only why I think *Lost* is a great show, but why it matters that television scholars allow evaluative concerns into our writing. I am not suggesting that the field embraces a wholesale shift toward aesthetic criticism, and ultimately celebrating or denigrating programmes is rarely a worthwhile singular scholarly goal. But we can imagine an academic engagement with television that embraces its own subjective evaluations more openly, and foregrounds evaluative rationales as part of a critical analysis. The act of evaluation is one of the chief reasons why I and many other avid viewers consume media – we want to assess a show's quality and engage in friendly and playful debate over the relative values of both beloved and dismissed programmes. Currently television scholars can continue doing such evaluation only while off-duty, on barstools and blogs, but there is something more to be gained by incorporating explicit evaluative claims into our scholarship. We can help posit television as a more legitimate and culturally validated medium by highlighting what it does well with precision and rigor, thus rescuing 'poor old television' from its island of cultural devaluation and embracing the possibility of shows like *Lost* to achieve greatness.

Notes

This chapter is an expansion and revision of thoughts previously published in 'The loss of value', *Flow* ii/5 (2005), available at *http://flowtv.org/?p=577*, and 'The value of *Lost*', *Flow* ii/10 (2005), available at *http://flowtv.org/?p=435* and presented at The Flow Conference, Austin Texas, October 2006. Thanks to the many who commented on, challenged and helped me refine my positions.

1   Jeremy G. Butler, *Television: Critical Methods and Applications*, 3rd edn (Mahwah, NJ: Lawrence Erlbaum Associates, 2007), p.ix.

2   Susan J. Douglas, *Where the Girls Are: Growing up Female with the Mass Media* (New York: Times Books, 1994).

3   Charlotte Brunsdon, 'Is television studies history?', *Cinema Journal* xlvii/3 (spring 2008), pp.127–37.

4   See Stuart Hall and Paddy Whannel, *The Popular Arts* (New York: Pantheon Books, 1965); Dick Hebdige, *Subculture, the Meaning of Style* (London: Methuen, 1979); and Raymond Williams, *Marxism and Literature* (Oxford: Oxford University Press, 1977).

5   See Michael Bérubé, *The Aesthetics of Cultural Studies* (Malden, MA: Blackwell, 2005); Simon Frith, *Performing Rites: On the Value of Popular Music* (Cambridge: Harvard University Press, 1996); and Alan McKee, *Beautiful Things in Popular Culture* (Malden, MA: Blackwell, 2006).

6   See Christine Geraghty, 'Aesthetics and quality in popular television drama', *International Journal of Cultural Studies* vi/1 (2003), pp.25–45; Jason Jacobs, 'Issues of judgment and value in television studies', *International Journal of Cultural Studies* iv/4 (2001), pp.427–47; Alan McKee, *Australian Television: A Genealogy of Great Moments* (South Melbourne: Oxford University Press, 2001); and Greg M. Smith, *Beautiful TV: The Art and Argument of* Ally McBeal (Austin: University of Texas Press, 2007).

7   '*Lost* to conclude in 2009–10 television season', ABC Television press release, 7 May 2007, available at *www.abcmedianet.com/assets/pr%5Chtml/050707_01.html*.

8   This idea of the narrative's assumed purpose was inspired by Greg Taylor's discussion of aesthetic evaluation. See Greg Taylor, 'But is it any *good*? Evaluative assessment reconsidered', unpublished manuscript presented at Middlebury College, 18 October 2007. Thanks to the author for sharing this work prior to publication.

9   See Steven Johnson, *Everything Bad Is Good for You: How Today's Popular Culture Is Actually Making Us Smarter* (New York: Riverhead Books, 2005).

10   Gary Troup, *Bad Twin* (New York: Hyperion, 2006).

11   Jason Mittell, 'Narrative complexity in contemporary American television', *The Velvet Light Trap*, 58 (2006), pp.29–40.

12   See David Bordwell, *Narration in the Fiction Film* (Madison: University of Wisconsin Press, 1985) for the defining analysis of the narrational mode of both Hollywood and art cinema, and David Bordwell, *The Way Hollywood Tells It: Story and Style in Modern Movies* (Berkeley: University of California Press, 2006) for an account of contemporary cinematic narrative strategies.

13   See Jason Mittell, 'Film and television narrative', in David Herman (ed.), *The Cambridge Companion to Narrative* (Cambridge: CUP, 2007),

pp.156–71, for further analysis of 'Walkabout' and *Lost*'s narrative techniques.

14   This survey research was conducted for Jonathan Gray and Jason Mittell, 'Speculation on spoilers: *Lost* fandom, narrative consumption, and rethinking textuality', *Participations* iv/1 (2007), available at *www.participations.org/Volume%204/Issue%201/4_01_graymittell.htm*. The most cited reasons for watching were 'I want to discover the answers to the island's mysteries' (91%), 'I enjoy the suspenseful plot' (90%), 'The show surprises me' (77%) and 'The show is unlike anything else on the air' (75%).

VIII. Chain of Events:

Regimes of Evaluation and Lost's Construction of the Televisual Character

Roberta Pearson

Desmond Hume (Henry Ian Cusick) told Charlie Pace (Dominic Monaghan) that he was going to die. Desmond had repeated visions of Charlie's death and saved his life on several occasions. But Desmond knew that he couldn't change the preordained chain of events. Charlie would eventually meet his death, if not in one way, then in another. In the episode 'Greatest Hits' (3.21), Desmond relates to Charlie a vision he has had of 'Claire [Emilie de Ravin] and her baby getting into a helicopter. A helicopter that ... lifts off ... leaves this island.' But for this to happen, Charlie must die: 'If you don't, none of it will happen. There won't be any rescue. I'm sorry, brother, but this time ... this time you have to die.' Charlie does finally succumb, keeping his promise to protect Claire and her baby, Aaron. Before facing his impending death he reminisces, writing a list of the 'five best moments of my sorry excuse for a life. My greatest hits. You know ... memories. They're all I've got.' The producers grant the tortured Charlie absolution in a series of flashbacks that reconcile him to his predetermined fate. Here, in reverse order of importance, are Charlie's 'greatest hits':

5) Hearing his band Driveshaft on the radio for the first time, which inspired him to continue his pursuit of rock-god status.

4) His father teaching him to swim at the holiday camp Butlins.

3) His brother Liam (Neil Hopkins) giving him a family heirloom ring. Liam thinks Charlie has a better chance of producing off-spring than he does: 'The ring has to stay in the family, Charlie. So please, take it ... Pass it on to your little one someday.'

2) Driving away a mugger who was trying to steal a woman's purse. The grateful woman calls him a hero.

1) Meeting Claire on the island the night after the crash. Charlie tells her, 'We'll sleep under the stars and before you know it the helicopters will come and take us all home.'

Lost's writers continually play with the theme of free will versus destiny, but Charlie's free will consists only of choosing to embrace the future these flashbacks foreshadow, with each past event pointing directly to his pushing the yellow button in the Looking Glass Hatch and drowning. His achieving rock-god status leads to his flying to Australia and boarding Flight 815 for the return trip; his childhood lessons enable him to swim into the hatch; his brother's injunction makes him see Aaron, to whom he leaves the ring, as his heir and descendant; his pleasure at being called a hero makes him want once more to be heroic and his attachment to Claire and the baby makes him want to ensure their rescue. Details in two of the flashbacks confirm that Charlie's destiny, like that of all the other characters, has from the first been entangled with the island and the other Losties: as he learns to swim, someone in the background says, 'Hurry up! Desmond, come on!'; the imperilled woman is Sayid's (Naveen Andrews) former love Nadia (Andrea Gabriel), who at some point before or after encountering Charlie also encounters Locke (Terry O'Quinn).

Like Charlie, Tony Soprano (James Gandolfini) has occasion to ponder free will versus destiny. In the 'Down Neck' (1.7) episode of *The Sopranos* (HBO, 1999–2007), Anthony Jr (Robert Iler) seems to be following uncomfortably close in his father's footsteps, with he and his mates breaking into the church sacristy and getting drunk on the communion wine. Characters are quick to draw implicit or explicit parallels between Anthony Senior's and Junior's behaviour. The school psychologist (David Beach) says, 'Anthony sometimes has trouble following the rules ... weighing consequences ... at times doesn't think before he acts.' Livia (Nancy Marchand), Tony's awful mum, informs the assembled family, 'Oh, his father was the same way. I practically lived in that vice principal's office.' Tony, leaning toward a biologically determinist view of his son's future, takes the problem to Dr Melfi (Lorraine Braco), his therapist. 'My son is doomed, right?' Melfi disagrees, articulating the doctrines of free will and American exceptionalism. 'People have choices,' she tells her client. When he remains unconvinced, she continues, 'This is America.' I would argue that Tony's free will derives not from the country but from the story world that he inhabits. As a character in a hermeneutically driven narrative, Charlie has no free will. As a character in a character-driven narrative, Tony does (or gives the appearance within the diegesis of so doing, although extra-diegetically the character's creators exercise complete control).

There are, naturally, no absolute, hard-and-fast distinctions between hermeneutically driven and character-driven narratives; all 'realist' narratives fall somewhere on the spectrum between the two extremes. Some texts, such as murder mysteries, tend to emphasise the resolution of narrative enigmas, while others, such as the novels of Henry James, tend to emphasise the exploration of character. *Lost* positions itself toward the resolution end of this spectrum, while *The Sopranos* positions itself toward the exploration end. To make this distinction clearer, consider the different purpose of flashbacks in *Lost* and *The Sopranos*. In *Lost*, subjective flashbacks, like Charlie's in 'Greatest Hits', must connect to the series' overarching hermeneutic. All past events are directly tied to present events; it seems nothing about a character's past is irrelevant to the plot. In *The Sopranos*, subjective flashbacks may parallel or provide the necessary backstory to present events, but they don't immutably tie individual character arcs directly to an overall narrative arc or hermeneutic. New information may be highly relevant to character development but irrelevant to plot development (to the degree, of course, that the two can be separated).

In 'Down Neck', as Tony worries that A.J. may learn the real meaning of 'waste management', a series of flashbacks reveals how he discovered his own father's mob connections. In therapy, Tony wonders what his life would have been like had his father not 'gotten mixed up in the Mob': 'Maybe I'd be sellin' patio furniture in San Diego or some shit.' The flashbacks offer the viewer fuller access to Tony's thoughts and emotions – his worries about A.J.'s future, his rather muted qualms about his choice of profession – but they do not point toward a fixed destiny. Tony is killing people in New Jersey rather than selling patio furniture in California because he has chosen to do so, not because an overarching mythology demands that he do so. *The Sopranos'* flashbacks illuminate the character's interiority, but they don't necessarily advance the plot in terms of connecting directly to present-day developments. *Lost'*s subjective flashbacks must advance the present-day plot by relating to the series' big questions: Why has the island gathered all the Losties together? What is the island's ultimate secret?

Jason Mittell tells us in this volume that it is the responsibility of television scholars to make 'arguments as to why a programme might be seen as more valuable following particular criteria, and how those criteria function culturally'.[1] Different kinds of texts require different regimes of evaluation. Tony Soprano may possess more of the depth and complexity traditionally valued by literary theorists than Charlie Pace, or any of the other Losties for that matter, but this does not make *The Sopranos* an intrinsically 'better' text than *Lost* or the Mafiosi inherently 'better' characters than the castaways. Characters are good or bad, in an evaluative rather than a moral sense, to the extent that they serve the needs of their story world. Tony Soprano is a great character in New Jersey, but might be a bad character on *Lost'*s mysterious island. He would certainly be a very different character had he to conform to the requirements of the *Lost* story world, which is much more tightly constructed around narrative enigmas than *The Sopranos*.

Is Lost Perceived as a Hermeneutically Driven Narrative?

Below I will provide a structuralist analysis of a *Lost* character to illustrate how the programme ties together character traits, backstory and the present to create a complex narrative unique in television drama. I argue that every element of the *Lost* characters is directly connected to the show's central narrative enigmas: what is the secret of the island and why are all the Losties there? Every scrap of information the producers provide about the characters may potentially illuminate the enigmas: what happened in their pre-island lives, which of their fellow castaways each of them has previously encountered and so forth. Before developing this argument further, however, I want to provide some extra-textual evidence to show that the hermeneutic has played a major role in *Lost*'s production and reception.

As Stacey Abbott (Chapter II) shows in this volume, the producers initially courted cult fans, emphasising the mythology that these viewers prize. Since achieving mainstream success, however, they have tended to foreground character over mythology in a bid to avoid the cult label that might imperil their mainstream status and ratings numbers. Said Damon Lindelof:

> The mythology is very important and we don't throw it away piece-meal. But at the same time, we approach every episode as, this is a Jack [Matthew Fox] episode; we're going to explain a little more why the guy needs to fix things all the time and let the island story support that obsession.[2]

Carlton Cuse also refers to the 'characters first, island second' position: 'We want the characters to focus on primarily their relationships with each other. We always view the show as a character show with a mythology frosting over the top.' Cuse thinks that 'there's a much larger audience that's much more interested in who is Kate [Evangeline Lilly] going to choose than the details about who Alvar Hanso is'.[3] He credits the show's wide appeal partially to the flashbacks, which he believes audiences enjoy for their development of the characters not their contribution to the hermeneutic:

> The flashback stories are the emotional core of the series and give a much broader audience access. There's a genre audience that enjoys the mythology, but the broader audience wants to know more about the characters and the flashbacks and go back to the seminal events in their lives.[4]

Attempting to appeal both to cult fans and to a wider audience, the producers have multiplied precedents and influences. Cuse has characterised the flashbacks as 'little *New Yorker* short stories'.[5] Those little short stories have over the years been penned by such literary giants as Ann Beattie, John Cheever, Vladimir Nabokov, John O'Hara, Philip Roth, John Updike and J.D. Salinger. Cuse makes a clear bid for cultural respectability by placing *Lost* within traditional

bourgeois regimes of evaluation that have always favoured charac-
ter-centred 'literature' over hermeneutically centred 'fiction' such as
mysteries and thrillers. However, the producers also cite texts, some
firmly canonical, some less so, whose authors have met or failed to
meet strong audience demands for satisfying narrative resolution.
Referring to the prominence of *Our Mutual Friend* in the second season finale, Cuse told the *New York Times* that Dickens

> was writing chapter by chapter for newspapers ... We often think:
> 'How much did Dickens know when he was writing his stories? How
> much of it was planned out, and how much was flying by the seat of
> his pants because he had to get another chapter in?'[6]

Cuse and the other producers have also cited more popular precedents. The *New York Times* said that Lindelof and Cuse often refer to
the *Harry Potter* books, wanting 'each season, like each book in J.K.
Rowling's series, to pose questions and answer them while at the same
time maintaining a larger mystery that holds the audience'.[7] And as
Abbott and others have pointed out, the producers repeatedly point to
Twin Peaks (Lynch/Frost Productions, 1990–1) and *The X-Files* (Twentieth Century Fox Television, 1993–2002) as cautionary tales, with
both series disappointing their once avid viewers by failing satisfactorily to resolve their mythologies. Despite their repeated invocations of
the importance of character, the producers seem well aware that the
show's enduring reputation will rest on providing convincing answers
to the central narrative enigmas.

As Cuse has admitted, 'All the questions we get asked are about
the mythology.'[8] The text seems to encourage a hermeneutically based
reading strategy, at least among those most active of viewers who
leave public traces of their interpretations – ranging from fans asking Cuse questions to television critics writing in major publications
to academics. *Time Magazine* named *Lost* one of the hundred greatest
television shows of all time:

> In a way it's a misnomer to call *Lost* one of TV's best shows – it's a
> fine show on the level of character and writing, but what makes it a
> classic is that it's the finest interactive game ever to appear in your
> living room once a week. An elaborate fractal pattern of intersecting
> stories concerning plane survivors on a not-quite-deserted island, a

secretive international organization and a monster made of smoke, *Lost* only begins with the 60 minutes you see on TV. Its mysteries, clues and literary–historical allusions demand research, repeat viewing, freeze-framing and endless online discussions.[9]

It is the interactive game, the mysteries, the mythology and the hermeneutic that warrant *Lost*'s inclusion in the all-time greats list, not its fine characters and writing. Mittell praises *Lost*'s unity of purpose: 'Every episode, every flashback, and every character's story can be understood as contributing to a larger understanding of the nature (or artifice) of *Lost*'s island locale.'[10] In other words, it's about the hermeneutic, stupid.

Mittell, along with another contributor to this volume, Jonathan Gray, co-authored 'Speculation on spoilers: *Lost* fandom, narrative consumption and rethinking textuality', in which they sought the opinions of *Lost* fans active on the Internet.[11] Respondents were asked to rank their reasons for watching and their primary reason for watching the show (Table 1).

Table 1. Pleasures of spoiler fans (n = 150)

	Reasons to watch (%)	Primary reason to watch (%)
I want to discover the answers to the island's mysteries	91	28
I enjoy the suspenseful plot	90	24
The show surprises me	77	1
The show is unlike anything else on the air	75	9
I find it exciting	71	3
I enjoy the innovative way the show tells its story	68	9
I am invested in the relationships that exist or could form between characters	38	4

As you can see, interest in the characters ranks far below interest in the hermeneutic. As Gray and Mittell conclude:

> There is no doubt that the chief reason that *Lost* fans consume the show and its cross-media experiences is to crack its secrets. Discovering the answers to the island's mysteries was our respondents' most commonly shared reason for watching the show and most cited primary rationale...[12]

This is not to claim, of course, that many of the fans aren't interested in the characters; but are they interested in the characters independent of their relationship to the hermeneutic? In the process of preparing this chapter, I trawled many *Lost* websites looking for episode summaries to jog my memory. The webmasters often identify episodes as 'Jack-centric' or 'Locke-centric', highlighting the character flashbacks of the week. The site *www.lost.about.com* details flashbacks character by character, even presenting them twice, once in story and once in plot order. It also includes elaborate maps of the characters' pre-island relationships, data which turn up in less elaborate form on the official ABC site. All this user-friendly character information seems addressed to the myriads of Internet fans who devote hours online attempting to decipher *Lost*'s central narrative enigmas, not to those who wonder whether Kate will end up with Jack or with Sawyer. Undoubtedly many viewers do desire the resolution of unresolved sexual tension as much, if not more, than the resolution of the central narrative enigmas, as attested to by fan Internet chatter and fiction. Nonetheless, a large percentage of viewers clearly read *Lost* as a hermeneutically driven narrative in which characters and character development take second place to the mythology.

STRUCTURALIST ANALYSIS OF CHARACTER CONSTRUCTION

Extra-textual evidence can only get us so far. The preponderance of evidence indicates the centrality of the hermeneutic to *Lost*'s reception, but formalist analysis can more precisely delineate *Lost*'s narrative innovation of inextricably linking character and hermeneutic. Character is a notoriously slippery concept; narratologists have tried for decades to explain how a mere textual construct can achieve person-like status in the minds of readers and viewers. In an essay in *The Cambridge Companion to Narrative*, Uri Margolin provides as good a definition of a fictional character as any:

> a contingently created, abstract, cultural entity, depending essentially for its existence on actual objects in space and on the intellectual activity of authors and readers. On this view, characters are invented or stipulated by a human mind, and generated in particular cultural and historical circumstances through the use of language, following certain literary-artistic conventions. They are ultimately semiotic constructs or creatures of the word, and it is the socially and culturally defined act of fictional storytelling that constitutes and defines them. [13]

Margolin advises that

> [to] find out what properties a given character possesses or what claims about him are true, there is only one route to follow: examine the originating text, what is explicitly stated in it and what can be inferred from it according to standard procedures.[14]

However, like most narratologists, Margolin considers only written and not moving-image fictions. The Losties are semiotic constructs but they are creatures of televisual codes, not of the word. Examining the originating text might entail a close analysis of every aspect of *Lost*'s *mise-en-scène*, editing, sound and graphics. Given that the *Lost* text constituted 60 episodes at the time of writing (with the airing of further episodes in the USA from the end of January 2008) this would be a daunting, if not impossible, task that would also make for rather boring reading. Luckily for both author and readers, my argument does not require a detailed close analysis of this nature. As I stated in a recently published essay:

> Television characters are not like holograms. Each tiny fragment does not contain the sum of the whole, but rather becomes fully intelligible only when juxtaposed with all the other tiny fragments in all the other scenes in all the other episodes in which the character appears. Television characters are to some extent autonomous beings, autonomous, that is, of the televisual codes and individual scenes/episodes that construct them, existing as a whole only in the minds of the producers and the audience. It is here that the characters

take on the quasi-human status so baffling to literary theorists, but so obvious to television producers and audiences. Anatomising the televisual character requires identifying the elements that constitute a character abstracted from the design of the text and existing in the story, that is, in the minds of producers and audiences, rather than conducting a close textual analysis of individual scenes/episodes/codes.[15]

Producers and viewers conceive of characters not as bundles of televisual codes but as fictional persons whose identities are defined by similar properties to those of actual persons. Televisual codes combine to create six key character properties or components: psychological traits/habitual behaviours; physical traits/appearance; speech patterns; interactions with other characters; and environment and biography (backstory).[16] The function of these components varies from story world to story world; as I have already indicated Lindelof, Cuse *et al.* of *Lost* use biography differently from David Chase *et al.* of *The Sopranos*. I want to substantiate this claim by breaking a *Lost* character down into his/her constitutive components – but which Lostie should I submit to my forensic analysis?

Personal preference biases me toward Locke, whom I find in some ways the most intriguing of the characters. Locke is also the perfect character with whom to explore my hypothesis. Of all the Losties, only Locke wants to stay on the island, his desperation driving him to prevent rescue by blowing up the submarine and killing Naomi (Marsha Thomason). The Others, who seem to know all the secrets, acknowledge Locke's unique affinity with the island. Both Ben (Michael Emerson) and Richard (Nestor Carbonell) tell him that he is special and his appearance causes great excitement among the other Others. The island also acknowledges his uniqueness, granting him insights not vouchsafed to his companions: a dream points him to the Pearl Station; a sweat-lodge induced hallucination convinces him to save Mr Eko (Adewale Akinnuoye-Agjabe) and a vision of Walt (Malcolm David Kelley) inspires him when he lies dying in the Dharma mass grave. Readers may object that Locke, who as Abbott says, 'comes to represent the cult mythology of the series', fits my hypothesis all too perfectly.[17] Take Mr Eko, for example. Ivan Askwith states that the unexpected departure of Akkinuoye-Agbaje to pursue a film career left unanswered many questions about his character.[18] Locke clearly

constitutes an ideal case in which the producers have so far successfully pursued the strategy of tying character to overarching narrative
enigmas.

Let us examine Locke through the six-element character tem-
plate:

1) Psychological traits/habitual behaviours

The Locke in the flashbacks is in many ways a completely different man
from the Locke on the island. Flashback Locke (F-Locke) is lonely, an-
gry, depressed and purposeless. Island Locke (I-Locke) is a much calm-
er and more focused man, although he can still exhibit intense rage
or depression when thwarted or disappointed. F-Locke was a follower
rather than a leader; a police psych profile predicted that he would be
amenable to coercion. I-Locke is confident and self-assured, to such
an extent that he contests Jack for leadership of the Losties. F-Locke
doesn't seem particularly untrustworthy or violent, but I-Locke will
do anything to achieve his ends, including lying and killing. I-Locke
displays habitual behaviours that F-Locke seems to have developed,
although we don't know where or when. I-Locke has hunting, tracking and survival skills. He is familiar with knives, guns and military
armaments. He knows about native American rituals, hallucinatory
drugs and carpentry. In addition to war games, he is a chess and back-
gammon player. He can even predict the weather. And he and Hurley
(Jorge Garcia) both like Twinkies (a shared taste that no one has as yet
identified as a clue to the island's mysteries).

2) Physical characteristics/appearance

John Locke, like all television characters, is conflated with the actor
who embodies him. Both F-Locke and I-Locke must look and talk like
Terry O'Quinn; the actor's facial configurations/expressions, body pos-
ture/gestures and vocal quality/mannerisms all contribute to character
meaning. Actor and character must inevitably share many characteristics, but some can pertain solely to the actor or to the character. For example, Terry O'Quinn is bald and ambulatory, but F-Locke sometimes
has hair and, post-defenestration, is non-ambulatory. As with Locke's
psychological traits, the island effects a major change of physical characteristics: I-Locke can miraculously walk again.

3) Speech patterns

Characters must have speech patterns (accent, overall tone, favourite phrases, professional jargon) suited to their race, gender, age and occupational identities. Tony's New Jersey accent, profanity and mob lingo all help to define the character in *The Sopranos*. The hallmark of both F-Locke and I-Locke's speech is a mysticism/spiritualism suitable to a man seeking faith and purpose. His characteristic tone is established in his first flashback episode, 'Walkabout' (1.4). He tells boss Randy (Billy Ray Gallion) that a 'walkabout is a journey of spiritual renewal where one derives strength from the earth and becomes inseparable from it'. He aspires to be like Norman Croucher, a double amputee who climbed Everest because 'it was his destiny'. He tells the Australian travel agent (John Simon Jones) that he must go on the walkabout: 'This is my destiny!' His mysticism is most marked when speaking about the island. After first seeing the monster, he tells Jack, 'I've looked into the eye of this island and what I saw was beautiful.' In relation to Charlie's heroin addiction he says, 'What I know is that this island might just give you what you're looking for, but you have to give the island something.'

4) Interactions with other characters

As with real people, fictional people derive identity partially from the social roles that they enact in the home, in the workplace and (sometimes) on mysterious islands. Tony's personality is increasingly shaped by the pressures of heading both the Family and his family, with the juggling of the two roles contributing to his panic attacks and need for therapy. As with psychological traits, the island effects a transformation upon Locke's social roles and interactions. In flashbacks occurring closest in time to the narrative present, F-Locke is a lowly worker in a cube farm, having to justify himself to the odious Randy. But I-Locke is clearly near the top of the Losties' hierarchy, even contesting Jack for leadership. F-Locke seems always to have been rather a loner, aside from his brief affair with girlfriend Helen (Katey Sagal). After his break-up with her and the subsequent disbanding of the marijuana commune, his only companions are his role-playing games (RPG) mates and phone-sex Helen. I-Locke initially establishes fairly close relationships with some of his fellow castaways, supporting

Charlie's efforts to kick his drug addiction and building a cradle for
Claire's baby, for example. But his interactions become more instrumental, as when he works with Boone (Ian Somerhalder) to open the
Hatch or teams with Mr Eko to push the button. At the end of season
three he goes off with the Others, although his informing Sawyer of
their plan to abduct the pregnant or potentially pregnant Losties indicates a residual concern for his old friends.

5) Environment

The design of the sets or the choice of outdoor locations adds much
to the viewer's knowledge of a character; the contrast between the
dark, shabby 'Bada Bing' back room and light-flooded, gaudy mansion
encapsulates the tensions involved in managing Tony's two families
in *The Sopranos*, for example. As with almost all aspects of the Locke
character, there is again a strong contrast between pre- and post-island life. F-Locke inhabits an environment suited to the protagonist
of a neo-realist or American indie film, with everyday spaces such as
low-rent apartments and cube farm break rooms. I-Locke inhabits
an environment suited to a hero (or perhaps villain?) of more exotic
genres; the romantic, action-adventure location of the island and the
vaguely science-fiction setting of the Hatch.

6) Biography

Locke has been a clerk in the toy section of a department store, a home
inspector and a regional collections supervisor for a box company, but
the flashbacks primarily delineate his tragic personal life. Raised in foster care, Locke knew neither of his biological parents. He meets them
in adulthood, when his mother and his father, Anthony Cooper (Kevin
Tighe), combine in a scam to persuade Locke to donate a kidney to his
father. Cooper disappears after the successful transplant, leaving Locke
sans both parent and organ. Trying to deal with his rage over his father's
rejection, he attends an anger management group where he encounters Helen. The two move in together but the relationship ends when
Locke, ignoring Helen's warnings, falls victim to another of his conman
father's scams. Locke then joins a marijuana-growing commune, which
he unwittingly betrays to an undercover policeman. He wants to save
his friends by disposing of the narc, but lacks the will to kill.

Locke again becomes involved with his father when the son of Cooper's most recent victim, a wealthy widow, visits him. When Locke threatens to expose him, Cooper throws him out an eighth-storey window, crippling him. While working for the box company, Locke determines to fly to Australia to go on the walkabout, but the tour company send him back to the USA on the fateful Oceanic Flight 815.

Like Charlie's, Locke's past has intersected with that of the other Losties. His mentally disturbed mother was once hospitalised at the same institution as Hurley and Libby (Cynthia Watros). While working as a home inspector, Locke encountered Sayid's girlfriend, Nadia. Hurley has investments in the box company and Randy used to be Hurley's boss. Anthony Cooper was the conman who caused the death of Sawyer's parents. It seems as if every aspect of Locke's biography, culminating with Helen's leaving him, his unwitting betrayal of the commune and his crippling, led him to board Flight 815. These events led directly to the spiritual crisis that he hoped that the walkabout would resolve – and that the island may yet resolve.

As this delineation of the six components of the Locke character shows, habitual behaviours, speech patterns and biography do not vary between F-Locke and I-Locke. However, speech patterns and biography anticipate his island destiny. His habitual behaviours (whether hunting boar, tracking Others or blowing up the Flame Station by beating the computer at chess) well suit him to his new home. Some of these behaviours, such as game playing, stem from his constant longing for a higher purpose and meaning, while he seems to have learned hunting and tracking skills from his father. His psychological traits, physical characteristics, interactions with others and environment all radically change between narrative past and present; he goes from pathetic loser to convinced visionary, from paraplegic to ambulatory, from follower to leader and from a mundane city to a mystical island. The island and its secrets are fundamentally connected to every component of the Locke character, and, perhaps to a lesser degree, to every component of all the *Lost* characters.

Lost's producers have created a unique set of characters with a different, or rather additional function to their counterparts in other television story worlds. The structuralist analysis of the Locke character illustrates the ways in which each component of the character has direct relevance to the series' central narrative enigmas. However, *Lost*'s character innovation can be seen most clearly in the deployment of biography and psychological traits.

REGIMES OF EVALUATION

This returns us to the question of different regimes of evaluation that I raised at the outset. How does *Lost* differ from other texts and how should we evaluate it? *Lost*'s deployment of character biography distinguishes the show both from other hermeneutically centred genres and from other serial narratives. Other hermeneutically centred genres such as mysteries, thrillers and procedurals do tie character biography to the central hermeneutic; events in the characters' pasts often provide the motivation or method for a crime. These genres usually take episodic form, however; individual short stories, novels or television episodes may be part of a series that features a cast of recurring characters but each individual text resolves a specific and contained hermeneutic. In these cases, biographical elements that contribute to solving the contained hermeneutics pertain to the one-off and not the recurring characters.

Serial narratives, at least serial television dramas and comedies, tend to use character biography for two purposes. First, biography augments character. *Lost*'s flashbacks, as well as connecting to the central narrative enigmas, illuminate the behaviour and motivations of the character foregrounded in the narrative present of a particular episode. Charlie's 'Greatest Hits' flashbacks not only point to his inevitable fate, for example, but help the audience to understand why he so readily embraces it. Locke's flashbacks delineate the desperation that led to such fervent commitment to the island (and to such excessive despair when, at the end of season two, he believes that the island has let him down). Second, biography introduces the novelty and divergence necessary in a long-running programme. Newly introduced elements of character biography often serve to instigate a new plot line, which may be contained within a single episode or spun out over several episodes, and which may or may not have a lasting impact upon the character. For example, Tony Soprano's sister Janice (Aida Turturro), seen in flashback as a child in season one's 'Down Neck', shows up as an adult in the narrative present of season two. Her presence initiates plot developments, like the killing and disposal of Richie Aprile (David Proval). By contrast, *Lost*'s flashbacks don't initiate independent plot lines, but directly connect to the established mythology. Locke's long-lost father not only cripples his son in the flashbacks but reappears in the narrative present at a crucial point in the Locke character's relationship with the Others and with the island.

Lost's deployment of psychological traits distinguishes it from other serial television dramas. Margolin tells us that:

> Some stories by definition involve change, at least some of these known properties of any character are not enduring but time-bound, and the character's total property set inevitably gets modified over time. The standard distinction between static and dynamic characters is based on the (non)-occurrence of major changes in a character's psychological features.[19]

This modification of a character's total properties often takes the form of a narrative arc that culminates in a life-altering epiphany (as, for example, with Ebenezer Scrooge's move from selfishness to altruism in Charles Dickens' *A Christmas Carol* or Macbeth's from loyalty to ambition to existential despair in the Shakespearean play). A dynamic character who experiences such an epiphany is often judged as superior to a static character who does not. But the requirement for a certain degree of stability and repetition shapes the narrative arc of the central characters of serial television dramas, denying them life-altering epiphanies that would threaten the series' format. Betty (America Ferrera) in *Ugly Betty* (Touchstone Television, 2006–) cannot revert to her former innocence and leave the magazine *Mode*. Dexter (Michael C. Hall), in his own show, cannot settle down with his girlfriend and stop killing killers. And Tony, whatever his inner conflicts, cannot renounce the Mob.

The central narrative premises of most serial television dramas demand a certain degree of character stasis, whereas *Lost*'s central narrative premise demands a certain degree of character dynamism. The island, whether possessed of supernatural powers or not, clearly effects changes upon its inhabitants both physical and psychological, and these changes are related to the central narrative enigmas. Just as I-Locke's psychological traits differ from F-Locke's, so must the psychological traits of all the I-Losties differ to some extent from those of the F-Losties: Charlie must move from selfish drug addict to selfless hero, and Sawyer from lone-wolf conman to an increasingly responsible member of the castaway community and so forth.

Lost's hermeneutically driven narrative thus requires characters who experience core changes to psychological traits while *The Sopranos*' character-driven narrative requires characters who maintain a core stability of psychological traits. To illustrate this point, consider the murderous parents present in both narratives: Livia implicitly consents to Junior's (Dominic Chianese) whacking Tony and Anthony Cooper throws Locke out of an eighth-storey window. Tony's actions upon learning of his mother's betrayal are consistent with his established psychological traits and habitual behaviours; he seeks revenge by smothering her. He fails, but even had he succeeded he would have remained fundamentally the same person; Livia's death would not magically have resolved his psychological conflicts. Locke must deal with his father's betrayal by radically altering his established psychological traits and habitual behaviours to become the killer he had previously refused to be. In 'The Brig' (3.19), Ben tells Locke that he must shoot his father to prove that he's ready to accept what the island offers him:

> You're still crippled by the memories of the man you used to be before you came to this island. And you'll never be free, until you release the hold that your father has over you. As long as he's still breathing, you'll still be that same sad, pathetic little man that was kicked off his walkabout tour because you couldn't walk.

Locke can't do the deed directly, but accomplishes the murder indirectly through Sawyer, thus completing the magical transformation of psychological traits that the island has begun to effect upon him. The man who wouldn't kill the narc to save the commune kills Naomi to save the castaways (or so he believes).

If character consistency is judged better than character change wrought through a *deus ex machina* device then Tony is a better character than Locke and *The Sopranos* a better text than *Lost*. Alternatively, if dynamic characters are judged better than static characters then Locke is a better character than Tony and *Lost* a better text than *The Sopranos*. But these texts are not inferior or superior to each other – they are simply different from each other. *The Sopranos* is a character-driven narrative that revels in the complexity and ambiguity arising from continued internal conflict. The famous cut to black that ends the last episode of *The Sopranos* leaves Tony pretty much where we found him in the pilot, worrying about getting whacked or being indicted. Some deplore this non-ending as a cheap stunt, but I would argue that whacking or indicting Tony would have undercut the show's central narrative premise. Neither the law's imprisoning him nor the Mob's killing him will resolve those inner conflicts that drove so much of *The Sopranos*' narrative. The *Sopranos*' greatness lies partly in its extensive exploration of a character who changes very little over the course of six seasons, who remains as complex at the end as he was at the beginning: a loving father and husband, who is also a serial adulterer, and a brutal thug who is also a man of honour.

Despite Mittell's advocacy in this volume (see Chapter VII), *Lost*'s greatness is yet to be proved. Critical judgments will undoubtedly depend on whether or not Lindelof, Cuse, *et al.* can deliver on their promise to come up with a persuasive explanation for the island's plenitude of mysteries; they must successfully resolve the many chains of events currently in play. In the season one finale, 'Exodus' (1.24), Locke explains to Jack why opening the Hatch is so important to him:

> I'm a man of faith. Do you really think all this is an accident? That we, a group of strangers, survived, many of us with just superficial injuries? You think we crashed on this place by coincidence? Especially this place? We were brought here for a purpose, for a reason – all of us ... The island brought us here. This is no ordinary place ... Boone was a sacrifice that the island demanded. What happened to him at that plane was a part of a chain of events that led us here. That led us down a path. That led you and me to this day, to right now ... The path ends at the hatch. The hatch, Jack. All of it happened so that we could open the hatch.

Locke here articulates one of *Lost*'s central narrative enigmas: why are each of the Losties on the island? Answering that question requires definitive resolution of each of their individual character arcs. *Lost*'s final episode cannot cut to black, leaving the characters facing uncertain futures. *Lost*'s greatness may lie partly in its extensive exploration of characters who change a great deal over the course of six seasons and successfully resolve their inner conflicts at the end.

As I said when first raising the question of evaluation, characters can be judged good or great partly by how well they fit the needs of the story worlds they inhabit. The structuralist analysis of character components I have conducted enables a more precise assessment of the fit between character and story world. *The Sopranos* first requires biography that gives rise to independent plotlines and second characters with relatively static psychological traits whose arcs culminate in ambiguity. *Lost* first requires biography that connects to central narrative enigmas and second characters with relatively dynamic psychological traits whose arcs culminate in certainty. To the extent that the characters of both texts' characters fit these criteria, they are good characters. Texts can be judged good or great partly by the innovation of their storytelling forms. The contingencies and pressures of producing a weekly television series may frequently come between intention and realisation, but *Lost*'s producers can still lay claim to a significant narrative innovation, a unique construction of the televisual character.

Notes

My thanks to Jonathan Gray and Angela Ndalianis for feedback on a draft of this chapter.

1   See Chapter VII, p.123.

2   Maureen Ryan, '"Lost" producers talk about setting an end date and much more', *The Watcher*, available at *http://featuresblogs.chicagotribune.com/entertainment_tv/2007/01/lost_producers_.html*, posted 14 January 2007.

3   Ibid.

4   Mark Cotta Vaz, *The* Lost *Chronicles: The Official Companion Book* (London: Transworld, 2005), p.55.

5   Ryan: '"Lost" producers talk about setting an end date'.

6   Kate Arthur, 'Our mutual friend: Dickens, Challah and that mysterious island', *www.nytimes.com/2006/05/25/arts/television/25lost.htm?_r=1&oref=slogin*, 25 May 2006.

7   Ibid.

8   Cotta Vaz: *The* Lost *Chronicles*, p.55.

9   James Poniewozik, 'The 100 best TV shows of all-time', *Time*, available online at *www.time.com/time/specials/2007/article/0,28804,1651341_1659192_1652600,00.html*.

10 See Chapter VII, page 125.

11 Jonathan Gray and Jason Mittell, 'Speculation on spoilers: *Lost* fandom, narrative consumption and rethinking textuality', *Participations* iv/1, available online at *www.participations.org/Volume%204/Issue%201/4_01_graymittell.htm*.

12 Ibid.

13 Uri Margolin, 'Character', in David Herman (ed.), *The Cambridge Companion to Narrative* (Cambridge: CUP, 2007), p.67.

14 Ibid., p.68.

15 Roberta Pearson, 'Anatomising Gilbert Grissom: the structure and function of the televisual character', in Michael Allen (ed.), *Focus on CSI* (London: I.B.Tauris, 2007), pp.42–3.

16 Ibid., pp.39–56.

17 See Chapter II, p.16.

18 See Chapter IX, p.165.

19 Margolin: 'Character', p.73.

IX. 'Do You Even Know Where This Is Going?':

Lost's Viewers and Narrative Premeditation

Ivan Askwith

When Matthew Fox appeared as the guest host of *Saturday Night Live* in early December 2006, his status as the most recognizable lead on one of US network television's most discussed dramas all but guaranteed the inclusion of a *Lost*-centric sketch. When the sketch finally appeared, however, it was set not on a mysterious island but in a corporate elevator, and found Fox – as himself, rather than in his role as Dr Jack Shepard – fielding a series of questions, theories, insults and romantic advances from an ensemble of *Lost* viewers eager for answers about the show's many mysteries. Upon entering the elevator and seeing Fox, the first of these viewers declares, 'I got a theory about your show' and then pauses for dramatic effect, before announcing, 'You guys got *no* idea what's goin' on on that island!' Fox, demonstrating patience that has presumably been refined through hundreds of similar real-life interactions, smiles politely and assures his antagonist that the writers do, in fact, know what's going on. Several minutes later, the passenger turns to Fox and points out that the elevator ride has been enjoyable, because, 'stuff is actually happening. Unlike your show, where stuff only *pretends* to happen.'[1]

About a month later, another *Lost*-related sketch appeared on the online humour site *SuperDeluxe.com*. Entitled 'Writers of *Lost*', the clip depicts a group of four strung-out, hyperactive thirty-something white males sitting around a conference table, desperately attempting to plot out *Lost*'s next major narrative arc.[2] The punchline, of course, is that the writers haven't the faintest notion of where *Lost*'s plot is headed, nor how to explain most of the significant developments that have occurred on the show to date. In an attempt to focus the discussion, the head writer asks his team, 'What's the one big loose end that we have yet to deal with?' The answers come in rapid succession:

> 'Smoke monster?'
> 'The Dharma initiative.'
> 'Eye patch guy!'
> 'The polar bears?'
> 'Locke's occasional crippledness?'
> 'The number sequence?'
> 'Who the Others are?'
> 'What the Others *want*.'
> 'Why the Others want *who* they want.'
> 'Why Hurley remains fat ... on a virtually foodless island?'

Frustrated with this approach, the writers decide to generate new ideas and eventually settle on the introduction of a new character: a witch who has reversed time, so that for the next two years the writers can simply submit their previous scripts with the page orders reversed. Sighing with relief, the head writer concedes that the solution is a brilliant short-term fix, but warns the team that, 'in two years, we've gotta get serious about this'.

It should go without saying that sketch comedies and satirists are going to take aim at mainstream entertainment and therefore that parodies of *Lost* are to be expected. What I find remarkable about the two sketches described above, then, is their deliberate focus not on the content or characters of *Lost*, but on the creative planning process – or lack thereof – that occurs behind the scenes. In general, television writing rarely generates discussion, except among a show's most devoted fans. Yet in each of these sketches the humour is derived from an open acknowledgement of a growing fear: that *Lost*'s writers and showrunners have no long-term plan, or – even worse – that the writers might be 'making it up as they go along'. Even Carlton Cuse, *Lost*'s co-showrunner, has conceded that there is 'an underlying anxiety (among fans) that ... we don't know what we're doing'.[3]

While the *SNL* and SuperDeluxe sketches make light of this anxiety, it is not exactly a laughing matter. Audience scepticism about

Lost's long-term plan has very real consequences, both commercial (as more viewers abandon the series in fits of frustration) and artistic (since *Lost*'s creative legacy will eventually hinge, in large part, on whether the writers were able to finish what they started). An increasing number of viewers have given up on the show since *Lost*'s sophomore season, insisting that its inexplicable twists and turns – which were often the best thing about the first season – were now beginning to serve as proof that the writers had no long-term plan in mind, and that the show's endless mysteries would never be resolved in a satisfying manner.

As a long-time viewer and fan I am invested in that question, but I am far more intrigued by a less obvious mystery: understanding the logic that has driven me, like so many other *Lost* fans and antifans, to assume that the eventual 'worth' of the show will hinge on whether or not the writers had a long-term plan when the show began, and the extent to which that plan has been followed. This chapter attempts to answer – or, failing that, to explore – two related questions: first, the reasoning that leads viewers to believe that a clear, premeditated narrative plan is essential to the show's success, and second, the specific factors that might explain why *Lost* finds itself facing this insistent critique when many other shows do not. Before exploring these questions, however, I would like to review several of the complaints most frequently voiced about *Lost*'s lack of a premeditated narrative plan. These complaints, undoubtedly not as irrefutable as their proponents believe, are nonetheless worthy of consideration, helping to explain how *Lost*'s narrative structure establishes – and struggles to fulfil – viewer expectations and demands.

The most common criticisms of *Lost* tend to fall into four overlapping categories:

1) Too many questions, too few answers

If viewers believe that *Lost*'s mysteries have no real answers, it might be because the show asks far more questions than it answers. Rather than providing meaningful answers and closure, *Lost*'s writers often answer questions not with explanations, but more questions.[4] And while the show's most dedicated fans find this pleasurable, an increasing number of viewers and critics have suggested that it is evasive, and are beginning to perceive the show's endless stream of new questions as a diversion – presumably from the perceived fact that *Lost*'s writers have no meaningful or logical explanations for their existing mysteries.

2) Redundant flashbacks and the endless middle

A great deal of criticism also focuses on *Lost*'s uneven pacing, with the harshest attacks focusing on the show's signature flashbacks. In many cases, this simultaneous unveiling of past and present can provide powerful narrative satisfaction, with flashbacks providing crucial information to contextualize a survivor's otherwise inexplicable actions and motives. Yet as *Lost* moved into its second season and the audience grew familiar with each of the survivors, some flashbacks began to appear more redundant than revealing.[5] To cynical viewers, such episodes hinted at two troubling possibilities: either the writers were stalling for time, in order to develop answers to *Lost*'s existing mysteries, or being forced to prolong the show's run, in order to give ABC more seasons of their lucrative drama.

3) Convenient inconsistencies

Numerous viewers have attacked *Lost*'s writers for resorting to sudden, inexplicable lapses in characterization and logic. For example, when Jack is reunited with Kate (Evangeline Lilly) after his capture by the Others ('The Man from Tallahassee', 3.13), viewers have good reason to expect that he will provide some explanation of where he has been, or what he has been doing. Instead, he refuses to tell Kate anything, or to explain his reasons for doing so. And while there might be a logical narrative explanation for such decisions (such as protecting Kate), viewers may opt for the strategic explanation: that Jack's silence is being used to either protect *Lost*'s secrets, or – far worse – to cover up the fact that *Lost* has no secrets to protect.

4) Meaningless signifiers

At every level, *Lost* seems to offer clues to viewers hoping to unravel the show's mysteries: characters are named for famous philosophers and intellectuals; many scenes feature significant works of literature and music; and recurring visual motifs emphasize themes such as dualism and white-versus-black dichotomies. However, while such details appear to be loaded with hidden significance, audiences are beginning to fear that *Lost*'s penchant for symbolism and reference constitutes little more than misdirection. As such signifiers come and go with little or no explanation sceptical viewers begin to interpret such clues as mere diversions, or, even worse, as cheap attempts to construct the appearance of meaning where there is none.

Nowhere has this concern been more apparent than with 'Hurley's numbers', a cryptic string of numbers that seem to possess some sort of mystical or cosmic significance. During *Lost*'s first two seasons, the numbers appeared to function as a marker, linking otherwise disparate moments and details in a complex web of relationships and associations. The numbers were obviously linked to the island and the survivors of Oceanic 815, leading viewers to expect an explanation of their significance. It came as a shock to *Lost* devotees, then, when co-showrunner Lindelof answered a question about the ultimate meaning of the numbers by musing:

> I think that that question will never, ever be answered. I couldn't possibly imagine [how we would answer that question]. We will see more ramifications of the numbers and more usage of the numbers, but it boggles my mind when people ask me, 'What do the numbers mean?'[6]

To many viewers, this was a damning moment for *Lost*, an admission from the co-creator that the writers hadn't pre-determined the answer to one of the show's most compelling mysteries. According to the writers, however, the origin of the numbers was a relatively low priority, since – at least according to Lindelof – most viewers would find this information 'very uninteresting, because ultimately our characters don't give a shit about the origin of the numbers'.[7] While this might be true – although at least in Hurley's (Jorge Garcia) case, we can argue that it is not – the fact remains that the show's heavy emphasis of the numbers has compelled much of the audience to view them as an important element of *Lost*'s greater mysteries.

The single most compelling indictment against *Lost*, however, came not from the show or an interview with *Lost*'s showrunners, but from ex-writer David Fury. Speaking to *Rolling Stone* after his departure from the series, Fury insisted that:

there was absolutely no master plan on *Lost*. Anybody who said that was lying. They keep saying there's meaning in everything, and I'm here to tell you no – a lot of things are just arbitrary. What I always tried to do was connect these random elements, to create the illusion that it was all adding up to something.[8]

Fury's statement offered an ironclad confirmation of viewers' fears and frustrations. The lack of a master plan suggested that the numerous references, clues and suggestions would never add up to answers and made a mockery of the fans' post-episode analysis, debate and speculation. The show writers, with good reason, were both hurt and incensed by Fury's statement. But while Fury's comments might have damaged the audience's faith in *Lost*, they also set the stage for debate over a problem that lies at the heart of this discussion – the fact that adhering to a pre-meditated narrative plan hasn't always been an option for US network television writers.

'TELEVISION DOESN'T WORK THAT WAY'

Responding to Fury's statement online, *Lost* writer Javier Grillo-Marxuach insisted that there was always a master plan for the series. Far more important, however, was Grillo-Marxuach's reasoned defence against the *Rolling Stone* accusations, in which he challenged Fury's explanation as a crass oversimplification of the conditions that govern network television writing and production. As he pointed out:

The truth about all television shows ... is that they are slightly amorphous living beings. They develop over time and things that work or don't work are used or discarded accordingly ... That's how good television is made – if some part of your plan doesn't work, you rework it until it does.[9]

Grillo-Marxuach also outlined a number of pragmatic factors that can encourage, or in some cases require, deviation from a show's original plan. Yet, as he points out, these deviations don't necessarily pose irreconcilable problems, and in some cases they can even result in notable improvements. For example, when Michael Emerson was cast as Henry Gale/Ben Linus, his character was only slated for a three-episode arc culminating in the revelation that he was one of the Others. Impressed with his performance, the writers expanded his role and made him their leader, a part that was once envisioned as a separate character.[10] Similarly, the fact that Locke (Terry O'Quinn) had formerly been wheelchair-bound stemmed from a spontaneous suggestion by Lindelof during scripting; and when viewers failed to accept the abrupt introduction of Nikki and Paolo, the writers penned 'Exposé' (3.14), an episode that integrated them into *Lost*'s diegetic history then literally buried them alive. Each of these deviations from *Lost*'s original plan represent conscious choices from the writing room and reflect proactive attempts to improve the show. However, pragmatic realities and unavoidable pressures have also forced *Lost*'s writers to accommodate other changes. These inescapable pressures reflect two simple truths about US network programming. First, television, unlike literary fiction, is not the product of a single creative vision, but of grand-scale collaboration between performers, writers, technicians, marketers and a host of other creative professionals. Second, television is an industrial product, refined to serve specific commercial purposes, and subject to the same logistical and financial constraints as any business. On the most basic level, this means that *Lost* is subject to the standard requirements that govern all network programming: each episode must adhere to a six-act structure, allowing for commercial breaks, and end with a hook that will draw viewers back for the next instalment. Similarly, each season should end with a cliffhanger strong enough to retain viewer interest until the next season begins. The standard requirements of production also force *Lost* to adhere to strict budgets and timelines, respond to network concerns, cater to scheduling conflicts, and work around resource, location and actor availabilities.

These pragmatic realities have had significant implications for *Lost*, with the most notable example being the sudden and somewhat premature death of Mr Eko in 'The Cost of Living' (3.5), which left numerous questions about the character unresolved. The writers had hoped to explore the character in greater depth, but when actor Adewale Akinnuoye-Agbaje insisted that he be released from his contract to pursue a film career, the showrunners had no choice but to oblige.[11] On the other hand, forced narrative deviations can also prove serendipitous: to wit, Jack Shepard was originally destined to die in the final moments of *Lost*'s pilot episode, leaving

Kate to lead the survivors. Concerned that this was too significant a violation of the audience's trust, ABC insisted that Jack survive, and he went on to become one of *Lost*'s most popular characters.

While such changes might not always be ideal for *Lost*'s narrative integrity, it is an oversimplification to raise them as proof that the show's writers have no long-term narrative arc. The important question, said Grillo-Marxuach in his response to Fury's assertions, is:

> Does [the act of] making these adjustments, accommodating new ideas that enrich our series, and letting the show be a creative process that allows for new development mean we are lying when we say we have a master plan? You tell me.[12]

The answer, at least according to Stephen King, is a resounding 'no'. Writing in *Entertainment Weekly* before the show's second season, King argued that

> The creators themselves may not know why the numbers on Hurley's winning lottery ticket are replicated on the side of the hatch ... but who cares? The chief attributes of creators are faith and arrogance: faith that there is a solution, and the arrogance to believe they are exactly the right people to find it.[13]

Yet King also posed a specific challenge, declaring that *Lost*'s showrunners' single most important obligation is knowing when to end the series, rather than continuing to fill episodes 'with years of ponderous flashback padding'. To fulfil this obligation, *Lost* would need to push back against what King described as 'The Prime Network Directive: Thou Shalt Not Kill The Cash Cow'.[14] Singling out *The X-Files* (Twentieth Century Fox Television, 1993–2002) as a cautionary tale, King suggested that the biggest threat facing serialized television narratives is the traditional network approach to programming, which involves renewing a show until it no longer attracts viewers, then cancelling it with little warning. While this approach poses no significant narrative threat to more traditional, stand-alone episodic programming, it can be crippling to shows like *Lost*, since it is impossible for the writers to determine a proper narrative pace without knowing – or having the right to decide – when their own show will end. Lindelof has lamented this exact problem, explaining:

The reality is that Carlton, myself, J.J. [Abrams], the creative brains behind the *Lost* universe, we could all band together and say, 'We're ending the show after three seasons because that's the arc. They get off the island, and we reveal all the things we want to reveal.' And the network would say, 'No, you won't.' They will hire somebody and do *Lost*, with or without [us].[15]

Even if the writers are not entirely to blame for *Lost*'s narrative short-comings – and there are several reasons to think that they're not – the viewer's experience and expectations remain the same: storytellers are expected to tell good stories, to keep their promises and to answer whatever questions they introduce. If *Lost*'s writers can't meet those expectations, viewers will feel cheated for investing their time and emotions in a show incapable of delivering on its own promises.

Why do viewers (myself included) worry so much about whether *Lost*'s writers have been following a deliberate plan and assume that the show's success hinges on successful resolution of its many mysteries? Viewer insistence on narrative premeditation is not unique to *Lost*. Evidence suggests that audiences bring similar expectations to most serial narratives and mysteries. As Hayward explains, the serial consumer 'learns to predict, to look for clues, to compare notes with other readers in an attempt to unravel the mystery and predict the narrative outcome',[16] a practice that Jason Mittell (see Chapter VII) refers to as 'forensic fandom'. If the practice of forensic fandom is based in large part on the satisfaction that comes from making accurate predictions, it is logical that serial audiences will expect such narratives to adhere to an implicit set of 'rules' that reward effort and attention.

When a storyteller fails to provide clues that foreshadow the eventual outcome of the narrative – or worse yet, provides clues without knowing the eventual outcome of the narrative – readers may feel that the author is violating a significant clause in what Hayward describes as 'the serial contract': 'Authors should not intentionally mislead the audience but should provide enough clues to enable intelligent and alert readers to anticipate future developments and take pleasure in correct guesses.'[17] Without knowing in advance how a story's narrative will evolve, it becomes impossible to provide meaningful clues. Their absence renders the practice of forensic fandom futile.

Yet it is also clear that some serial fictions require premeditated narrative more than others: audiences demand far more narrative planning from the writers of *Lost* and *Twin Peaks* (Lynch/Frost Productions, 1990–1), for example, than for *Buffy, the Vampire Slayer* (Mutant Enemy, 1997–2003) and *Babylon 5* (Babylonian Productions, 1994–8). While the audience expectation of narrative premeditation is not unique to *Lost*, there are at least four possible factors that encourage *Lost*'s audience to approach the show with different expectations than the audiences of most other serialized television programmes.

1) Lost *is structured and written more like a novel than a television series*

In many regards, *Lost* is the most novelistic show ever to air on US broadcast television. Despite functioning as a week-to-week serial, *Lost* has placed a near-unprecedented emphasis on strict continuous serialization. Each episode of the series functions not as an independent narrative unit, but as a sequential link in a chain that stretches from the first episode to the last, framing the entire series as a singular narrative, rather than an overlapping series of related narratives. As a result, the show quickly becomes (and remains) inaccessible to viewers who have not seen most or all of the previous episodes of the series. This being so, it seems that the previous episodes are all essential to understanding the meaning and context for the 'present' episode of the show. Unlike *Buffy*, for example, where a good season of the show could retain its lustre even if a subsequent season was disappointing, *Lost* has linked the 'meaning' and 'value' of all episodes together, so that each new episode adds to the overall work, and re-contextualizes the significance and value of the earlier episodes.

Lost's showrunners have often noted that *Lost* has 'a beginning, a middle, and an end'.[18] And this claim alone – that the show has 'an end' – made *Lost* an anomaly in US television, where most writers must be prepared to infinitely defer resolution until their show has been slated for cancellation. For most television programmes, the entire run of a series (with the brief exception of the pilot and finale) is intended to serve as 'an endless middle'. Much of the satisfaction of watching an episode of *Lost* hinges on the viewer's expectation that the mysteries will eventually be solved in a satisfying and meaningful fashion – a process that mirrors what Peter Brooks has described as 'the anticipation of retrospection'.[19] If at the end of the day (or in this case, the end of the series) this hasn't happened, those episodes become less pleasurable both to remember and to watch, since their pleasure was predicated in large part on the promise of eventual fulfilment and revelation.

As mentioned earlier, Lost also sets itself apart from most television programming through the liberal and frequent use of literary devices such as symbolism, repetition and inter-textual reference (such as the juxtaposition of white and black, tight close-up shots of an eye opening and Hurley's ubiquitous number sequence).[20] It is possible that most of Lost's recurring motifs and elements have no great significance in the show's overarching narrative. In interviews, however, Lindelof has implied that such details are included as 'easter eggs' to reward attentive viewing and generate discussion. This could be seen as a significant violation of the viewer's trust. In his analysis of narrative structure, Brooks has suggested that, 'an event gains meaning by its repetition' and that the repetition of elements in a text '...allow the ear, the eye, the mind to make connections, conscious or unconscious, between different textual moments, to see past and present as related and as establishing a future that will be noticeable as some variation in the pattern'.[21] Even if the writers intend otherwise, Lost's extensive use of recurring elements and motifs carries the inherent promise that their implied connection will eventually be fully revealed. In the absence of such revelations, viewers may feel that their efforts have been wasted and their trust violated.

2) Lost *insists that 'everything happens for a reason'*

Perhaps it would be easier to overlook such suggestive use of repetition if it were not for Lost's insistence that 'everything happens for a reason', a claim that was appropriated as a tagline during the show's second season. The claim is also rearticulated within the show itself on a regular basis by John Locke, who – like many viewers – spent much of the show's first season insisting to both his fellow survivors and the audience that 'each one of us was brought here for a reason'.[22] Yet, like the audience, Locke's faith in a greater meaning begins to waver as the series wears on. Searching for the pattern that might explain the series of coincidences and misfortunes that have defined his life, Locke progresses from his self-professed status as 'a man of faith' (season one) through a state of disillusionment and existentialist despair (season two) before returning to his initial convictions (season three). In 'Further Instructions' (3.3), when he reaffirms his faith and whispers, 'I'm sorry ... I ever doubted you. Sorry I gave up on my faith in the island', we might argue that the audience is witnessing an act of wish fulfilment, with the writers pleading for a similar concession from viewers who had lost faith in the show's narrative plan.

Lost has brought this challenge upon itself, however. The insistent claim that 'everything happens for a reason' makes causality an essential structuring device, central to deciphering the most enigmatic aspects of the show. But causality implies that the majority of the events and details in *Lost* are included for reasons that will eventually be revealed. These expectations are consistent with the often-cited dramatic principle of 'Chekhov's gun'. Russian playwright Anton Chekhov insisted on multiple occasions that the inclusion of a noticeable detail in a narrative requires the eventual clarification of its significance: 'If you say in the first chapter that there is a rifle hanging on the wall, in the second or third chapter it absolutely must go off. If it's not going to be fired, it shouldn't be hanging there.'[23] On this principle, our narrative pleasure relies upon the assumption of eventual understanding of the motives behind Locke's apparently inconsistent or self-defeating actions. The provision of an eventual explanation for initially inexplicable events and decisions provides one of *Lost*'s most distinctive narrative pleasures. However, the lack of clarification of a character's motives diminishes the viewer's ability to believe in both story and character.

In promising that everything happens for a reason, *Lost* also implies that careful analysis of the show's minor details will provide viewers with greater insight into the island's mysteries. As a result, critics often describe *Lost* as 'the first television program that owes its soul to video games',[24] with the show's wealth of suggestive details and references compelling its most dedicated viewers to multiple viewings of each episode in search of missed clues. In some cases, the desire to parse *Lost*'s subtle references has also driven viewers to do 'homework' that extends well beyond the show's textual bounds. Just before *Lost*'s second season, one of the show's writers informed the *Chicago Tribune* that Flan O'Brien's *The Third Policeman* (1940) would appear in an upcoming episode, and that viewers familiar with the book – which 'was chosen very specifically for a reason' – would 'have a lot more ammunition in their back pocket as they theorize about the show'.[25] According to the fan-edited *Lostpedia.com*, the book went on to sell more copies in the three weeks after the episode's airing than in the six years preceding it.[26] Nor was this a one-time occurrence: a number of online communities, including such mainstream media sources *The Washington Post*, have formed active '*Lost* Book Clubs' that convene during the hiatus between seasons, in order to read and discuss texts that have made suggestive appearances on the show.[27] If *Lost* fails to deliver on the claim that 'everything happens for a reason', many viewers may feel that their efforts were in vain.

3) Lost's non-linear chronology creates unique expectations

Narratologists often draw a distinction between *fabula*, the actual order in which the narrative's events take place, and *sjuzet*, the sequence in which those events are related to the reader. These terms are particularly useful for untangling *Lost*'s complicated non-linear narrative structure, which jumps between 'the present' (life on the island), 'the past' (character-specific flashbacks) and, beginning with the third season finale, 'the future' (life after rescue).[28] Tzvetan Todorov has suggested that detective stories make the relationship between *fabula* and *sjuzet* most apparent, telling the story not from the chronological beginning (when an act of crime is committed) but from the mid-point (when an investigation begins). The narrative then moves forward through time, as the detective carries out an investigation, but also backwards through time, as the detective reconstructs the hidden events that culminated in a crime. Detective stories 'end' only when they have arrived at the 'beginning' (that is, when the audience understands the act that set the narrative in motion).

Lost's narrative is similar to, if more complicated than, traditional detective stories. If the characters themselves fail to act like detectives – much to the frustration of those viewers who believe that the survivors would be more concerned with solving the island's mysteries – there is no question that *Lost*'s viewers are positioned as detectives. Nor is there any question that solving *Lost*'s mysteries will require viewers to reconstruct events that took place before the crash of Oceanic 815. Many of *Lost*'s most powerful moments result from the show's experimentation with *sjuzet*, with each flashback ostensibly providing new details that recontextualize some or all of the viewer's previous theories. *Lost*'s narrative teaches us that we must decipher the past in order to understand the present. Yet in doing so, *Lost* offers an implicit promise that the past *will* provide meaning to the present, and as such, that the past was written before the present. For *Lost*'s experiments with *sjuzet* to be compelling, the viewer must believe that the *fabula* ('what actually happened') has been pre-determined.

We can distinguish between two kinds of questions that arise in *Lost*: questions about the past and questions about the future. Questions about the past (such as, 'What is the island?', 'Who are the Others?', 'What is the smoke monster?') become the basis for understanding the present. We can't understand what we are seeing, or have already seen, without answers to bring logic and meaning to the narrative and to turn a random sequence of enigmatic details and conflicts into a meaningful series of logical narrative events. Cuse has suggested that, '[*Lost*] is like a mosaic. There are tiles in the present, in the past and now in the future as well. When all the tiles are in place, the story of *Lost* will be complete.'[29] Cuse makes an implicit promise that a clear and meaningful picture will emerge from the eventual juxtaposition of all of *Lost*'s narrative fragments. For example, at some point *Lost* will need to reveal who the Others are and explain their motives, information that should justify a series of otherwise inexplicable actions from the show's first three seasons and answer questions such as:

- Why did the Others send spies to infiltrate the survivor camp, despite knowing that the survivors were innocent victims rather than hostile agents pursuing an agenda?

- Why did the Others first appear in tattered rags and bare feet and construct a fake camp when they had access to modern clothing, supplies and technologies?

- Why did the Others not simply explain their situation and agenda to the survivors during their first encounter on the island?

Since *Lost* implies that 'everything happens for a reason', answering each of these 'sub-questions' will require a more compelling explanation than 'it was more dramatic to keep them mysterious'.

Questions about the future, on the other hand (such as 'Will Kate settle down with Jack or Sawyer (Josh Holloway)?', 'Will Charlie (Dominic Monaghan) kick his heroin addiction?', 'Will the survivors get off the island, and if so, at what cost?') do not carry this same burden since the answers do not need to be pre-determined. Our own experiences – our personal narratives – help us accept that the future has not been written, and is still subject to change. However, the past's being uncertain and flexible casts doubt forward into the present. Viewers' most pressing concern is not whether the writers know where *Lost* is going, but whether they know where *Lost* began.

The introduction of flash-forwards potentially makes *Lost*'s nonlinear narrative even more problematic. Until the final moments of the third season, the audience's experience of *Lost* involved the relatively straightforward experience of 'now' and 'earlier'. The introduction of the flash-forward device, however, poses the showrunners an even greater challenge: recontextualizing the narrative 'present' as the 'future's past'.[30] Just as audiences have always demanded that *Lost*'s flashbacks eventually add up to a coherent and logical 'present', the show's remaining episodes now face the additional burden of depicting a present that adds up to, and explains, the flash-forwards.

4) *Lost is a serial narrative being developed in a period of transition*

It is important to recognize that some of the challenges facing the show have less to do with *Lost* itself, and more to do with the act of writing serial fiction for audiences who have not yet formed specific criteria for evaluating such narratives. While it is tempting to imagine that *Lost*'s writers are facing new challenges that result from the show's far-reaching ambition, historical precedents suggest that the complicated (and sometimes adversarial) relationship between serial fiction writers and audiences is inherent to the genre itself. As Cuse has pointed out, even Dickens – often credited as the first successful serial writer – faced similar challenges and pressures:

We often think: 'How much did Dickens know when he was writing his stories? How much of it was planned out, and how much was flying by the seat of his pants because he had to get another chapter in?'[31]

It might be some comfort to Cuse to know that *Lost*'s parallels to Dickens extend far beyond the imperative to meet weekly deadlines. Victorian audiences and critics often expressed frustration when reviewing the individual instalments that made up Dickens' novels. Jennifer Hayward found that even *Our Mutual Friend*, which *Lost* incorporates as the final novel that Desmond plans to read before he dies, was subject to such criticism, noting that, 'During its run ... many reviewers complained repeatedly about its complexity, saying that the novel was too full of subplots, minor characters who persisted in taking centre stage, and narrative strands not fully worked out.'[32]

The existing scholarship on Dickens also proves useful when assessing the unique challenges of writing serial fiction – challenges that are as pertinent to Lindelof and Cuse today as they were to Dickens almost two hundred years ago. In particular, Butt and Tillotson have observed that

Writing in serial involved maintaining two focuses. The design and purpose of the novel had to be kept constantly in view; but the writer had also to think in terms of the identity of the serial number, which would have to make its own impact and be judged as a unit.[33]

As Dickens himself noted in the 1837 preface to *The Pickwick Papers*, 'every [instalment] should be, to a certain extent, complete in itself, and yet ... when collected, should form one tolerably complete whole'.[34] Today, television viewers hold serial dramas such as *Lost* to a similar standard, evaluating them not just as instalments in a longer work, but as individual units of narrative in their own right.

Recognizing this challenge, Lindelof and Cuse have attempted to explain their plans for the show through reference to a more recent serial narrative, J. K. Rowling's *Harry Potter* saga. What differentiates *Lost* from the *Harry Potter* books – and, for that matter, from *Our Mutual Friend* – is the fact that Dickens and Rowling both enjoyed a freedom that Lindelof and Cuse have not: knowledge of a predetermined end-date, and with it, the ability to understand how each instalment would function as part of an eventual whole. Even without this freedom, *Lost*'s writers find the structure of *Harry Potter* useful in explaining their approach to plotting, with Cuse suggesting that, 'each season is … a book, like the *Harry Potter* series. Each one has its own character and shape.'[35] Thus, *Lost*'s first season was about the crash of Oceanic 815 and the survivors, the second about the hatch and the third about the Others.

Nevertheless, without determining an end date, as Rowling did for *Harry Potter*, the question remains: can a television show, forced to perpetuate itself for an undetermined period of time until it is cancelled, be successful in following a long-term narrative arc? At least two precedents exist to suggest that it can: *Buffy* and *Babylon 5*. *Buffy* structured each season around a villain, or 'Big Bad', who would be introduced, developed and defeated. While *Buffy*'s characters participate in a specific ongoing narrative, with each episode of the show existing on a firm timeline, each season feels very much like a distinct chapter or volume in a larger work. *Buffy* viewers can argue that certain seasons were better than others, but one bad season doesn't taint the entire series. *Babylon 5* took a different approach. Series creator J. Michael Straczynski claimed to have planned the five-season arc of the series before shooting the first episode, but, similar to the *Harry Potter* series, in which each volume covered a single year of Harry's education, each season of *Babylon 5* encompassed a full year of diegetic time. Thus even when narrative threads remained unresolved at the end of a season, the audience was presented with a clear governing logic for the show's structure.[36]

Not all television serials have been as successful in developing individual seasons as self-sufficient narratives, as the eventual narrative shortcomings of *Twin Peaks* make clear. While there are many theories to explain the abrupt disappearance of *Twin Peaks*' audience during the show's second season, one plausible explanation concerns the structural design of the central narrative. While it is true that *Twin Peaks* (particularly in its second season) introduced a range of character-specific mysteries and plots, the show was never able to escape from the first season's near-exclusive emphasis on finding the answer to a singular question, who killed Laura Palmer? For much of the audience, the resolution of this core question became 'the point' of the series, with anticipation of this eventual answer providing the show's dominant pleasure. When *Twin Peaks* identified Laura's killer (2.9) and shifted its genre from detective procedural to soap opera, many of the show's remaining viewers lost interest, believing that the show had transformed into something fundamentally different from that with which they had first engaged.

These examples suggest that *Lost*'s viewers may feel frustrated because they cannot yet decide whether the show's division into distinct chapters and volumes is valuable in itself. Unlike *Buffy*, *Harry Potter* or *Babylon 5*, the distinctions between *Lost*'s seasons often seem more useful to the writers than the audience. As one critic has complained, the experience of watching *Lost* sometimes leaves the audience with the impression that, 'like small children playing with toys, [the writers] drop each mystery after a few minutes and then run to the next one, hoping viewers will follow'.[37]

It is of course possible that *Lost*'s writers have made the conscious choice to write for long-term rather than first-run network viewers; on more than one occasion Lindelof and Cuse have admitted that the show is often written and shot with the DVD audience in mind. Just as many Victorian readers preferred to wait until Dickens' serialized novels were released as bound compilations,[38] an increasing number of *Lost*'s viewers have abandoned the show's week-to-week broadcasts in favour of binge-viewing on DVD. While *Lost*'s ratings declined in the show's second and third seasons, the show's second-season DVD sales broke all previous records,[39] and the third season ranked as the most popular time-shifted television series for 2007.[40] Producers face the same dilemma as Dickens, having to design a narrative to cater to multiple modes of consumption. Also, *Lost*'s audiences and critics face the same dilemma as Dickens', trying to evaluate the success and artistic merit of a serial narrative prior to completion.

EPILOGUE

Just before the end of *Lost*'s third season, ABC issued a press release to announce the 'bold and unprecedented' decision that *Lost* would run for three more seasons and end in 2010. According to Stephen McPherson, president of ABC Entertainment, this was a necessary decision: 'Due to the unique nature of the series, we knew it would require an end date to keep the integrity and strength of the show consistent throughout, and to give the audience the pay-off they deserve.'[41] Of course, ABC's decision – which flies directly in the face of King's 'Prime Network Directive' – was motivated by more than mere artistic integrity. As Lindelof and Cuse explained in interviews throughout the previous year, *Lost* was bound to continue losing viewers until it offered an end date, and with it, the implied resolution of all its mysteries. The decision to announce a finite run for *Lost* served both commercial and artistic needs.

A few weeks prior to the show's fourth-season premiere, Matthew Fox sat down with *Entertainment Weekly* to share his thoughts on the importance of the announcement:

> I was happy. Damon [Lindelof] said it to me best once: 'It's like running a marathon and you don't know how long it is.' If he has a story in his mind, how does he tell that story if he doesn't know how long the book is. I'm telling you, the story is going to charge and move rapidly in the next 48 episodes. One of the knocks on the show is that it hasn't moved fast enough. Part of that was because Damon felt like he didn't know when to let it go. Now he knows.[42]

After *Lost*'s first season, critics and writers suggested that the show's most important contribution was that it cleared the path for a new wave of television programmes with rich details and complex, rewarding narratives. If Fox is right, and *Lost*'s final three seasons demonstrate the importance of an established end date in developing a coherent and compelling serial narrative, the show may accomplish something even more important. It may provide the precedent for a new era of television narratives that have the freedom to end.

Notes

For their insightful comments on earlier versions of this chapter, particular thanks are due to Jonathan Gray, Elizabeth Wiltsie, Anton Markin and Jason Mittell.

1   'Matthew Fox', *Saturday Night Live*, 2 December 2006.

2   'Writers of *Lost*' at *www.superdeluxe.com/sd/contentDetail.do?id=D81F2 344BF5AC7BB29A4AEDE0D956F45CC7B35FAFE1B8CD6*>, 4 January 2007.

3   '"*Lost*" creators: we know where we're going', available at *www.cnn. com/2007/SHOWBIZ/TV/01/16/television.lost.reut/index.html*>, 16 January 2007.

4   This trend has also prompted viewers and critics alike to compile cata-logue-length lists of the show's unresolved narrative threads. The most often cited of these is IGN's 'Top 50 *Lost* Loose Ends', available at *http:// tv.ign.com/articles/745/745595p1.html*, 13 November 2006.

5   Few episodes have been accused of padding *Lost*'s run more often than the Hurley-centric 'Tricia Tanaka is Dead' (3.10), often referred to as 'Hurley and the Van'. While the present action focuses on Hurley find-ing and reviving an abandoned Dharma Initiative van, the flashback seems to offer little more than a new refrain for the well-worn theme of Hurley's bad luck. Although the introduction of the van is paid off both in the past, when its origin is explained in the Ben-centric flashback ('The Man Behind The Curtain', 3.20), and in the present, when it is used in a surprise attack on the Others ('Through The Looking Glass', 3.22), 'Tricia Tanaka' is generally cited as the closest thing to a stand-alone episode of *Lost*.

6   Michael Ausiello, 'Ask Ausiello', available online at *www.tvguide.com/ Ask-Ausiello/051116*, 15 November 2006.

7   S.T. Collins, 'The Lost Boy', *Wizard Entertainment*, available at *www.wiz-arduniverse.com/television/lost/003243877.cfm*, 6 February 2007.

8   G. Edwards, 'The Secrets of *Lost*', *Rolling Stone*, 6 October 2005.

9   Javier Grillo-Marxuach, entry at *LiveJournal.com*, 1 October 2005.

10 Ed Martin, 'Damon Lindelof and Carlton Cuse on the challenges of writ-ing *Lost*', available at *www.mediavillage.com/jmentr/2007/02/08/jmer-02-08-07*, 8 February 2007.

11 See Eric Goldman, 'How will *Lost* end?', available at *http://tv.ign.com/ articles/755/755527p1.html*, 16 January 2007.

12 Grillo-Marxuach: entry at *LiveJournal.com*.

13 Stephen King, '*Lost*'s soul', *Entertainment Weekly*, available at *www. ew.com/ew/article/0,,1100673,00.html*, 9 September 2005.

14 Ibid.

15 K. O'Hare, 'The journey of "*Lost*"', available at *http://tv.zap2it.com/ tveditorial/tve_main/1,1002,271%7C99441%7C1%7C,00.html*, 8 January 2006.

16 Jennifer Hayward, *Consuming Passions: Active Audiences and Serial Fic-tions from Dickens to Soap Opera* (Lexington, KY: The University Press of Kentucky, 1997), p.77.

17 Haywood: *Consuming Passions*, p.56.

18 K.D. Thompson, 'Lost creators promise no disappointments in finale', *The Houston Chronicle*, 24 May 2006, available at *www.chron.com/disp/ story.mpl/ent/3885172.html*.

19 Peter Brooks, *Reading for the Plot: Design and Intention in Narrative* (New York: Knopf, 1984), p.22.

20 Few US network programmes use a comparable level of symbolism and repetition; in this regard, *Lost* has more in common with 'high-end' HBO programmes such as *The Sopranos* and *Six Feet Under*.

21 Brooks: *Reading for the Plot*, p.99.

22 See, for example, 'Exodus, Part 2' (1.24).

23 Cited in S. Shchukin. *Memoirs* (1911), via Wikipedia, 'Chekhov's gun' at *http://en.wikipedia.org/wiki/Chekhov's_gun*.

24 Jennifer Buckendorff, 'Fans play TV series "Lost" like an interactive video game', *The Seattle Times*, 10 January 2006, available at *http://seattletimes.nwsource.com/cgi-bin/PrintStory.pl?document_ id=2002730079&zsection_id=2002113064&slug=lostgame10&date=200 60110*.

25 P.T. Reardon, 'Literary publisher gets mysterious role on ABC's "Lost"', *The Chicago Tribune*, 21 September 2005, available at *http://metromix. chicagotribune.com/search/mmx-0512260133dec26,1,6483098.story*.

26 See 'Third policeman', at *http://lostpedia.com/wiki/Third_policeman*.

27 Liz Kelly, 'Join the "Lost" book club,' *Washington Post*, 11 July 2007, available at *http://blog.washingtonpost.com/celebritology/2007/07/lost_ book_club.html*.

28 Confusing matters further, *Lost*'s showrunners have clarified that the 'future' depicted at the end of the third season is not the end-point of the series, and that an additional act will take place even farther into the future. This means that the 'future' depicted in 'Through the Looking Glass' (3.22) will also, at some point, be recontextualised as 'present' and/or 'past'.

29 Alan Stanley Blair, 'Cuse: It's Time To Change *Lost*,' available at *www. syfyportal.com/news424521.html*, 7 December 2007.

30 The easiest escape from these challenges would be to introduce time-travel and the prospect of multiple narrative realities, an option which appears to have been explored through Desmond's time-travel in 'Flashes Before Your Eyes' (3.8).

31 Kate Arthur, 'Dickens, Challah and that mysterious island', *The New York Times*, 25 May 2006, available at *www.nytimes.com/2006/05/25/ arts/television/25lost.html*.

32 Hayward: *Consuming Passions*, p.82.

33   John Butt and Kathleen Tillotson, *Dickens at Work* (London: Methuen, 1957), p.15.

34   C. Dickens, *The Pickwick Papers* (London: Penguin Classics, 1999 [1837]), p.6.

35   Todd Gilchrist, 'Interview: Carlton Cuse', available at *http://dvd.ign.com/articles/726/726981p1.html*, 21 August 2006.

36   The example of *Babylon 5* also reinforces the argument that network television programmes have to be flexible enough to account for unexpected change. Even the existence of a clear five-year plan was not enough to ensure that *Babylon 5*'s narrative would unfold according to a masterplan. Facing the prospect of cancellation due to low fourth-season ratings, Straczynski was forced to speed up his plans, and compressed his fifth season plans into the second half of the fourth season. When *Babylon 5* was renewed for a fifth and final season, his original plot had already been completed, forcing him to quickly generate an additional season's worth of narrative.

37   A. Dehnart, 'Why "*Lost*" has lost me as a viewer', available at *www.msnbc.msn.com/id/14911832MSNBC.com*, 8 October 2006.

38   Hayward: *Consuming Passions*, p.37.

39   Thomas K. Arnold, '"*Lost 2*" finds way to top of DVD sales', *The Hollywood Reporter*, available at *www.hollywoodreporter.com/hr/search/article_display.jsp?vnu_content_id=1003121876*, 14 September 2006.

40   Nielsen Company, 'The Nielsen Company issues top ten US lists for 2007', press release, 11 December 2007, available at *www.nielsen.com/media/2007/pr_071211a_download.pdf*.

41   ABC, '*Lost* to conclude in 2009–10 television season', press release, 7 May 2007, available at *www.abcmedianet.com/web/progcal/dispDNR.aspx?id=050707_01#*.

42   D. Snierson, '"*Lost*": Matthew Fox flash forwards to season 4', *Entertainment Weekly*, 11 January 2008, available at *www.ew.com/ew/article/0,,20169281_4,00.html*.

X. Lost in Genre:
Chasing the White Rabbit to Find a White Polar Bear

Angela Ndalianis

Over the last few years television, and the fictional shows that occupy its spaces, have become a driving force of experimentation: within the formal structure of the shows themselves; in terms of the advances they have encouraged through collaborations with newer, digitally reliant technologies; and also in generating alternate narrative scenarios within new media formats that extend the audience's experience of a specific television narrative. Shows like *Lost, 24* (Imagine Entertainment, 2001–) and *Heroes* (Jackson Films, 2006–) have all played significant, even groundbreaking, roles in creating storytelling strategies that extend the fictional spaces of their TV universes into the media worlds of mobile phones, podcasts, comic books, novels and the Internet. As I have argued elsewhere, the conglomeration of the entertainment industry and its reliance on new communications technologies has resulted in an industry that has multiple media interests.[1] The outcome has been new convergences between diverse entertainment forms, and these configurations have formal repercussions. While the academic community has begun to explore the ramifications of cross-media story extensions in relation to their impact on the cinema, few have explored the current transformations that television shows like *Lost* signal in light of the cross-media adventures that they favour.[2]

Embracing the era of viral marketing head-on, the extension of *Lost*'s narrative system (and here I refer also to the audio-visual stylistic elements of the show) into mobisodes, computer games and the alternative reality game (ARG) 'The *Lost* Experience' – with its associated network of websites, YouTube videos, novels and on-site visits to 'real' geographical locations across the world – suggests that additional narrative 'meaning' becomes increasingly reliant upon an audience that is capable of embracing multiple-media 'texts' in order to extract more complex layers of meaning (but, not always crucial meaning) from the phenomenon that is the television series. The series of innovations that have been generated by *Lost*'s producers have taken the combination of story extension and marketing as an integrated unit into new directions. The series truly has been a phenomenon in ingenious marketing that weaves its viewers deeper into its frustratingly addictive story structure. This chapter explores the implications of such changes, specifically from the perspective of generic definition and process. How does genre manifest itself in *Lost* and its affiliated satellite stories, and does the series reflect a shift in the processes that generate and create genres?

Lost's creators are renowned for their delight in playing with genre 'rules' through generic mixing. In his earlier work on *Alias* (Bad Robot, 2001–6), J.J. Abrams thrust his protagonists into spy thriller, drama, romance, science fiction (SF) and supernatural conventions, enmeshing them into frenzied and convoluted narrative threads from which there was no escape. Carlton Cuse had sharpened his teeth on *The Adventures of Brisco County Jr* (Boam/Cuse Productions, 1993–4), a show that experimented by merging the western, SF, comedy and drama. Under the watchful eye of that other genre-mixer Joss Whedon, David Fury refined his generic expertise on *Buffy the Vampire Slayer* (Mutant Enemy, 1997–2003) and *Angel* (Mutant Enemy, 1999–2004) before moving to *Lost* (and subsequently to *24*). And while having worked on more 'vanilla' generic pieces such as *Crossing Jordan* (Tailwind Productions, 2001–) and *Nash Bridges* (Carlton Cuse Productions, 1996–2001), Damon Lindelof's work on *Lost* has exposed his own penchant for generic 'impurity'.

In addition to creatively remapping the conventions of the reality TV show *Survivor* (Mark Burnett Productions, 2000–) and the *Robinson Crusoe* castaway survivor tradition most recently updated in the film *Cast Away* (Robert Zemeckis, 2000), *Lost* is riddled with *Thirty-Something*-esque drama both on the island and in the mainland flashbacks: the romantic on-again/off-again scenarios between Jack (Matthew Fox) and Kate (Evangeline Lilly), and Sawyer (Josh Holloway) and Kate; the tragic love shared by Shannon (Maggie Grace) and Sayid (Naveen Andrews); the dreadful death of Boone (Ian Somerhalder); Charlie's (Dominic Monaghan's) pathetic attempts at kicking his drug addiction; the identity-shattering relationship between Jack and his father (John Terry); the high-drama lead-up to Sun (Yunjin Kim) and Jin's (Daniel Dae Kim) marriage; the drama involving Sun's powerful father (Byron Chung) and Sun's tragic love affair; and – the story that would have to win the prize for most heart-wrenching in the show – Locke's (Terry O'Quinn) pitiable desire for fatherly love, which leads to his loss of a kidney and inability to walk.

Lost also draws on a supernatural, fantasy and horror heritage from diverse media. From the world of television it draws on *Alfred Hitchcock Presents* (Shamley Productions, 1955–62), *Twilight Zone* (Cayuga Productions, 1959–64), *The Prisoner* (ITC, 1967–8) and *The X-Files* (Twentieth Century Fox Television, 1993–2002) – series that surprised, shocked and horrified viewers week after week with the revelation of unnatural and uncanny phenomena that flew in the face of everyday logic. In literature there is evidence of influence from the Stephen King novels *The Stand* (1978) and *The Langoliers* (1990), both of which became TV movies,[3] and both of which confronted the reader with apocalyptic scenarios triggered by the presence of human-inspired evil. There is also *Lost Horizon* (1937), Frank Capra's own hybrid film about a group of plane crash survivors who find themselves in a strange and threatening land, and, of course, *Alice's Adventures in Wonderland* by Lewis Carroll (1865),[4] which takes its young hero into a strange, and sometimes frightening, land that refuses to function according to the laws of the 'normal' world.

As is necessary in horror, we have a monster: the supernatural (or, is it?) black mist that eventually brings about the destruction of Mr Eko (Adewale Akinnuoye-Agbaje). *Lost* is also replete with themes that are typical of horror – in particular, that of the collapse of identity, system and order that is triggered by a threat to the culturally demarcated borders that define the rules of society and 'normality'. The monster's entry into the social order and the 'thing' that creates that monster in the first place frequently questions the foundations of human nature.[5] Locke, Mr Eko, Jack, Charlie, Sawyer, Kate, Sayid – these and many other characters in the *Lost* ensemble undergo serious, soul-searching explorations that test the very limits of their identities.

Horror is also notorious for undermining the wholesomeness and 'naturalness' of the family as institution. From apocalyptic horror films such as *Night of the Living Dead* (George Romero, 1968) and *Texas Chainsaw Massacre* (Tobe Hooper, 1974) to the many not-so-happy families that litter the world of Stephen King's small-town communities, to the snake-sacrificing, clone-reproducing, interbreeding family units that run across the 9-year history of *The X-Files,* the family unit as supposed building block of civilization itself is ruthlessly questioned.[6] Following this tradition, especially through the flashbacks that paint vivid pictures of the familial histories of the main characters, *Lost* reveals a reactionary streak that is typical of the horror genre by making a strong case for the family as a destructive social force as opposed to a positive force that is integral to civilization.

Perhaps *Lost*'s most interesting relationship, however, is to the SF genre. It deliberately teases the viewer with fixing its affiliation with science fiction, only to then deny this association or, at least, delay the fuller development of that association. The *Island of Dr Moreau*-like experiments and mysterious creatures that are repeatedly withheld from view (especially in season one) clearly situate the series within the tradition of mad science. In the book *Film/Genre* – one of the most astute explanations about the process of genre – Rick Altman explains that the semantic elements are the shared building blocks of a genre that includes 'common topics, shared plots, key scenes, character types, familiar objects...'.[7] In SF and SF–horror television (and films) of recent years, key semantic components of the genre's corpus across both media have included:

- mad scientists and radical technological advancements (*Battlestar Galactica* (various, 2004–8), *Stargate SG-1* (Sony Pictures Television, 1997–2007), *Dr Who* (BBC, 1963–85, 2005–));

- ethically problematic experiments that tamper with the laws of nature (*Stargate Atlantis* (Sony Pictures Television, 2004–), *Mutant X* (Fireworks Entertainment, 2001–4));

- Big Brother surveillance (*Farscape* (Jim Henson Productions, 1999–2003), *Babylon 5* (Babylonian Productions, 1993–8));

- genetic and psychological experiments using morally abhorrent technology (*Dark Angel* (Twentieth Century Fox
Television, 2000–2), *Andromeda* (Fireworks Entertainment,
2000–5)); and

- 'Big Bad Corporations'[8] and government organizations
whose operations are clouded in mystery and rely on technological advances whose real purpose is obscured in the
official face they show to the world (*The 4400* (Renegade 83,
2004–), *Space: Above and Beyond* (Twentieth Century Fox
Television, 1995–6)).

The collision between religious belief systems that require leaps
of faith versus unwavering conviction in the rationality of science as
found in SF TV shows like *Stargate SG-1*, *Farscape*, *Andromeda*, *Battlestar Galactica* and *The X-files* (which is itself a horror/SF/comedy/
drama hybrid) is also present in *Lost*. Most dramatically, Mr Eko's
faith in a higher, mystical force and Locke's obsessive worship of the
'power' of the Island stands in sharp contrast to the rationality of
characters like Jack, Sawyer and Kate. This conflict is played out to
the max in the apocalyptic narrative that threatens to destroy hu-
mankind and whose mystical and supernatural properties are being
countered (supposedly) by the Dharma Initiative's maniacal belief in
the outcomes of science and technology. All it takes, according to the
Initiative, is mathematics – or rather, the re-evaluation of the mathematics delivered by the 'Valenzetti Equation', which purported to
represent the date of humanity's destruction (a fact hinted at in the
series and developed more fully in 'The *Lost* Experience').[9]

Relying on the writings of Darko Suvin, Jan Johnson-Smith suggests that a major structural component of science fiction is 'cognitive
estrangement' that frequently leads to the speculation about the actual or possible nature of reality – something that is at the very centre
of *Lost*.[10] The interplay between the supernatural horror and SF horror dimensions of the series is fascinating in this respect in that the
audience is frequently left uncertain as to which of the two subgenre
realities they are experiencing. Is the dark-mist monster, for example,
a product of supernatural forces or is it the creation of mad science?
Is it explainable by fantastic means or by rational means? Are the individual backstory dramas of the characters integral to the SF and/or

horror elements of the series or do they belong to an alternate generic realm? The generic 'solution' frequently lies somewhere in the show's future.

Altman argues (and, as will be discussed here, he later expands upon and revises) that the semantic elements can only make sense and produce generic meaning when placed within a syntactic structure that allows for the extraction of central themes, character relationships and the narrative concerns of the genre.[11] For example, the semantic blocks of illicit corporations that misuse technology, genetic experiments, Big Brother surveillance and experiments on people fit comfortably within the syntactic structure of science fiction. These semantic combinations produce syntactic meaning which explores the relationship between science, culture and nature. Most frequently, the human abuse of science and attempt to adopt the role of god and creator, as mentioned above, brings into play another thematic that explores scientific rationality against the backdrop of more ethereal and mystical religious belief systems. Consider, for example, the binaries of science/religion that are integral to shows like *Battlestar Galactica*, *Star Trek: Deep Space Nine* (Paramount Television, 1993–9) and *Farscape*.[12]

However, using the serial possibilities of television to strategic ends,[13] the innovation and frustration of *Lost* lies in the fact that it persistently withholds the syntactic connections and conclusions that can produce such generic meaning. An experimenting scientist, for example, can belong to the genres of drama, SF, SF–horror and horror; this iconic character even appeared in an episode of the sitcom *Gilligan's Island* (CBS Television, 1964–7), a series that also notoriously influenced the creators of *Lost*.[14] The 'meaning' of the block of information that is the mad scientist, however, and the role it serves in the larger syntactic picture, is fluid in the series. The viewer is persistently taunted with semantic blocks of information that can belong to horror, drama, reality TV or SF, but often the actual relationship between the semantic and syntactic elements are denied for weeks on end – or (God forbid!) until the series' concluding episodes.

Paralleling an observation made by Rick Altman in relation to the film industry, David Fury in interviews has stressed the fact that television networks and genre don't mix;[15] and the ABC network, in particular, made clear its aversion to the *Lost* writers' stabilizing the series' genre affiliations – in particular, with science fiction. Clear generic identity implies a fixity that also (it is assumed) fixes and potentially reduces a show's audience. *Lost*'s strategically fluid approach to genre has the potential for attracting a wider audience that is not driven by specific genre tastes. However, as Jason Mittell explains, the increased mixing of genres in series like *Buffy the Vampire Slayer* and the subsequent lack of generic 'purity' does not mean that genres and genre analysis are no longer important. We 'must look instead to the multiplicity of genres evoked in any instance. Through the prevalence of generic mixing and niche segmentation, genres may be even more important today than in previous television eras.'[16] He continues: 'the practice of generic mixture has the potential to foreground and activate generic categories in vital ways that "pure" generic texts rarely do'.[17]

Additionally, while the networks may have an aversion to genre, this is not necessarily the case for the writers and audience. While I agree with Mittell that genre is extremely important in television today, and that understanding its mode of operation foregrounds the culturally specific and 'historically contingent' process of genre, I do not share his view that the genre mixing that is manifest in shows like *Lost* is only different in matter of degree when compared to the genre combinations of earlier series like *The Flintstones* (Hannah-Barbera, 1960–6) and *Dragnet* (Mark VII, 1951–9). The extent of generic fusion and the level of reflexive manipulation of conventions that take place today are the product of different institutional practices compared with those of the 1950s and 1960s. They *are* 'historically contingent' and require a reconsideration of the methods of genre analysis that should be applied to them.

Intra-, inter- and cross-media generic exchange has always been integral to generic process. However, the primary consideration from the perspective of genre analysis has been the way similar and other genres from within and beyond one medium feed back into specific or multiple examples of a genre text. The movement is centripetal: generic codes, intertextual sources, allusions and other influences are directed back into the text so that the audience (and genre theorists) may then respond to and extract meaning from it. So far, it is this centripetal movement that has been of concern in this chapter, and which concerns the majority of genre theories. But what happens when the generic process spills beyond the boundaries of the text that is *Lost* and continues its articulation of genre meaning(s) beyond the television series? What if, in other words, the movement were a centrifugal one that was reacting to the centripetal process that generates the TV series *Lost*?

Consider ABC's decision to release 'The *Lost* Experience' ARG alongside the second season of *Lost*. Labelled a 'game' and influenced by one of the earliest forays into viral marketing and strategizing in entertainment culture – Steven Spielberg's 'Beast' game that preceded the release of the film *A.I.* (2001) – it is that and so much more.[18] Viral marketing relies on social networking:[19] the recent example of viral marketing for the forthcoming film *The Dark Knight* (Christopher Nolan, 2008) is a case in point. A huge viral-blitz campaign has witnessed the appearance of (amongst other things) a website supporting the political campaign of Harvey Dent, whose image was, over months of increased word-of-mouth viewer access, slowly defaced with graffiti Joker-eyes and the Joker's red-rimmed diabolical smile – over time this again metamorphosed into the 'real' Joker, or rather, the Heath Ledger version that will appear in the new film.[20] By adapting the 'rules' of viral marketing, which rely on targeting an audience stealthily through word-of-mouth (primarily through a gimmick delivered on the Internet), the *Lost* team presented their content in the hope that 'players' would spread the 'experience' further and, even more so, bring their experience of 'viral *Lost*' back with them to inform their understanding of 'TV –*Lost*'. From here, an elaborate web of clues and possible conspiracies could be investigated by fans in the hope that they could solve many of the TV show's mysteries, including that of the elusive polar bear.

The ways in which the *Lost* team approached this viral campaign has major implications for our study of genre. The 'Experience' involved the audience becoming integrated into extended *Lost* stories, or, more precisely, 'snippets' of information that padded out and further explained details presented in the TV show; some unravelled on the web, some on television and some in the player's 'real' space. Hanso Foundation advertisements were aired during the commercial breaks for the *Lost* TV series, for example, and included a number to call that provided information about the Hanso Foundation website. Here players then discovered that the Hanso Foundation, through its funding of the Dharma Initiative (the secret science project apparently funded by the Hanso Foundation in the 1970s) was involved in the construction of facilities on the island that were depicted in *Lost*. Also, a fictional Oceanic Airlines website posted announcements about flight cancellations and players could check for the victims of flight 815. The site *ApolloCandy.com* appeared and promoted a chocolate bar named Apollo (which characters had been seen eating in the TV series) – and it was later revealed that the Apollo Candy Company was bought by Alvar Hanso, the founder of the Hanso Foundation. On *Lost,* it was disclosed that the character Gary Troup was an author who died in the crash of Oceanic Flight 815, but that before getting on the flight he had delivered a manuscript called *Bad Twin* to his publisher (characters in the show are seen reading the manuscript).[21] Not only is it possible to buy a copy of *Bad Twin* on *Amazon.com*, but the Hanso Foundation published newspaper advertisements (in 'real' newspapers) that condemned the novel. Additionally, a series of fictitious blogs, which were presented as being posted by 'real' people announced that some Apollo Candy bars had 'fallen off the back of a truck' and managed to make it to certain locations around the world, which meant that the avid fan could make their way to stores to claim their very own Apollo chocolate bar.[22] The character Rachel Blake, also known as Persephone, was introduced to guide players through 'The *Lost* Experience'. As a supposedly 'real' (but fictional) person who had exposed Hanso, she wrote blogs and had her own website, and she uploaded interview exposés with Alvar Hanso – the man behind the *Lost* mystery – onto YouTube. These conspiratorial leaks would do even Fox Mulder proud.

In *Lost Online Studies*, Sean Casey states that

> 'The *Lost* Experience' combines two literary techniques: frame storytelling and historical fiction. Frame Stories contain one or more stories within a framing story ... In this sense, 'The *Lost* Experience' is fiction in our world, and the television show *Lost* exists in the world created by 'The *Lost* Experience'.[23]

The 'experience' not only serves to generate and heighten the *Lost* mythology but it spills the generic process beyond the TV show's borders, placing it firmly within the wider social sphere. In addition to the examples outlined above, not only were television ads for Hanso presented by the 'real' company Sprite, but footage of an orientation video for Station 6 (The Orchid) bypassed the television show entirely: the video showed experiments with numbered rabbits that implied successful exploration of time travel – a semantic sign associated with science fiction. In other words, through 'the *Lost* Experience' the semantic blocks dealing with 'Big Bad Corporations', scientific experimentation that is ethically problematic, characters like mad scientists, research on time travel, and so on, are thrust into our more immediate social sphere – or, to use Casey's words, this information presents itself as a 'historical reality' that is firmly integrated into our reality.

These further pockets of genre information are available to the audience only if they are willing to follow the threads that exceed the limits of the TV series and, while it is possible to just watch the show and focus on that narrative universe, following the alternate story paths offers denser layers of story and genre activity that in turn fosters more obsessive immersion in the fictional world. Significantly, the various extended pieces of semantic information highlight the SF traits more forcefully by providing intricate details about the Dharma Initiative and the intentions of the Hanso Foundation than are provided by the TV show.[24] Also, the producers and writers of the series have made clear that they consider 'The *Lost* Experience' to be an integral part of *Lost*'s mythology. Damon Lindelof has commented:

> I would say in terms of all the ... background that we did, in terms of the Valenzetti equation and explaining the formation of the Hanso Foundation and doing the other films ... we'd consider that stuff canon to the show. Where there'd have to be wiggle room is the Rachel Blake story where she's in the real world, in the outside world as we define it, the show *Lost* might be defined in an entirely different outside world so we can't vouch for the overall fit ability and veracity of everything that Rachel was doing. But we can say that all the factoids that she was uncovering were vetted, in fact many of them were written by us personally so they are canon.[25]

'The *Lost* Experience' participants play a far more active role in seaming together an overall syntactic logic to *Lost* as an entire media experience that seeks to attain a level of *Lost*-literacy not offered by the TV show alone. In interviews, Lindelof has acknowledged the impact that computer games had on the original conception of the TV series: certain parts of 'The *Lost* Experience' operate like the Easter Eggs, or hidden messages, that are planted by game designers in many computer games – messages that reward the persistent fan for their zealous activity and engagement with the *Lost* universe. Likewise, as is the case with games, 'The *Lost* Experience' allows the player to access and interact with blocks of story and genre information in such a way that it creates the illusion that the player will be an integral part of how the story unravels. Adopting a quest role familiar to gamers, in a very real sense, 'The *Lost* Experience' player appears to become active in the process of plot development. For example, participants in the 'Experience' gather information (about Hanso, the Dharma Initiative, the roles performed in each of the hatch facilities, suddenly unveiled conspiracies, etc.) and bring this information back to their experience of the TV series, therefore padding out particular story clusters and the genre information they contain. However, not only does this give the viral-*Lost* participant further levels of understanding when compared both to the diegetic characters and viewers of TV-*Lost*, but it also integrates them far more actively into the generic process in that the viral-*Lost* participant possesses blocks of generic information that is withheld in TV-*Lost*.

Celia Pearce has explained that game narratives are emergent in that they are always in the process of becoming. As such, the narratives are playing with the player as much as the player plays with them.[26] This is precisely the sensation that 'The *Lost* Experience' bargains on: the illusion that players are contributing to an emergent narrative and, in turn, to its genre identity. Henry Jenkins has also explored the concept of narrative in and as process in games. In particular, he takes issue with the 'conceptual blind spots' that prevent ludology theorists (theorists who favour 'play' over 'narrative' theory) 'from developing a full understanding of the interplay between narrative and games'. He continues:

> First, the discussion operates with too narrow a model of narrative, one preoccupied with the rules and conventions of classical linear storytelling at the expense of consideration of other kinds of narratives, not only the modernist and postmodernist experimentation that inspired the hypertext theorists, but also popular traditions which emphasize spatial exploration over causal event chains or which seek to balance between the competing demands of narrative

and spectacle. Second, the discussion operates with too limited an understanding of narration, focusing more on the activities and aspirations of the storyteller and too little on the process of narrative comprehension.[27]

Computer games and viral entertainment encounters like 'The *Lost* Experience' have the potential for affecting their participants in very real and immediate ways, and the reason for this is clear when considered in light of Jenkins' observations. Beyond the linear story, the 'spatial exploration' that entails the exploration of websites, additional televisual material such as advertisements and actual geographic locations becomes a crucial component of the generic identity of *Lost*. And as Jenkins explains with regard to games, the participants' activity in the process of 'narrative comprehension' – and, in turn, generic comprehension – is as significant as that of the storyteller's. Quoting Michel de Certeau, Jenkins makes a case 'for spatial relations as the central organizing principle of all narratives: "Every story is a travel story – a spatial practice".'[28] Viewing a world like the one we see in TV-*Lost*, no matter how engaged we are with the characters and the predicaments that befall them, the spatial practice is one that lies solely in the domain of the characters. The audience looks on at the characters who navigate their spaces and experience their emerging narratives. When viral-*Lost* enters the equation, however, players become actively involved in this spatial practice, collecting clusters of information and bringing them into their experience and understanding of the television show.

This has interesting ramifications not only for *Lost*'s emerging narrative but also for the genres that it (potentially) contains. Continuing with de Certeau's analysis of narrative spaces, Jenkins explains that

> De Certeau is thus interested in analyzing and documenting the process by which we 'mark off boundaries' within the narrative world, by which characters map, act upon, and gain control over narrative spaces. Just as narratives involve movement from stability through instability and back again, narratives also involve a constant transformation of unfamiliar places into familiar spaces. Stories, he argues, are centrally concerned with 'the relationship between the frontier and the bridge, that is, between a (legitimate) space and its (alien) exteriority ... The story endlessly marks out frontiers. It multiplies

them, but in terms of interactions among characters – things, animals, human beings' … Plot actions, he argues, involve the process of appropriation and displacement of space, a struggle for possession and control over the frontier or journeys across the bridges that link two spaces together. As De Certeau … notes, the central narrative question posed by a frontier is 'to whom does it belong?'[29]

Given the active role participants play in the emerging narrative, they actually compete with TV-*Lost*'s characters for access to information. The frontier that de Certeau discusses includes information about: the forces that led to the plane crash; the role played by the Hanso Foundation and the Dharma Initiative both in the events occurring on the island and beyond the island in the world the characters lived; particulars regarding the Initiative's experiments; and information about the end of the world, such as what will bring it about and what can delay it. This and so much more information is riddled with generic codes and, as mentioned above, 'The *Lost* Experience' not only provides a great deal of this background information but it also delivers a more stable genre identity. Furthermore, 'The *Lost* Experience' marks off a frontier that contains information that is primarily in the possession of the 'Experience' participants rather than the TV show's protagonists. In terms of understanding the forces that control the predicament that *Lost*'s castaways are in, if we were to seek an answer to the questions posed by de Certeau – to whom does the frontier belong? – the answer would have to be the player/viewer who is external to TV-*Lost*'s main narrative universe.

In *Film/Genre*, Altman revises his semantic/syntactic model to also encompass what he labels 'pragmatic' structures that include 'usage dispersion' that is less fixed and almost impossible to contain in any analysis of the process of generic meaning production. In focusing on pragmatics, Altman considers 'not only various spectator groups, but producers, distributors, exhibitors, cultural agencies, and many others' that conjure a multiplicity of often conflicting views and readings of the semantic and syntactic structures of genres.[30] This 'multiplicity' is integral to a genre's identity. 'The *Lost* Experience' and other innovative practices that have adopted strategies such as those typical of viral storytelling offer a new example of this more unstable and erratic space of meaning production. Viral-*Lost* participants extract, circulate and contribute to *Lost*'s generic meaning in ways that differ dramatically to the modes of engagement embraced by 'pure' TV-*Lost* viewers – or, in fact, to the meaning intended by the ABC studios or the writers.

In many respects, what we are witnessing in these extended modes of engagement is a method of appropriation more typical of fan culture.[31] In *The Practice of Everyday Life* Michel de Certeau makes an important distinction between the concepts of 'strategy', which is a tool applied by social institutions to affirm and reproduce their power, and 'tactics', which are the tools of individuals who generate their own voice within the system. Extending de Certeau's concept of 'poaching' to fan culture, Henry Jenkins described poaching as a process whereby fans develop 'tactics' in order to reclaim 'original' texts such as television series and transform them into new and extended creations that are stamped with the identity of the fan. Television networks like ABC have recently begun to fine-tune this lesson that they actually poached from the fans by generating creative alternatives to their own original texts and offering community-based experiences that are typical of fan and cult culture – 'The *Lost* Experience' being a classic example. However, in poaching this process from fan culture, ABC has transformed 'tactics' back into 'strategies' that are part of an official culture and the 'original text'. In doing so, they have opened up further contested spaces by transforming the role of viewer to one that can also encompass active participation in the narrative and generic process.

Is the television viewer's experience and interpretation of *Lost*'s engagement with genre more authentic than that of a viewer who has also been a '*Lost* Experience' participant? Whether the answer is in the affirmative or not, one thing is definitely clear: the boundaries of our critical models must expand and become more flexible in order to embrace these new and dynamic story extensions that test the limits of traditional genre analysis.

Notes

1   See Angela Ndalianis, *Neo-Baroque Aesthetics and Contemporary Entertainment* (Boston: MIT Press, 2004).

2   On the film cross-media convergence see Henry Jenkins, *Convergence Culture: Where Old and New Media Collide* (New York: New York

University Press, 2006); Ndalianis: *Neo-Baroque Aesthetics*; and Andrew Darley, *Visual Digital Culture: Surface Play and Spectacle in New Media Genres* (London: Routledge, 2000).

3   *The Stand* was released in revised form in 1990 and the mini-TV series (directed by Mick Garris) was released in 1994. The impact of King's novel and the mini-series version has been frequently stated by the creators of *Lost*. *The Langoliers* was one of the four stories published in *Four Past Midnight* and the TV film, directed by Tom Holland, was aired in 1995. For a detailed account of the influences on *Lost* see Lynnette Porter and David Lavery, *Unlocking the Meaning of Lost: An Unauthorized Guide* (Naperville: Sourcebooks, 2006).

4   Lewis Carroll, *Alice in Wonderland* (London: Macmillan, 1865).

5   On the conventions of horror see Steven Jay Schneider and Tony Williams (eds), *Horror International* (Detroit: Wayne State University Press, 2005). Unfortunately, very little has been written on the horror genre in television and despite sharing some of its conventions and themes with the horror film and horror comics, television has developed an approach that is unique to its medium.

6   For further information on the horror film's concerns with the family unit, see Vivian Sobchack, 'Bringing it all back home: family, economy and generic exchange', in Gregory A. Waller (ed.), *American Horrors: Essays on the Modern American Horror Film* (Chicago: University of Illinois Press, 1987), pp.175–94.

7   Rick Altman, *Film/Genre* (London: British Film Institute, 1999), p.89.

8   A term coined by Fred Glass in 'The new bad future: *Robocop* and the 1980s' sci-fi films', *Science as Culture* 5 (1989), pp.7–49.

9   According to the 1975 orientation film (the 'Sri Lanka Video', which is unveiled by Rachel Blake, the character in 'The *Lost* Experience' who posts the video online), the Valenzetti Equation, a mathematical equation developed by the Princeton University mathematician Enzo Valenzetti, 'predicts the exact number of years and months until humanity extinguishes itself'.

10   See Jan Johnson-Smith, *American Science Fiction TV: Star Trek, Stargate and Beyond* (London: I.B.Tauris, 2005), pp.24–5.

11   See Altman: *Film/Genre*, especially pp.219–21.

12   On the religion–science duality, see Vivian Sobchack, *Screening Space: The American Science Fiction Film*, (Chapel Hill: Rutgers University Press, 1997), and on SF television see M. Keith Booker, *Science Fiction Television* (Westport: Praeger, 2004).

13   On seriality and television, see Lucy Mazdon and Michael Hammond (eds), *The Contemporary Television Serial* (Edinburgh: University of Edinburgh, 2005).

14 The episode, of course, is 'The Friendly Physician' (2.29), in which a mad Frankenstein-like Dr Boris Balinkoff performs experiments on the *S.S. Minnow* castaways, swapping their minds and placing them in different bodies – and even giving one of the castaways the mind of a chicken! For more on the comparisons between *Gilligan's Island* and *Lost*, see '*Lost* update, *Gilligan's Island* comparison' at *www.lotgk.com/lost/20070103lost. asp*.

15 See David Lavery, 'Get *Lost* in a good story: serial creativity on a desert island', *Flow TV: A Critical Forum on Television and Media Culture* iii/2 (23 September 2005).

16 Jason Mittell, *Genre and Television: from Cop Shows to Cartoons in American Culture* (New York and London: Routledge, 2004), p.xiii.

17 Ibid., p.153.

18 For further information about *A.I.* and 'The Beast', go to the Cloudmakers website (*www.cloudmakers.org/*) and see Robin Clewley, 'Robot sites a web of deception', *Wired* v/5 (2001).

19 Jeffrey F. Rayport first coined the term 'viral marketing' in 1996. See 'The virus of marketing', *Fastcompany* (December 1996), available online at: *www.fastcompany.com/online/06/virus.html*. See also Ralph F. Wilson, 'The six simple principles of viral marketing', *Web Marketing Today*, 1 February 2005, available online at *www.wislonweb.com/wmt5/viral-principles.html*.

20 At the time of writing the site is still available at *http://ibelieveinharveydent.warnerbros.com/* but the graffiti and the new Joker are no longer visible.

21 You can access interviews with Gary Troup on the fictitious show 'Book Talk' on YouTube. He is interviewed by the show's host, Laird Granger, and they discuss the controversy surrounding Troup's mysteriously out-of-print first book, *The Valenzetti Equation*, as well as his new novel, *Bad Twin*. Available at *http://youtube.com/watch?v=HtrcVTOkq14*. The real author of *Bad Twin* is Laurence Shames (who also had creative input from some of the *Lost* writers).

22 In Australia this was the '*Lost Ninja*' site (*http://au.blogs.yahoo.com/lostninja/*), hosted by Channel 7, the station that airs *Lost*. By going to the comic bookstore Minotaur and asking 'What did one snowman say to the other?', you would be presented with an Apollo chocolate bar.

23 Sean Casey, 'Frame story/historical fiction: understanding The *Lost* Experience', *Lost Online Studies* i/3 (2006), available online at *www.loststudies.com/1.3/frame_story.html*.

24 Add to this other details that circulate within the social sphere – the fact that the *Lost* reruns have been picked up by the Sci-Fi Channel, that J.J. Abrams will direct the next *Star Trek* film and that Damon Lindelof will

produce it – and *Lost*'s association with science fiction becomes even stronger as far as (some) public interpretation of *Lost*'s genre affiliation.

25 See 'BuddyTV interviews *Lost*'s Damon Lindelof and Carlton Cuse – and gets answers!', Buddy TV, available at *www.buddytv.com/articles/lost/ buddytv-interviews-losts-damon-4766.aspx*, 7 March 2007.

26 Celia Pearce, 'Story as play space: narrative in games', in Lucien King (ed.), *Game On: The History and Culture of Videogames* (London: Laurence King, 2002), p.118.

27 Henry Jenkins, 'Game design as narrative architecture', in Noah Wardrip-Fruin and Pat Harrigan (eds), *First Person: New Media as Story, Performance, Game*, (Cambridge: MIT Press, 2004), pp.12–21.

28 Henry Jenkins in Mary Fuller and Henry Jenkins, 'Nintendo® and New World travel writing: a dialogue', in Steven G. Jones (ed.), *Cybersociety: Computer-Mediated Communication and Community* (Thousand Oaks, CA: Sage, 1995), pp.57–72, available online at *www.stanford.edu/class/history34q/readings/Cyberspace/FullerJenkins_Nintendo.html*. Jenkins quotes Michel De Certeau from *The Practice of Everyday Life* (Los Angeles: University of California Press, 1984), p.115.

29 Jenkins in Fuller and Jenkins: 'Nintendo® and New World travel writing', pp.126–7.

30 Altman: *Film/Genre*, p.210.

31 In fact, in his blog Jenkins observes that Jesse Alexander, Executive Producer of *Alias, Lost* and *Heroes*, admitted in an interview for *Wonderland* to reading Jenkins' book *Convergence Culture* and to seriously considering his analysis of transmedia storytelling as it relates to fan culture. In particular, he discusses the cult show *Heroes*. See Jenkins' blog at *www.henryjenkins.org/2007/07/catching_up_on_fan_culture. html*. For the original interview, go to *www.wonderlandblog.com/wonderland/2007/06/hollywood-games.html*.

Part III
Representation

XI. Lost in the Orient:
Transnationalism Interrupted

Michael Newbury

In the *Lost* episode 'Stranger in a Strange Land' (3.9), Jack Shepard (Matthew Fox), the reluctant leader of a mini-global community of airline crash survivors on a South Sea island, flashes back to a romance he once shared with Achara (Ling Bai), a beautiful Thai tattoo artist. Immediately following the title credits, viewers are thrust into Jack's flashback. The camera pans from left to right, crossing open ocean with monoliths rising from it while seagulls shriek. It passes the trunks of one or two palm trees, reaching a grass hut on the beach. The movement stops and Jack, very clearly not in the land of white, Western modernity, steps into the frame from the right. He is dressed more or less as a Western tourist in a loose-fitting, pinkish-purple, button-down shirt and baggy khaki shorts. After surveying the scene with some sense of satisfaction that he is, indeed, a stranger in a strange land, he makes a long, slow, dramatic arc with his arm, raising sunglasses from just below his waist to his eyes. Jack is an *isolato*, a Westerner alone in an 'Orient' that promises him escape.

Viewers of the show know Jack to be the embodiment of almost everything white and Western, but also to be a little rebellious against conventional authority. He is handsome, white, male, a child of privilege, a gifted neurosurgeon, well schooled and practised in the benefits of technological progress and modern medicine. When confronted with the mystical or inexplicable powers of the island inhabited by the crash survivors, Jack typically takes the posture of the man of reason, insisting on rational explanations in the face of John Locke's (Terry O'Quinn) embrace of faith. Nevertheless, Jack also has a profoundly strained relationship with authority and convention, perhaps most fully suggested by the constant friction we see between him and his alcoholic father (John Terry), who happens also to be the chief of neurosurgery at the hospital where both men work. Jack is impulsive and will not be told what to do. He is shown to disregard the presumed limits of medical science, sometimes with remarkable success. The elaborate tattoo on his shoulder (not to mention his alien presence on a remote Thai beach) measures Jack's unconventionality, even if he stands on that same beach as the embodiment of the authority he sometimes resists.

We see no other tourists, or even accommodations for them, as Jack descends to the sand. The local inhabitants, who are mostly manipulating fishing nets and carrying baskets in this distinctly premodern economy, ignore him. A local boy (Shannon Chanhthanam) selling soda, however, greets him as 'Docta' Jack. Jack, able to afford a staggering sum in the context of this isolated economy, pays the boy extravagantly – in US currency. When the boy offers what seems to be a form of thanks, Jack good-naturedly and condescendingly tells him, 'You know, I can't understand a word that you're saying, right?' He likes this boy. He likes being the only white man on the beach. He likes the authority that he carries with him by virtue of his masculinity, money, modernity and whiteness. Jack is the avatar of a prosperous, mobile, technologically advanced global order. The boy selling sodas (along with Jack) lets us know that this 'primitive' beach may some day be on its way to joining that larger economy, even if it hasn't joined it yet.

For all of Jack's skill and self-confidence, though, he cannot assemble the simple kite he wants to fly. He needs, it turns out, the help of Achara, who sits girlishly giggling, hiding behind windblown bangs in a halter top with a neckline plunging almost to her navel. Their attraction to one another is immediate and utterly non-verbal, signified by soft, slow piano music and a series of wistful shots and counter-shots in which neither speaks. In fact, the two manage to put the kite together and get it into the air using only gestures and touch to communicate, and it is almost a full minute before Jack and the viewer learn that Achara can speak English. Over the remainder of the episode, Achara and Jack play out a version of the oft-repeated *Madame Butterfly* narrative.[1] Achara, the beautiful, sensuous Asian woman turns herself over to a passionate sexual affair with Jack, the white Western man, the embodiment of globalization and imperial power, which lasts about a month. The 'Orient', it seems, has offered Jack everything he might have hoped for, expected, or felt entitled to. In the end, however, Jack transgresses against local customs in a kind of figurative rape scene, forcing Achara to give him a tattoo and to exercise her mysterious 'gift' of seeing into people. She tells Jack what he already seems to know: 'you are ... a leader ... a great man'. The next day, a gang of local men including Achara's brother (Siwathep Sunapo), less heroic in every way than Jack, beat him on the beach where his love affair began. They force Jack to leave, pushing back the global tide he represents, as Achara looks sadly on, yearning for Jack and all he brings with him, tearful that her land's traditions and the relatively primitive men who enforce them have aborted her romance.

This series of flashbacks ought to be understood as a fairly conventional recurrence of a popular and profoundly gendered orientalism, a repetition of one of the most routinized narratives through which masculinized and racialized American power has imagined its assertion (and even the invitation to assert itself) over a prostrate, feminized, mystical Orient. Such orientalist imaginings, as we shall see, are an altogether persistent part of *Lost's* narrative and visual vocabulary. Indeed, with characters who once moved freely across national borders and around the globe stranded by a plane crash on an island, one of *Lost's* most notable efforts seems to be the imaging forth of a transnational model of community, a seeming understanding of the formulation of racial and national identities less in intra-American and more in global and diasporic terms.

However, *Lost's* imagining of transnational subject formation is also peculiar, at least if we try to theorize it in ways consistent with current scholarly and even popular discourse on the matter. If we are to understand identities as formed at multiple geographic points and across national boundaries in an age of electronic information exchange and frequent travel across borders, then what are we to make of an unnamed, unreachable island thoroughly cut off from exchange, migration and movement? If many of the survivors of this crash once moved readily around the globe, interacting with multiple nations and cultures before boarding Oceanic flight 815, one could hardly imagine a more apt metaphor for the halting of global motion than a trans-

Pacific plane breaking into pieces, crashing, and depositing survivors on an uncharted and supernaturally undiscoverable island.[2]

Not only is our mini-community of transnational globetrotters cut off from geographic movement and communication, it is also temporally displaced, shifted backward in time to confront a bipolar world of rigidly imagined borders and identities associated with cold-war culture. The Dharma Initiative and the Others, past and present inhabitants of this island, live in something vaguely similar to cosy 1950s subdivisions complete with lawn furniture. They move through labs and hatches resembling cold-war era bomb shelters frozen in the styles of the 1970s. The cold-war Others, the normatively white natives of this South Pacific island, are a resident monster that must be confronted by our mixed group of contemporary international migrants and tourists. The Others, in fact, demand very literally that the crash survivors stop moving around and observe borders, warning several times that if they leave a demarcated territory, ugly conflict will follow.

While one might, in the current political context of 'global terrorism', expect to find in an enemy the habits of terrorists, the Others of *Lost* live and function much more fully through images and practices aligned with the nation-state than they do through familiar representations of the terrorist, insurgent or even dissident. They bring forth not so much the imagistic vocabulary of contemporary threats but offer instead a problematic and malevolent recent past. On the island, the Others control virtually all means of technological and military power, including an impressive, almost panoptic, apparatus of surveillance. When they infiltrate the survivor community or recruit outsiders to their cause, they do so not with sleeper cells of racially distinguishable foreigners hiding at the margins of society but with individuals who bear all the markings of white professionals: Ethan (William Mapother), Goodwin (Brett Cullen), Richard (Nestor Carbonell) and Juliet (Elizabeth Mitchell). Oceanic 815 is distinctly not blown up or hijacked; captives held by the Others are never executed or displayed but incarcerated and surveilled; likewise when Ben (Michael Emerson) wants to show a crucial contemporary event on television to prove to Jack that the Others have ongoing contact with the mainland, we see the final out of the World Series, that most traditional, even nostalgic – and whitest – of major US sports events.

So *Lost*, we might say, pits our survivors from a contemporary era of transnational flow and migration against a cold-war population that insists on the dualistic nature of self, nation and globe, a realm of clearly demarcated selves and Others. At the same time, however, if the crash survivors suggest a contemporary idea of movement across borders, they also routinely do violence to the idea of subject formation beyond the terms of nationhood and racial oppositions. We can see this arrest of transnational flux, for example, in 'Stranger in a Strange Land' – an episode which is far less a tale of cultural or physical migration and far more an imagining of the static imperatives of racial, gender and national separation. Achara's and Jack's identities are no doubt formed in comparison to one another – female/Asian/mystical/conquerable versus male/White/rational/conqueror – but Jack and Achara are formed *only* by essentialized points of contrast and separation; they lack points of contact, interpenetration and mobility across each other's borders, even in their most intimate moments. At one point, Jack interrupts their lovemaking to say, 'It might be nice, after a month of you coming and going whenever you want, to find out something about you.' 'Stranger in a Strange Land' teaches us, in the best mode of *Madame Butterfly*, that East is East and West is West.

In the apparent conflict between the cold-war-oriented, exaggeratedly white and malevolently suburban Others and the racially and nationally mixed group of flawed but plucky crash survivors, both groups turn out to be surprisingly locked in to highly stabilized and oppositional versions of racial and national identity. *Lost*, I would suggest, only *seems* to push us toward a world in which identities flow freely across racial and national borders. In the end, it offers instead an imagining of what it would mean to disrupt the discourse and fact of migratory movements with persistent cultural memories and reminders that reinforce racial and national distinction.

What we get in *Lost* is the heroic discourse of a transnational community that stabilizes and unifies itself through shared hostility toward the bipolar politics of the cold-war 'Others'. But this hostility to the sterile, white and bipolar past is coupled with the persistent disruption of multinational unity by flashbacks that reify national, racial and class-based distinctions. The only hope for overcoming the divisions urged forward by these memories is to suppress the flashbacks, the places from which movement began, to keep the question of one's origins largely secret from fellow survivors. The show, then, insists upon and idealizes the possibility of a contemporary multinational, multiracial community, in a utopian rejection of the past as embodied by the Others. At the same time, *Lost* acknowledges the imperative to suppress the articulation of deeply remembered racial and national distinction in the achievement of this ideal. The utopian vision of a multinational, multiracial, cross-class contemporary community, in short, is one in which the crucial markers of national, racial and class difference are subordinated to or erased by a sense of common purpose in battling the white past.

In crucial ways, then, I will argue that *Lost* features more a narrative of assimilation than a narrative of multinationalism or transnational affiliation. The community of survivors is defined less by global movement than it is by a privileged, even mythological, narrative of multicultural absorption into American nationhood. The point I would like to emphasize, though, is how profoundly *national* this imagined racial community is. The survivors of *Lost*, become, through their persistent contrast with the Others, less a transnational community and more an idealized sign of the USA's complete racial tolerance in a post-cold-war world, an instalment in the ongoing and utopian myth that the USA tells itself (and the world) about its presumptively nonracialized and nonimperialistic essence.

THE GLOBALIZATION OF US MULTICULTURALISM

That *Lost* is calculatedly engaged in the consideration of globalisation and transnational movement has everything to do with the emergent technological and economic imperatives of the television industry. During a period of technological convergence in which the dominance of traditional television networks has been weakened by cable, satellite and various modes of digital recording and circulation, robust foreign distribution looms ever larger in determining the economic success of 'American' mass culture. *Lost*, with its self-conscious assemblage of a multiracial, multinational cast, its primary setting on an island apart from any named national territory, and secondary settings scattered across multiple continents, offers rich possibilities for global audience appeal and identification. Indeed, *Lost* has by any measure been among the most internationally successful shows to come out of the

USA or any other nation's television industry. Its conspicuous avail-
ability on outlets such as iTunes and ABC's website and the various
other aspects of 'The *Lost* Experience' have only enhanced the show's
international visibility. *Lost* has aired in more than 180 countries and
is among the most popular shows broadcast in many of them.[3]

The show's global distribution and fan base speak irrefutably to
its international popularity but also to a set of ideological possibilities that attach themselves readily to the economics of global television. Seen from one perspective, *Lost* (and possibly other shows that
achieve similarly broad international appeal) marks the increasingly
blurred boundaries of national audiences; from another perspective,
however, it presents a striking opportunity for the projection of US
nationalism into living rooms around the world. *Lost*, as I will argue,
does offer a vision of transnational movement and the possibility of
affective identification with the show to a multinational audience. It
does so, however, in a way that inescapably puts the USA at the centre
of the global order while situating other nations as satellites orbiting
its periphery.

My point here is not so much that J.J. Abrams, ABC, or any others who might be called the originators of *Lost* seek conspiratorially
to colonize the globe through visions of internationalism that place
the USA at the global centre, but rather that *Lost* presents an oddly
utopian and familiar story of world migration *toward* Americanness,
toward the USA conceived (however tendentiously) as a nation of multiracial harmony. That American cultural forms of many kinds have
long and repeatedly told the privileged story of harmonious immi-
grant assimilation to a liberal democratic state that tends to assume
white privilege is hardly a new discovery. As Mae Ngai argues, such
stories of assimilation and absorption, whatever facts of history they
may ignore, structure US conceptions of virtuous citizenship. They
are stories that allow for the reconciliation of a fraught, contentious,
often racially divisive history into a story of US exceptionalism, a vision of the nation as endlessly and uniquely generous, open, non-rac-
ist and non-imperialist. They are stories, in short, that position the
USA as an example of tolerance and harmony to the rest of the world.[4]
Such stories and the negotiations they undertake may be particularly
necessary at the current moment, as the US military stalks the globe
in search of terror, often leaving destruction in its wake, but these

accounts of idealized racial harmony and absorption are hardly unique to the present day.

What may be most striking about *Lost* in this context is that strategies for selling global television through affective appeals to international audiences become simultaneously strategies for generating *international* identification with the utopian myth of a US melting pot on a global scale. In *Lost*, as I will argue, the world is refigured through the lens of an idealized (and strangely imperialistic) American multiculturalism. *Lost*, at least through its first three seasons, presents a globalized version of American multicultural reconciliation.

In this way, *Lost* works as a mass-mediated form very much in the complex and contradictory fashion outlined by Frederic Jameson in 'Reification and Utopia in mass culture'. It imagines forth the markers of a culturally concrete and problematic past to allow for the collective negotiation of a movement away from it, the achievement of a solution (in this case) to the social contradictions presented by persistent problematics of race and imperialism.[5] Crucially, however, in a way that Jameson does not discuss, *Lost* offers an exercise in global exportation and community formation, an affective, emotional appeal to a multinational audience to see itself as part and parcel of an American utopian vision.

CRASH SURVIVORS AND COMBAT PLATOONS

The group of survivors in *Lost* functions very much like the heroic platoons of Hollywood combat films. Since the 1940s, the combat film has tended to focus on a multi-ethnic, multi-class unit that stands for the diversity of the USA. The platoon must overcome the internal racial and class differences that threaten to divide its members' intimacy and interdependence on one another every bit as much as it must overcome a formidable, often racialized enemy. In the quintessential Second World War versions of the form, the multi-ethnic fighting unit emerges with a sense of shared nationality that melts away personal matters of racial, regional, class and ethnic difference. Diverse emblems of American masculinity are brought into a mythical figuration of nationhood united against a formidable foe, who, it turns out, really *is* threateningly different by race and nature.[6]

Understanding the survivors of *Lost* through this paradigm of a melting pot heated by the shared hatred of a racialized enemy makes a certain amount of sense, but it also has significant complications. To begin with, our melting pot is no longer national but global, with the survivors of the crash hailing from South Korea, England, Australia, Brazil, Iraq, Nigeria and the USA. From within the USA we have a white neurosurgeon, a Latino lottery winner, a white clerk from a box manufacturer, a black construction worker/artist and his son, and so on. In the demographics of this group, no other nation can claim anything like that level of diversity, and each is represented instead by only one or two individuals. Finally, in a stark divergence from the classic combat film, about half of those stranded on the *Lost* island are women.

I do not mean to suggest that the community in *Lost*, anymore than a platoon in combat films, functions without persistent friction and even death, but these frictions are largely subordinate to the ragtag multiracial, multinational alliance that the survivors share in opposition to the cold-war whiteness of the Others. Indeed, explicit spoken racial and ethnic tensions in *Lost* are intensely diminished when compared with the epithets and conflicts present in some versions of earlier combat films and narratives. This platoon is much more likely to squabble over limited or unusual resources: diamonds, guns, or a heroin stash, for example. Only one character, Sawyer (Josh Holloway), ever drifts toward racial jokes and epithets, and those in the community of survivors clearly see such language as the embodiment of backward Southern whiteness, of prejudices that this contemporary multiracial community cannot imagine itself to hold. Furthermore, with the battles in the concluding episodes of season three, the conflict between the survivors and the Others has grown increasingly and more explicitly militarized than at any other point in the show's history.

So what *Lost* imagines for us is a kind of *globalized* platoon in which differences of race, nation, class and even gender are subordinated to a sometimes tenuous but also shared sense of purpose that intermittently breaks down based on conflicts that are almost never explicitly racialized – Locke's obsessions, Charlie's (Dominic Monaghan) drug addiction and Sawyer's hoarding of consumer goods all lead to disputes of various kinds. Members of this group have their differences but, like a good platoon, they know they need to survive; they need to fight off the Others who *are* intrinsically different from the identity they share as global citizens in a multiracial, multinational community. *Lost*, borrowing from the logic of the combat film, paradoxically internationalizes the reach of nationhood, melting together not just groups from within the defined borders of the USA; instead, it offers a metonymic representation of the entire world coalescing, but in a way that is manifestly led by contemporary Americans. Jack Shepard, in particular, will lead the struggle against the cold-war past. The multinational, multiracial dynamics of this community simply become absorbed into the disproportionately expansive representation of an American diversity led by a handsome, upper-middle-class, white neurosurgeon on the survivors' beach.

Even Iraqis, subject to the USA's imposing military force, represented here by the character of Sayid (Naveen Andrews), are ready to play their part in the shared effort, to engage in combat against a cold-war past with Americans who do not even seem to remember the Persian Gulf War of the 1990s. In his memories, Sayid speaks Arabic and moves through the sinister spaces of the Iraqi secret police; he knows the intimate violence of torture as no other among the castaways does, and, when his hands are tied, he can break an enemy's neck using only his legs. But Sayid harnesses these violent and sadistic impulses in the name of supporting Jack and the platoon of castaways. By the end of season three, Sayid's self-sacrificing dedication to the cause of the unit only intensifies, as he fully acknowledges Jack as the community's leader after brief doubts and expresses his unqualified willingness to die for the sake of his comrades and to spare Jack, the community's most treasured human asset.

The *Lost* survivors, then, are the ultimate in imagined communities, a nation that transcends and absorbs not just different ethnicities, languages and folk within its borders, but that absorbs every nation in the world, creating the paradoxical vision of a global nation defined not by reference to differences from other nations but by references to its distinction from the USA's cold-war, normatively white past. This unit of once transnational travellers has become not just a multinational community; rather, it has settled into a more or less stable geography isolated on the beach, a representation of US multiculturalism. This multiculturalism is, of course, fraught with potential conflicts, divisions and leadership vacuums that need to be filled by Jack as 'shepard' to his ragtag flock, but, as we are frequently reminded verbally and visually, the community also has its complicated beauty and harmony. One of the show's most typical devices for weekly closure is to pan across the beach showing the castaways as a community, or to offer a montage of shots that let us know just how fully tenuous, diverse, but unified they are as a group. The shared intimacy of such shots stands in stark contrast to the cold, unemotional, racially homogenous and authoritarian scenes we get of the 'Others', deviously plotting in hatches surrounded by medical equipment and surveillance technologies, or in the paradoxically sinister comforts of life in a subdivision.

FLASHBACKS, RACE AND NATION

So far I have been suggesting that the survivor community in *Lost* is, in fact, the vision of a world community guided by an understanding of US multiculturalism and forged from the sense of a shared enemy in the imagined past. It is also a community in which personal interests, far more than racial, national, class or gendered differences, point to the difficulty of holding the group together. Identities on this island are not formed and known crucially by transnational movement, however much those surviving may have travelled before being stranded and however diverse their places of origin and race may be. Instead, they are a unit cast together in circumstances that make their pasts unknown, and, to some extent, irrelevant to one another as they are forged into a conflicted but shared identity. As John Locke, the man reborn as the *tabula rasa* theorized by the philosopher whose name he bears, puts it: everyone starts new on the island, with a clean slate. No one in the survivor community is formed by motion across borders or transnational contact, because all such crossings are literally impossible in this context of enforced isolation.

However, one of *Lost*'s most striking conventions is to spend a considerable amount of time in flashbacks, taking characters backward in time and off the island on which they find themselves trapped. None of the survivors has the possibility of communication or contact with homelands in the present, but all of them are in constant contact and exchange with memories of their cultural and geographic pasts,

pasts defined by key terms such as race, nation, class and gender that remain largely hidden from the group. These same pasts, however, are known to the audience. The show, in fact, feels duty-bound to remind viewers over and over of this ironic discrepancy in knowledge. For example, Juliet who competes with Kate (Evangeline Lilly) for Jack's attentions, points out that Kate knows almost nothing about him, not where he was born, or that he was married, divorced and so forth. Viewers know all of this. No one will believe that Hurley (Jorge Garcia), the least glamorous figure on the island, is in fact a multimillionaire, though the audience knows that to be true.

Again, this mode of narrating, especially in this context, echoes one of the most prominent Second World War combat narratives, Norman Mailer's *The Naked and the Dead* (1948).[7] In *The Naked and the Dead*, the platoon is sent on a supremely dangerous recon mission by a politically manipulative commander. They must cross an imagined South Pacific island laden with alien, tropical threats in order to discover the troop movements of the racially abhorrent Japanese. The highest peak on the island, looming over the platoon wherever it travels, is given a nearly supernatural presence. The platoon is initially led by a young, white, Protestant officer who comes from a background of privilege, but the enlisted men come from a wide variety of ethnic, class and regional backgrounds – Jewish, Italian, Irish, Latino, poor rural southerners and so forth. The mission itself turns out to be an exercise in strategic absurdity, because the island is taken by the USA wholly independent of the platoon's sacrifice. The mythical purpose of the mission, however, bringing together in a shared sense of purpose and sacrifice the multicultural members of the platoon, is all the more foregrounded by the military futility of the reconnaissance gained. By the novel's end, the enlisted men who have survived the mission stand on a boat singing and laughing with each other, even as they feel betrayed and abused by corrupt and incompetent officers.

When, during their mission, Mailer wants to make clear the intensity of the social divisions among these soldiers that must be overcome, he inserts flashback chapters in which each of them provides his racial, ethnic and cultural history, a history never shared directly with others in the platoon. These privately remembered pasts situate characters very clearly within a context of racial, ethnic, class and regional difference rather than united effort, but that knowledge of difference is, of course, more fully known by readers than it is by other members of the platoon.

Flashbacks in *Lost* often work in similar ways to emphasize differences of racial, national or ethnic origin that seldom get elaborated upon in the present of the show. We already have, for example, Jack's memory of Achara to work with. When Jack remembers race and nation, he remembers them as signals of crucial, sensuous, mythical and insurmountable difference through the fantasy of *Madame Butterfly*. To articulate that memory, to publicize it and make it known on the island in the terms the audience sees it, would be in many ways to acknowledge race and nation within the community of survivors in ways that these characters do not, to point to them as a potential source of difference and conflict. For this community to work, it needs not to establish borders between its constituents and their multiple points of origin, but instead to soften or dissolve borders in favour of shared purpose. It needs to imagine a multicultural global community roughly analogous to an expanded vision of intra-American diversity. This is, after all, as viewers know even better than the characters themselves, a world in which every member of the mini-global community is mysteriously and mythically, and sometimes even genetically, tied together.

Jin (Daniel Dae Kim) and Sun (Yunjin Kim) provide us one more example of the way that flashbacks in *Lost* threaten to disrupt the vision of the multicultural Americanness that the survivor community embodies. If, when he plunges back into his memories, Jack Shepard is lost in the Orient of *Madame Butterfly* in a way that defines his radical and complete whiteness, modernity and Americanness, then Jin and Sun, when they move mentally back in time, are the captives of what I would like to call 1980s and 1990s corporate orientalism. Among others, *Year of the Dragon* (Michael Cimino, 1985), *Rising Sun* (Philip Kaufman, 1993), *Black Rain* (Ridley Scott, 1989) and various works of cyberpunk film and fiction, most notably William Gibson's Neuromancer[8] and Ridley Scott's LA in *Bladerunner* (1982), all image forth white racial fears of Asian invasion in these years. The texts, whether as fiction or film, uniformly link imperialistic Asian corporate power to both the 'Orient's' feudal, disindividuated and militaristic past and to mysterious and brutal structures of Asian organized crime. The USA, in its undisciplined business practices, its emphasis on individuality and its lack of sufficient ruthlessness, promises, in these accounts, to become an impotent colony as the East moves forcefully westward, buying landmarks, corporations and otherwise laying claim to US resources.

The most dramatically realized expression of this corporate orientalism is surely Michael Crichton's *Rising Sun* (1992)[9] and the movie that came out of it. Both versions give us an almost *Fu Manchu*-like tale of the Japanese corporate conquest of California, enabled partly in the movie by white US traitors to the race and nation. In the film, which is, if anything, more muted in its hysteria, Japanese businessmen understand what Americans do not: 'business is war'. They construct a high-rise in LA, which the film shoots dramatically projecting upward from below. The building is, we learn, built wholly from components imported from their mother country. Japanese businessmen relax from taking over US corporations by eating sushi off the naked bodies of beautiful white women. In fact, they keep a private brothel full of young US blondes, at least some of whom have been kidnapped or blackmailed into white slavery, so that the Japanese men yearning to conquer the USA on every front might satisfy that desire. All of these depredations upon the USA are facilitated not just by the powerful work ethic and disciplined business culture of the Japanese, but also through various kinds of nefarious and illegal acts: spying, crimes, cover-ups and so forth. The Japanese corporation, in short, is an extension of and takes its structural order simultaneously from organized crime and the ancient Shogunate, which is referenced quite directly in a dramatic scene of a traditional drum performance featured at a celebratory cocktail party atop the corporate high-rise.

Lost clearly borrows significantly from this mode of representing Asian corporate power in the back stories of Jin and Sun. In a series of flashbacks spread out over all three seasons, we learn that Sun's father (Byron Chung) heads an enormous heavy manufacturing business, though what that corporation specifically makes beyond automobiles remains murky. Clearly, though, Mr Paik's business practices link him tightly to organized crime. When Jin goes to work for him, he finds himself ordered to beat those who have interfered with the corporation's plans. When Mr Paik asks Jin to commit murder, he tries to quit, only to be told that he cannot leave his job. Neither he nor Sun can escape the father she obviously fears, because, as Jin responds to her proposal to start a new life: 'You think it's that simple? ... If we run away your father would—' do the apparently unspeakable. Even the fertility doctor consulted by Jin and Sun expresses his overwhelming fear of crossing Sun's father.

The feudal nature of Korean corporate capitalism is further emphasized by Jin's experience at the Seoul Gateway Hotel ('... and Found', 2.5). Here, a manager or executive hires Jin as a doorman after a thoroughly humbling interview in which the unbridgeable differences between their social positions are made apparent. Throughout this interview, the camera looks down on Jin as he averts his eyes and bows his head. The interviewer insults Jin's small town origins, unceremoniously rips a tag off of his necktie, tells him that he stinks of fish while warning him that the Seoul Gateway is one of the finest hotels in the city, and insists that a crucial part of the doorman's job is to refuse to 'open the door to people like you'. Not surprisingly, we learn later, Mr Paik and the owner of the Seoul Gateway 'do business' with one another. Korea is featured as a corporate culture in which caste is rigidly enforced and organized crime is everywhere.

However, if *Lost* clearly borrows from the vocabulary of 1980s and 1990s corporate orientalism, it also lacks the most urgently felt worry of such books and films. *Lost* never imagines the mixed-up gangland, Tong-style, shogunate-influenced corporate culture of Korea as a threat beyond its borders, least of all to white Westerners or the USA. Korean corporate capitalism is here contained in Korea and evidences absolutely no threat of global expansion, of absorption or conquest of the West. In fact, given that the Seoul Gateway hotel is one of the finest in the city, presumably catering to international business, one might be surprised that in all of the many scenes shot there, it is utterly impossible to definitively spot a Westerner.

Instead, the overwhelming authority and corruption of Korean capitalism threatens young westernized Koreans who might wish to migrate. Sun clearly hopes to step outside the traditional gender role into which she has been cast by her family; Jae (Tony Lee), Sun's lover, attended Harvard, majored in Russian literature, speaks English fluently, teaches it to Sun, and, in his heart, always hoped to remain in or return to the USA. But, as Jae tells Sun, 'You can't run away from your life', so he came back to serve, clearly more as an obligation than a heartfelt calling, as the general manager of the Seoul Gateway, one of nine hotels owned by his family. Both Jae and Sun resent the efforts of their parents to arrange a marriage between them and within their proper caste, and, instead of marrying, they carry on an affair. If Jae is less than fulfilled in his role as the manager of one of Seoul's finest hotels, Sun is miserable in her marriage, which her father dominates by controlling every move that Jin makes. She, too, would flee to the USA, not because Korean corporate power will follow her there, but because it represents a possibility for escape. Jae, for his part, commits suicide after being discovered in the affair and beaten by Jin, who has been ordered to kill him by Mr Paik for bringing shame to the Paik family.

If the orientalized corporations of Korea destroy Jae and bear heavily upon Sun, they treat Jin no more kindly. He is the son of a fisherman, the embodiment of a vanishing local economy of the type we see preserved for Jack's touristic pleasure when he meets Achara in Thailand. Jin moves to Seoul hoping to work his way up the corporate ladder, but is instead turned into the brutal and brutalizing servant of a corrupt, criminal and feudal corporate power that threatens always to destroy his marriage. Jin, like Sun and Jae, entertains the possibility of crossing from East to West, of running from Korea to the USA, only to learn from an anonymous Korean enforcer in an Australian airport's restroom that, if he tries it, Mr Paik will track him down. Rather than threatening the West with the colonization and absorption characteristic of 1980s and 1990s corporate orientalism, the Korean corporation in *Lost* makes any kind of westernization or westward migration impossible. Even in the context of corporate power, East is East and West and West. Those wishing to be Americanized will become the victims of borders and fences erected by the essentially feudal structures of Korean corporate power. Asian migration to the implicitly more tolerant, diverse and enlightened USA is not associated with 'yellow' imperialism in *Lost* as it is in the corporate orientalism of the 1980s and 1990s. Rather, migration to the USA and *assimilation* within it is the yearned for goal of Korea's best and brightest young adults. The backstory of Jin and Sun, then, is precisely not a tale of globalization and diaspora, but one of separation and isolationism, of the impossibility of young Koreans (however much they *yearn* to flee) moving beyond seemingly ancient borders of nation and race.

If, however, Jin's and Sun's flashbacks suggest identities firmly rooted within uncrossable national and racial borders, their memories play out against a story on the island that emphasizes interracial unity, the formulation of a globalized and unified multicultural nation. We are first introduced to Jin and Sun's backstory in an episode that also features Jin's apparently random and brutal beating of Michael (Harold Perrineau), one of only two adult, African American survivors of the crash. In the end, we learn that the beating is the product of cultural misunderstanding. Jin was transporting a watch worth tens of thousands of dollars; Michael found it in the wreckage after the crash; Jin assumed he had stolen it, and, to quote Sun, as 'a matter of honour', he attacked Michael. It would, of course, seem remarkable in a world not over-determined by symbolic and racial meanings that the *only* Asian male survivor should end up in heated and violent conflict with the *only* African American male on the beach over a matter of theft.

Whether one chooses to point to the often reported tensions between Korean grocers and black patrons in New York and Los Angeles, to think further backward to S.I. Hayakawa's simultaneous celebration of Asian American upward mobility and urging of blacks to stop protesting and follow that example, or move forward from there to former Japanese Prime Minister Yasuhiro Nakasone's suggestion that blacks and Hispanics inflict grave cultural and economic costs on the USA, one readily finds a discourse of racial trouble in which African Americans stand in a criminal or quasi-criminal relationship to a mythic ideal of the more disciplined Asian. As several scholars have pointed out in recent years, this casting of the model minority myth against African American and other minorities is by no means wholly an Asian American effort. Nakasone, after all, is Japanese and within the USA the interests of a white majority has been at times well served by setting Asian American and African American identities artificially against one another.[10]

In *Lost*, however, the complicated formation of this stereotyped conflict goes unremarked, and we get only a familiar representation of Jin's almost visceral and brutal distaste for the one African American man on the island. Heightening the racialized antagonism, Jin also clearly sees Michael as a sexual threat when he finds him speaking to his wife. This intense black–Asian conflict, though, is never explicitly articulated in racial terms, and *Lost* seems to present it primarily so that Jin, Sun and Michael can undergo a startling racial reconciliation – even as the three never seem to notice the racial enmity they represent. If the backstory of Jin and Sun points to the impossibility of East and West merging, this narrative of life on the island emphasizes melding into an interracial friendship and trust that promises the formation of a single, globalized, multicultural nation. It offers, in short, a utopian solution for a community of viewers to the problem of black–Asian conflict.

As the flashbacks to Korea continue into *Lost*'s second season, Michael and Jin form a fast friendship in their shared resistance to the Others, who kidnap Michael's son, Walt (Malcolm David Kelley). This shared intimacy unfolds as Jin very slowly learns the imperative of speaking some English – at least enough to say 'friend' when referring to Michael – since that is the language of the international nation of crash survivors. The interracial reconciliation that is simultaneously an elimination of international differences becomes even more dramatic when Jin runs into the forest searching for Michael accompanied only by Eko (Adewale Akinnuoye-Agbaje), a black character of Nigerian origin. Together, Jin and Eko find Michael and bring him back to the group of survivors. This multinational group of blacks and Asians represents not most crucially any kind of racial globalization or embrace of cross-cultural influence, but the reconciliation of racial and national differences in the shared community allied against the cold-war threat of the Others.

Lost, in its complicated narrative movements, trades in the language and representation of global migration and movement for the image of a melted-together US multiculturalism overseen primarily by Jack Shepard. This community is not utterly tidy in its representation of multiracial unity any more than are the combat platoons of Second World War movies. It is a motley group, filled with potential frictions to be overcome in the name of the greater good. As Jack tells the survivors early on, 'Find something to do. Every man for himself isn't going to make it.' Not only is Jack the leader of the settlement on the beach, the USA, with a population of survivors vastly more diverse than that of any other nation, is readily imagined in *Lost* as co-extensive with the world. Survivors here simply have to figure out how they fit into this nation that, in one of its privileged stories about itself, melts away the notion of nationality. The racialized, cold-war enemy on the other side of the island, the Others, provide the force against which the multicultural vision of the contemporary USA defines itself: a normatively white, cold-war past of subdivisions and bomb shelters. *Lost* imagines the day when the globe will be united against the self-acknowledged malevolence of this cold-war past in multicultural unity under God and indivisible. It imagines connection, unity and refuge from restless global movements on the one hand and the enforcement of rigid frontiers against an imagined past of bipolarity, separation and racial homogeneity on the other. It imagines the solution to problems of racial and national conflict by allowing a multinational audience to see the world as a nation in the image of American immigration mythology.

It notably dismisses – and even fails to acknowledge – alternative histories of global movement, war and migration, most obviously in its lack of reference to current global conflicts. The enemy here is provincial whiteness. The contemporary USA has moved past such social discriminations in the world of *Lost*, even if, away from the mysterious island, global warfare that is, in part complexly bound to racialized, imperial and nationalistic drivers occupies the front page of newspapers. Though we stand only at the end of season three and confront substantial uncertainty about the show's future narrative conventions, I like to imagine (with tongue in cheek) that at *Lost*'s conclusion all of the survivors will board a plane for Los Angeles, for the USA, where they will settle happily, because, as the show fantasizes for us in the very route of Oceanic 815, that is where the world *wants* to be headed anyway.

Notes

1   On the *Madame Butterfly* story see Gina Marchetti, *Romance and the Yellow Peril: Race, Sex, and Discursive Strategies in Hollywood Fiction* (Berkeley: University of California Press, 1994), pp.78–108; Mari Yoshihara, *Embracing the East: White Women and American Orientalism* (New York: Oxford, 2002).

2   The literature on the formation of transnational subjects is vast. For a brief, recent and readable example with some relevance to *Lost*, see Henry Yu, 'Los Angeles and American studies in a Pacific world of migrations', *American Quarterly* 56 (2004), pp.531–43.

3   Roberta Pearson, '*Lost* in transition: from post-network to post-television', in Janet McCabe and Kim Akass (eds), *Quality TV: Contemporary American Television and Beyond* (London: I.B.Tauris, 2007), pp.239–56; see also Chapter XI in this volume.

4   Mae Ngai, *Impossible Subjects: Illegal Aliens and the Making of Modern America*. (Princeton: Princeton University Press), pp.5–7. See also Bonnie Honig, *Democracy and the Foreigner* (Princeton: Princeton University Press, 2001).

5   Frederic Jameson, 'Reification and Utopia in mass culture', *Social Text* 1 (winter 1979), pp.144–6.

6   On the combat film and platoon see Jeanine Basinger, *The World War II Combat Film: Anatomy of a Genre* (New York: Columbia University Press, 1986); Richard Slotkin, 'Unit pride: ethnic platoons and the myths of American nationality', *American Literary History* xiii/3 (fall 2001), pp.469–98.

7   Norman Mailer, *The Naked and the Dead*, 50th anniversary edn (New York: Picador, 2000).

8   William Gibson, *Neuromancer* (New York: Ace Books, 1984).

9   Michael Crichton, *Rising Sun* (New York: Alfred A. Knopf, 1992).

10   See Frank Wu, *Yellow: Race in America Beyond Black and White* (New York: Basic Books, 2003), pp.39–78.

XII. We're Not in Portland Anymore:

Lost and Its International Others

Jonathan Gray

As many television scholars and producers have argued of late, television is in a transitional era. To Lynn Spigel and Jan Olsson, this is 'television after TV',[1] while Amanda Lotz writes of a 'revolution' in American television.[2] If this transitional time is notable for changes and innovations of form,[3] and of production, distribution, and transmission at local levels,[4] then it is also notable for its increasingly globalized nature. The age of the truly *national* broadcaster and of its one-size-fits-all logic is under threat, challenged from within national borders by narrowcasting and niche marketing, and giving rise to increased discussion of multiple public spheres,[5] not a singular, united public sphere.[6] Meanwhile, television regularly flows beyond its national borders, sometimes following transnational and diasporic audiences, sometimes as part of a general process of cultural interaction and exchange, and often as part of media multinationals' exerted attempts to establish textual and/or corporate beachheads on all foreign soil.

The state of national television is in flux, and certainly a great deal of current scholarship examines the specificities of how television travels, how it is received in foreign contexts, and how business models are changing to account for globalization.[7] To date, however, little has been said about how television programmes are imaging and imagining the world now that more of that world is likely to be part of their audience. If television is moving beyond the nation, how – if at all – are its texts adapting, not just as products that are distributed globally, but as narratives, and as sets of meanings? And since it is US television that is particularly successful and particularly aggressively plugged worldwide, how is it adapting?

A scan through US primetime television might suggest that little if any adaptation is occurring. Many US shows still care first, foremost and only about addressing an American audience. Not only do we have *American Idol* (Fremantle Media North America, 2002–), *America's Funniest Home Videos* (ABC Productions, 1990–) and *America's Got Talent* (Fremantle Media North America, 2006–), but many other shows focus solely on American characters in American places. Small-town family or teen dramas such as *7ᵗʰ Heaven* (CBS Paramount Network Television, 1996–2007), *Gilmore Girls* (Dorothy Parker Drank Here Productions, 2000–7), *Everwood* (Warner Bros. Television, 2002–6), *Dawson's Creek* (Outerbank Entertainment, 1998–2003) and *Smallville* (Tollin, 2001–) regularly appear to be set not only miles but many years away from a globalized world, following US television's long-established fascination with suburban life away from the global mix of the city. Yet even many shows set in the international cities of New York, Los Angeles and Miami have either shown little or no awareness of the global in the local, as with *Friends* (Warner Bros. Television, 1994–2004) or *Seinfeld* (Castlerock Entertainment, 1990–8) for instance, or have included foreigners largely as terrorists and criminals, as with *24* (Imagine Entertainment, 2001–) or *CSI: Miami* (CBS Productions, 2002–).

When US television does voyage outside the nation's borders, most often it does so in heavily orientalized terms, either exoticizing (as in travel, cooking or wildlife programmes) or reducing non-Americans to bad guys and their victims (as in *The Unit* (David Mamet Chicago, 2006–), *Alias* (Bad Robot, 2001–6), and the nightly news). US television shows have thus very rarely exhibited any awareness of addressing an international audience, and still too frequently present international settings and characters in ways that belittle them and that bolster Americans' self-image as the best people on the planet.

Within this framework of Othering and exclusion, we can better understand how *Lost* was a stark break from business as usual when it hit the air in 2004. *Lost* is, first, set outside the USA; second, filmed outside the contiguous 48 states, in Hawaii; third, its regular characters have included an Iraqi, an Australian, an Englishman, a Nigerian, two Koreans, a Frenchwoman and a Scot; and fourth, its cast has included Australians, white Brits, black Brits, a South Asian Brit, a Canadian, a Croat, a Brazilian and a Korean. It is thus, to date, US primetime television's most international show. And it has been successful, being a breakout hit of 2004 in the USA, still regularly in the Nielsen top 30 and also a huge success internationally. A 2006 study of 20 countries by Informa Telecoms and Media found *Lost* the second most popular show, behind only *CSI: Miami*.[8]

Importantly, too, its bold act of leaving the USA behind has inspired followers, with *Heroes* (NBC Universal Television, 2006–) premiering in 2006 – a show that, at the 2006 fall preview screenings at the New York Museum of TV and Radio, was introduced proudly by an NBC executive as 'very international, just like *Lost*' – and *Life is Wild* (CBS Paramount Network Television, 2007–8) premiering in 2007. This chapter will study *Lost*'s depiction of the world and its people outside the USA. As I will show, and as Chapter XI by Michael Newbury also details, *Lost* suffers from many orientalizing and belittling tropes. However, over time it has also challenged many of these tropes with remarkable skill. In particular, its gradual recoding of some of the island's international inhabitants, along with its poignant and ever-developing discussion of the nature of home and belonging, has offered a refreshingly complex rendering of the politics of belonging that, if all too rare, is fitting for globalized television and is an encouraging development for US television.

IRAQI TORTURERS, KOREAN GANGSTERS AND NIGERIAN WARLORDS: ORIENTALISM AND LOST

As Edward Said notes, European and US attempts to make sense of the rest of the world have long been characterized by a process of Othering. An Other is a psychological foil created as a repository for characteristics, ideas and urges that one wishes to disown, and hence Others serve as projections of that which we do not want to be. Not the products of honest research that they often purport to be, they are constructions and fictive renderings. Said notes their perpetuation through history, as yet more anthropologists, historians, scientists, artists and travellers merely replicate the same tired stereotypes, seeing in other people the difference and strangeness they expect to find. 'Knowledge' of the Orient, Said observes, '*creates* the Orient, the Oriental, and his world', so that '[i]t is Europe that articulates the Orient; this articulation is the prerogative, not of a puppet master, but of a genuine creator, whose life-giving power represents, animates, and constitutes the otherwise silent and dangerous space beyond familiar boundaries.'[9] The Other or Oriental becomes a caricature, meaning the actual human being is always spoken for, never allowed to speak for or of him or herself.

Orientalism and Othering are thus 'a set of constraints upon and limitations of thought', since they 'represent or stand for a very large entity, otherwise impossibly diffuse, which they enable one to grasp or see',[10] reducing complexities of difference to simple binaries. 'We' are the civilized ones, endowed with a code of honour, a respect for science and rationality, compassion, and above all individuality and profundity, while 'they' become the mass of irrational, barbaric savages or pitiable, laughable simpletons. Not only does Othering represent a failure to engage with those from other countries as real beings but, as Said notes, most insidiously, such binaries 'could prepare the way for what armies, administrations, and bureaucracies would later do on the ground, in the Orient',[11] 'justifying' imperial rule by positing an inherent lack in all of 'them' that 'we' did and do not share. While Othering as a mode of 'understanding' is common worldwide, as Said reminds us, when combined with real world power differentials between the Otherer and the Other, Othering easily begets imperialism.

Said's *Orientalism* stands out as a remarkable study of colonial history, but his continued work and criticism until his death in 2003 insisted that Orientalism was still a dominant mode of viewing the non-Western world. And while Said's own work focused on Orientalism directed towards the Middle East in history, literature and policy, many scholars have found Othering and Orientalism of all non-Westerners across the mass media. David Richards has charted the Orientalist gaze across a history of Western art, anthropology and literature.[12] Catherine Lutz and Jane Collins examine *National Geographic*'s systematic Othering in the mode of romanticizing the 'noble savage' and his or her 'primitive' customs and beliefs.[13] William O'Barr finds Othering a common element in advertising images of non-Westerners.[14] M. Shahid Alam, among many others, has studied the Orientalist gaze of international news.[15] Sunaina Maira and John Hutnyk have examined Western youth culture's love of all things Indian as Orientalist, so that, as Hutnyk argues, 'India becomes the biological/genetic/conceptual repository and archive for values, concepts, styles, and "life essence" considered absent in the individualistic "developed" West.'[16] Hutnyk has also penned a detailed study of how Western constructions of Calcutta, through maps, traveller's tales, film, photographs and tour books, result in visitors replicating the Calcutta they expect, rather than seeking out the complex realities of the city.[17] David Morley notes that the media's construction of nation and national identity has often relied upon images and notions of the foreign as the threateningly different.[18] And, as many studies of media representations of ethnicity within any given nation illustrate, Othering and Orientalism have become common lenses through which many media texts gaze at and make sense of (that is, project and construct) all manners of racial or cultural difference.

Turning to *Lost*, the show introduced several of its non-Western characters to us in heavily Orientalized terms. As Newbury in this volume shows, the initial treatment of the Korean couple Jin (Daniel Day Kim) and Sun (Yunjin Kim) by the script, camera and other characters is particularly illustrative. Early in season one, Jin comes across as a domineering, chauvinist husband, while Sun appears to be a submissive, diminutive presence living under his shadow. Many of *Lost*'s first images of Jin were of him giving orders to his wife, or reprimanding her in harsh tones. As importantly, several scenes depicted other characters *seeing* Jin give orders and sharing concerned looks, and we were thus invited to share, as part of the 'we', their Orientalist gaze and judgment of what at first appeared to be yet another one of 'them' – an East Asian sexist brute terrorizing his shrinking violet of a wife. Often Korean dialogue between the couple would go without subtitles, underscoring their foreignness and their difference, separating them from us as viewers as much as from the other islanders, and subordinating Jin and Sun to their fellow crash victims.

As correlate to Jin's language difficulties in particular, he became one of the show's sources for comic relief, as he would stumble through attempts to communicate with others. Here, knowing viewers could also appreciate the irony that Korean–American Daniel Dae Kim reportedly had to bone up on his shaky command of the Korean language for the role. Ironic, yes, but the resulting performance was thus clearly coded as one of an American aping a Korean character as penned by white American writers. Then, in 'House of the Rising Sun' (1.6), viewers were shocked out of seeing Jin as (solely) a comic element when he brutally beat Michael (Harold Perrineau), playing into role as the irrational, dangerous Oriental. Furthermore, if Jin appeared to act outside established Western rules of behaviour, by placing Jin and Sun in a repressive organized crime family, the producers painted Korea itself in broad, reductive strokes, as a place of uncontested male chauvinism, usury and with an absence of rational law or power structures. Sun, we learn, was learning English secretly, intending to escape to the USA, the promised land beyond the reach of Korean law, family and corruption.

Sayid (Naveen Andrews) and Mr Eko (Adewale Akinnuoye-Agjabe) are also initially presented in Orientalized terms, as will later be discussed, with the Iraqi torturer and the Nigerian warlord and drug smuggler respectively conforming closely to the long line of Orientalist depictions of the Arab world and to colonial narratives of the 'Dark Continent'. Beyond mere characters, though, as with Korea, foreign *places* are frequently depicted as inherently strange and dangerous. For example, the tellingly titled 'Stranger in a Strange Land' (3.9) that examines Jack's (Matthew Fox) time in Thailand is particularly steeped in the exotic. As Newbury in this volume (see Chapter XI) charts with rich detail, the episode reduces Jack's Thai lover to a combination of tourist sex trinket and mystic, offering Jack (the man of science and rationality) as the lone identification point through which we are invited to gaze at the exotic Thai setting around him, and building up to a scene that rocks between a rape fantasy and an Orientalized mystical sexual experience. Finally, the flashback ends with Jack being beaten by a group of voiceless Thai thugs, thereby referencing multiple other Orientalist tellings of the exotic beach tale, such as *The Beach* (Danny Boyle, 2000) or *Turistas* (John Stockwell, 2006), complete with the sense of local danger.

Jack's visit to Thailand occupies the flashback scenes of a single episode, but the general exoticization of Eastern spirituality pervades *Lost* through the Dharma Initiative. Dharma, the Sanskrit word for a general sense of order in life, and a central tenet of Hindu, Buddhist, Jain and Sikh belief and philosophy, is used in *Lost* to imbue the island-controlling Initiative with a strong air of Eastern mysticism. Lest the viewer miss the name's significance, Dharma's ubiquitous training video scientist, Dr Marvin Candle (François Chau), is South East Asian. Moreover, the Dharma Initiative's set sign-off is the Nepali and Hindi '*Namaste*' (meaning, 'I bow to you'), complete with the South and South East Asian sign of respect, greeting or farewell of placing the palms together. Even when Dharma's on-island representatives all appear to be white and American, the writers' choice to surround this experiment with the accoutrements of Buddhism introduces a sense of the unknown, the supernatural and the other-worldly.

Then there is Africa. With the second season addition of Mr Eko, the island now had a crash survivor from Nigeria. Eko's flashbacks tell a story of a nation/continent in strife, where a mission is desperately trying to help the struggling people, yet is helpless against a cold and bloodthirsty gang who regularly kill with no reason. Viewers would be familiar with this Africa from the news – a lawless, impoverished place run by 'tribal warlords' who smuggle drugs and kill for sport. *Lost* maintains a centuries-old Orientalist depiction of Africa as ruled by animalistic irrationality and cruelty, its depiction barely more nuanced than the bones through the nose or the cannibalism of earlier renderings. Even children become killers, which, while a thorough violation of the natural order, is sometimes understandable, given their residence in a supposedly kill-or-be-killed continent. Eko himself is seen as capable of turning off his moral compass to commit considerable violence. As with Thailand, Korea, and Iraq, Africa is depicted in Orientalized terms.

Admittedly, *Lost*'s world is a dark one, the USA included. Various flashbacks, for instance, show a USA in which the Mittelos Bioscience company can have Juliet's (Elizabeth Mitchell's) boss killed in plain sight in Miami. With few exceptions, however, *Lost*'s USA is still governed by law, and hence by a prevailing moral code and by rationality. Kate (Evangeline Lilly) is on the run from the law for killing her step-father, and along the way she falls in love with a cop. Ana-Lucia (Michelle Rodriguez) was herself a police officer, and her flashbacks deal with her desire to kill out of revenge, an urge that is coded as un-cop-like, and which leads to her mother/supervising officer recommending that she take time off. Locke's father (Kevin Tighe) and Sawyer (Josh Holloway) may have conned their way around the country, but they were on the move to avoid the law. Though unwittingly, Locke (Terry O'Quinn) leads an undercover agent to foil a commune's marijuana-growing operation. And even Jack's father (John Terry) must pay for his drunken gurney-side behaviour when Jack ensures that the hospital board relieves him of his duties. Thus, while Thailand, Korea, Iraq and Africa offer no sense of law, the US flashbacks frequently involve a tangible power of law, in stark opposition to the lack thereof in the Orientalized nations.

Lost also includes several white Others, who, though slightly stereotyped – as with Charlie (Dominic Monaghan), the Mancunian rocker suffering from drug addiction, Desmond (Henry Ian Cusick), the Scot who can identify brands of scotch at a distance, and Rousseau (Mira Furlan), the slightly crazy, non-team playing Frenchwoman – are spared the caricaturization of their non-Western counterparts. Australia, meanwhile, is depicted in a tellingly binary manner. On one hand is the lawful, familiar-looking (that is, USA-like) white Australia, complete with suburbs, fancy yachts and roadside pubs. On the other hand, we also see a mystical, exotic, indigenous Australia, home to a famed healer, and the intended site of Locke's spiritual quest of discovery. A powerful spirit is posited as resting over the Outback, and Locke's and Bernard's (Sam Anderson's) and Rose's (L. Scott Caldwell's) attempted encounters with this spirit pose it as indigenous.

Lost's gaze at the non-white, non-Western world frequently belittles, while relying on careless and clichéd tropes of ruthless murderers, unchecked aggression and lawlessness, or, by contrast, the exotic, mystical and seductive. These depictions make it important that the island is itself in liminal space, seemingly in an unknown location in the South Pacific and peopled not by Pacific Islanders but by Ben (Michael Emerson) and the white 'Others'. The island is positioned somewhere between the lawful, rational, scientific USA and the lawless, irrational, mystical rest of the non-white world, its ambiguous location exacerbating the uneasiness stemming from not knowing exactly what the island is and under what rules (if any) it operates. So too with the Dharma Initiative, who may seem partly based in 'Portland', yet who are surrounded by Buddhist terminology and fronted by a South East Asian in their videos. If *Lost*'s writers have set up an ongoing battle of science and faith, forcing the viewer to continually question which of the two, or how much of each, is at play in any given occurrence, their coding of the rest of the world as mystical, the USA as scientific, and the island and Dharma as somewhere in between amplifies the viewer's confusion. This liminality even extends to the filming location, since Hawaii is similarly both the USA and not the USA, both 'here' and 'there' (for more on Hawaii's liminality see Chapter V in this volume).

EDITING THE SCRIPT: CHALLENGING ORIENTALISM

In numerous ways, then, *Lost* may appear to conform to a pervasive Orientalism in US television. Jack's Thai adventure in particular seems wholly drawn from a colonialist narrative, and much of the depiction of Africa echoes colonial-era accounts justifying European 'civilization' of these 'barbarians'. However, at the same time, the show has also proven remarkably unconventional in dynamically challenging tired Orientalist scripts, and in self-reflexively debunking and replacing them. Somewhat characteristic of many 'progressive' depictions on television, *Lost*'s images at times take steps backward into regression and racism, yet at other times take bold steps forward in thoughtful and nuanced character development.

The character arcs and development of Jin, Sun and Sayid are especially worthy of closer analysis, since these figures have surpassed their initial stereotyping, both through the writing and the acting. As with any good mystery, and any good serial narrative, *Lost*'s novelty and narrative pleasures have often come from developing characters, and its writers have concentrated significant energy on shifting perspectives and on changing formerly comfortable truths. Viewers are turned into analysts who must try to piece together what is going on across time, since no character is who they at first appeared to be. In short, *Lost* frequently requires the viewer to re-evaluate not only individual characters, but also potentially the production of the stereotypes associated with those characters. Hence, while in the above section I argued that many of the show's non-Western characters and places are *initially* presented in Orientalized terms, part of the show's strength lies in its ability to recode these as it progresses.

Season one's flashbacks in particular specialized in offering character revelations: Hurley (Jorge Garcia) was a multimillionaire, Locke was paraplegic, and so forth. The second Jin and Sun flashback in '... In Translation' (1.17) similarly spun our understanding of Jin. Presented at first as the hired thug and domineering husband, Jin was revealed instead to be a man trying to do whatever necessary to be with his wife. Forced into being Sun's father's (Byron Chung) hitman, Jin took to roughing his marks up, but never killing them. His anger, meanwhile, was re-contextualized for us as a sense of failure. Viewers were invited to see that Jin's inability to communicate with the islanders extended to his inability to communicate with his wife, to whom we now saw that he was hopelessly devoted. For her part, the more that viewers learned of Sun's past – of her learning English behind Jin's back, of her plan to move to the USA, of her affair, of her dispatching of Jin's extortionist mother – the less and less she appeared a diminutive Asian stereotype. Aided further by a strong and nuanced performance by Yunjin Kim, Sun has become a confidante, friend and force of strength in the group. Thus, in Jin and Sun, we have seen an impressive metamorphosis, as both were introduced as stereotypes, yet both have subsequently transcended those types.

Following this episode, and the couple's eventual reconciliation, Jin and Sun have become two of the island's most endearing characters. While sexual tension simmered between multiple other pairings, Jin and Sun have taken their place as the island's beloved couple. Bernard and Rose are the largely desexualized 'cute' older couple, but Jin and Sun are presented both as objects for viewer sexual attractions *and* as objects for romantic identification. The writers often use their relationship as an emotional hook, as in season two's penultimate episode, 'Live Together, Die Alone (1)', in which the two are separated by Jin's determination to get Sun rescued and hence to voyage outwards on the raft. In such moments, we are no longer invited to look *at* them with an Orientalist gaze, but to identify *with* them and to feel for them, not as Koreans, nor even as non-Koreans, but as people. In short, then, over three seasons the two have developed into nuanced, fleshed-out characters. Sun's character development on the show is all the more impressive, too, since it reflects Yunjin Kim's triumph at becoming the first East Asian star to successfully transition to US television stardom.

Sayid's development as a character also speaks to a powerful transcendence of stereotype. To begin with, Sayid's role as torturer occupies peculiar semiotic space in *Lost*, for while at one moment Orientalizing him as a bloodthirsty Arab, it also contributes to fashioning him as the island's action hero. *Lost* shares a televisual moment with *24*, and the latter's Jack Bauer is notorious for his proclivity to torture. Both characters are depicted as *able* to torture anyone, but only *willing* to do so in dire circumstances. While we should be shocked to see that torture is now an acceptable skill in a hero's bag of tricks, political ramifications aside, in action-hero generic coding it speaks to their masculine resolve (even if Sayid, contra Jack Bauer, regrets having tortured people). As a result, Sayid has that most desirable of action-hero attributes: he is someone you don't want to mess with.

He is also yet another of the cast's heart-throbs. With straggly hair and muscular frame, and with his go-it-alone attitude, Sayid screams sex appeal. For a South Asian Brit playing an Iraqi, though, this is no easy feat, given centuries' old codings of non-white men as either sexually dangerous aggressors likely to take 'our women', or as effeminate and foppish. Sayid and Shannon's (Maggie Grace's) short-lived romance also joined Bernard and Rose's as a rare depiction of biracial romance on US television. Granted, Boone (Ian Somerhalder) objected to the relationship, but viewers knew enough to understand it as incestuous jealousy, not an outgrowth of racist sentiment per se.

By no means solely the hired muscle or hunk, either, Sayid is one of the island's smartest residents, gifted at working with electronics and blessed with a tactical mind. He is driven and, alongside Jack and Locke, one of the island's unquestioned leaders. He is emotionally intelligent, too, a savvy observer of the island's social dynamics, and personally wracked with guilt over his own past actions. Action-hero status, sex appeal, tenderness in romance, leadership, moral sense and intelligence: none of these fit the bill of a traditionally Orientalized depiction of an Arab man, and put together, especially in a post-9/11 television environment that is frequently hostile and crude in its depictions of Arabs, Sayid stands out as a unique character on US television. Indeed, the depth and subtleties of his character and the strength of his performance also avoid making him appear a crudely conceived 'perfect Arab' counter-stereotype.

In terms of casting, meanwhile, *Lost* has been notable for hiring numerous non-American actors to play non-American roles. The cast's visible internationalism and the rise of some non-American cast members into becoming stars of the small screen have in their own way ever so slightly displaced the USA and Americans as the natural, rightful and sole centres of big-budget global television.

THE OTHERS, THE ORIGINAL OTHERS AND THE OTHER OTHERS

A central task then becomes one of evaluating the ensuing entangled mess of caricature and character, belittling and developing, shallowness and profundity, Othering and identification. It would be easy to castigate the programme for its failures, and merely noting that it is 'trying' is not sufficient defence. As Chinua Achebe's broadside attack on Joseph Conrad's *Heart of Darkness* (1902) makes clear, trying is certainly not enough. Though Conrad's novel is often praised for questioning colonialism, as Achebe notes, along the way Conrad reduced the Africans to mere set paintings that served as the dark, fearful backdrop to a wholly white British journey into the recesses of the mind. Nevertheless, at the same time, *Lost* is not *Heart of Darkness*. Achebe's central critique of *Heart of Darkness* is that Conrad might criticize the colonial impulse, but in unproblematically reducing the Africans to backdrop, and in never truly challenging his narrator Marlowe's way of looking at Africa, 'he neglects to hint, clearly and adequately, at an alternative frame of reference by which we may judge the actions and opinions of his characters'.[19]

By contrast, I now want to argue that *Lost* does offer such an alternative framework. Till now, I have been tip-toeing around the fact that this chapter is about Othering in a show with a group referred to as 'the Others', and whose third season ended with the suggestion of there being 'original Others' and even 'other Others'. But let me now look beyond depictions of characters and places, and turn to thematics, facing the term 'Other' head-on and examining what *Lost* has said in its three seasons so far about Others, and how the show has developed its discussion of Othering, home and belonging.

When first previewing in the summer of 2004, one of *Lost*'s key narrative hooks was the fear of the Other. Previews showed the crash survivors trying to make heads or tails of their new environment, grouping together, and the preview then led up a bestial noise from the jungle, followed by Charlie's question, 'Guys, where are we?' Interest in the unknown in part sold the show, and in part drove the initial episodes, with some form of beast appearing to inhabit the island. Then, as fear of the beast subsided, a new and more viable threat was posed by the Others. Like classic bogeymen from children's tales, the Others came at night, dragging children and other survivors into the darkness. And thus was born one of the island's and show's prime dynamics and binaries: us and them, the Lostaways and the Others. The Others were seen as brutal, savage and primitive at first, with fleeting shots of them showing people in rags walking through the jungle; and, most importantly, they acted without any seeming reason, kidnapping, killing and infiltrating the camp through the personages of Ethan (William Mapother) and Goodwin (Brett Cullen). When Jack finally sets out to find them, he comes across a tribal scene of Others hiding in the shadows with torches, faceless but palpably threatening and real. Conrad's *Heart of Darkness* again comes to mind, as the Others, or rather, the Lostaway's conception of them, conforms entirely to the crudest form of Orientalism and Othering.

Along the way, however, numerous individuals and occurrences begin to challenge the stark binary. First, Sayid finds Rousseau (Mira Furlan), who we are led to believe might be an Other, but who turns out to have lived on the island alone for many years. Then in dramatic fashion, season two's premiere introduced us to Desmond, living in his hatch, but again, not an Other. All the while, the show's continual use of flashbacks, each week from a different person's perspective, and its common trope of beginning episodes with close-ups of characters' eyes, drew the viewers' eyes to the issue of *perspective*. Suspicions of unreliable narration bubbled up on the fan boards, as fans became more and more aware of the subjectivity of each flashback – as the episode opening scenes often seem to highlight, we know that we are seeing the island *through the Lostaways' eyes*. Carlton Cuse and Damon Lindelof cruelly refused to reveal greater truths, as instead we rarely learned anything about the island that one of the central crash survivors did not know. In the midst of this came Goodwin, the second Other infiltrator, yet a likeable character. Before being killed by the edgy Ana-Lucia, Goodwin offered the fascinating proclamation that the Others only took the good people, not the bad ones. And thus the whole edifice of the good guys versus the Others was brought into question. If the Others only took good people, maybe *they* were 'the good guys'? And with a growing number of anomalous characters polluting the stark binary of Lostaways and Others, the duality lost its hold.

Then season three continued this reversal. Just as season two began with our first look through a non-Lostaway's eyes, season three began by placing us in the Others' book-club meeting. A perfect image for quotidian middle-class life, the book club meet in an average suburban-style home, having a mundane discussion about the book of the week. Now 'we' as viewers, who had previously only been invited to join the Lostaways, were part of a new 'we', being offered a different perspective. As the season progressed, Juliet was offered as a new point of identification, especially through her pathos-filled flashbacks involving a sick sister and her desire to let her have a baby. And Jack, who had long been offered as a primary point of identification and reference for viewers, was befriending the Others. We even saw Flight 815's flight attendant at Camp Other, happily insisting that the children were safe and that all was fine.

What Goodwin had suggested – that the Others were not necessarily the bad guys – therefore now had purchase. Throughout season three, viewers were invited into a confusing game of guessing each character's motivations, and of sorting through their conflicted positioning as both bad guys and good guys. Even Jack became more standoffish, not only to his fellow survivors, but also to audience identification, thereby pushing viewers away from him, yet leaving us unsure of where to place our allegiances instead. We could still seemingly trust in certain characters' *intent* to 'do the right thing', but we could not be sure of what the 'right thing' actually was.

By the end of season three, the writers had thoroughly confused the formerly easy Lostaway–Other binary. Julia Kristeva has noted of society's reliance on us–Other binaries that

> living with the other, with the foreigner, confronts us with the possibility ... of being an other ... [which is] not simply ... a matter of ... accept[ing] the other, but of being in his place ... to imagine and make oneself other for oneself

and Homi Bhabha's theorizing of postcolonial hybridity similarly posits the importance of being able to see ourselves as others and others as ourselves.[20] Gradually, then, *Lost* has offered us this experience of 'being an other' and of 'making oneself other for oneself'. However, precisely because *Lost* has all along been a water-cooler show that demands decoding and unpacking with, dare I say, *others*, it self-reflexively challenged notions of perspective, calling upon the viewer to self-reflexively re-evaluate scripts of Othering, and of how and whether to trust the modes of seeing offered them. When twinned with the character arcs and development of Jin, Sun, Sayid, Eko and others who have broken out of stereotype, *Lost* has performed the impressive stunt of recalibrating numerous modes and tropes of Othering.

Some might argue that *Lost*'s voice would have been more resolute if it simply started without Othering in the first place. Ultimately this might lose the value of the experience and of the journey, however. Newcomb and Hirsch wrote of *M*A*S*H* (20th Century Fox Television, 1972–83) that an explicitly and firmly anti-war episode in which the characters deserted and went home would have ended the story; having viewers continually experience the wartime suffering of its characters, though, produced a more lasting anti-war message.[21] Similarly, Patricia Mellencamp posits that *I Love Lucy*'s (Desilu, 1951–7) continued depiction of Lucy Ricardo's (Lucille Ball's) subjugation to her husband's (Desi Arnez's) petty insistence on confining her to the domestic sphere might have heightened the experience of injustice for the viewer.[22]

Both examples here point to television's ability to craft multi-season narratives that offer audiences an experiential message across the show's life. Yet both shows were generically trapped within a sitcom formula that limits progression. As a serial drama, *Lost* can develop. And whether individual audience members follow suit or not, the show offers viewers an experiential trip through processes of Othering, to contestation of those processes, to thorough interrogation of perspective. As Glen Creeber argues, one of television's greatest, if underused, powers is to use narrative hooks over significant time to pull a viewer through new perceptual, experiential terrain.[23] If *Lost*'s early previews suggested it would be a show about interacting with the unknown in an unknown place, the show has lived up to this, offering ideas on how to conceive of belonging, home, ownership, rights over place, the good and the bad, the known and the unknown, and the local and the foreign, in an era of globalization.

'WE HAVE TO GO BACK'

Precisely because *Lost* is a developing narrative, and I write this chapter halfway through its six-season life, its writers may yet add other kinks. Such kinks might revert to Othering, leaving much of the above to appear as a rather optimistically naive wish-exercise. Nor, let me reiterate, have the writers transcended Orientalizing tropes, as their depictions of place are still particularly Orientalized.[24] Nevertheless, season three ends on a note that particularly illuminates our understanding of the show's take on home, belonging and other people. Instead of the usual flashback, the final episode, 'Through the Looking Glass (2)' (3.23), delivers a flash-forward, to a lost and scarred Jack. We learn that one of the characters has died, and the fan freeze-framing of the obituary saying that the dead man is survived by a teenage son suggests it is Michael. The funeral occurs at a roadside parlour, and only Jack attends, albeit standing at the back. Later, Jack calls Kate and asks to see her, and the two meet by an airport runway at night. Frantically, fighting tears, he explains that he thinks they were wrong, and that they need to go back to the island.

If, as Juliet's first flashback episode title and my own title suggest, the Lostaways and the Others found themselves 'not in Portland', playfully alluding to Dorothy Gale's famous observation to Toto in *Wizard of Oz* (1939) that 'we're not in Kansas anymore', Jack's statement offers a radically different message than did Victor Fleming's famous film. Throughout the first three seasons, nobody has been clicking his or her heels louder than Jack. As a crashed-on-the-island story, *Lost* has a generic imperative towards returning 'home'. And with its increasing interest in time, and with its stark division between flashbacks from home and scenes from the now of the island, this move home is figured as temporal, not just spatial. But whereas *Wizard of Oz* initially gives Dorothy her wish to leave home, only to lead to her eventual desire to return home, season three ends by granting Jack's wish to return home, only for him to desperately want out. Jack's 'home' is a world of sterile funeral parlours with nobody in attendance, and of intense isolation and alienation. It seems he feels most comfortable at an airport, a clear symbol for transit and movement.

Season three ends with a poignant message for post-national television – that home is neither so simple, so warm and comfy, nor so immutable as national television broadcasting has long imaged and imagined it to be. As David Morley notes, 'home' was a central concept for national broadcasters. Broadcasters addressed most audiences in domestic spaces, giving them a significant vested interest in posing home as a safe refuge away from the worries and dangers of all that was not-home. Projected out to the macro-scale of the nation, many broadcasters saw it as their duty to create the nation as home.[25] As Stuart Hall argues of the BBC, it was 'an instrument, an apparatus, a "machine" through which the nation was constituted. It produced the nation which it addressed: it constituted its audience by the ways in which it represented them.'[26] And, as was argued at the outset of this chapter, the act of constructing the national home often involves creating crude characterizations of Others and other countries that posit them as inferior foils to the superiority of the national home and its people.

Yet in Lost, the liminal space of the island may be preferable to national homes that are depicted as no safe-havens to which to return. The island is not Portland, and is not the USA – or Australia, Korea, England, Iraq, France, Nigeria or Scotland – but it might be a better home, as many of the Flight 815 survivors have realized. Extrapolating beyond the individual programme, this message has macro-resonances. Lost has proven to be a rare instance of a US primetime drama set outside the USA. Yet season three's ending goes further, suggesting that the USA may not be the natural, best and only home, and that home might lie instead somewhere beyond the nation's borders and, as a result, beyond the former national broadcaster's conceptual borders, in a hybrid liminal space such as the island's residents have experienced. Thus while Lost has been guilty of dividing the world into binaries of Orient and Occident, ultimately 'home' exists outside this binary, as do the island and its inhabitants. For a primetime US television programme to offer such a message – or for any television programme to offer such a message, for that matter – represents an intriguing step forward towards a post-national television.

Notes

1   Lynn Spigel and Jan Olsson (eds), *Television After TV: Essays on a Medium in Transition* (Durham, NC: Duke University Press, 2004).

2   Amanda Lotz, *The Television Will Be Revolutionized* (New York: New York University Press, 2007).

3   See Chapter III; Jason Mittell, 'Narrative complexity in contemporary American television', *The Velvet Light Trap* lviii/1 (2006), pp.29–40; Jeffrey Sconce, 'What if? Charting television's new textual boundaries', in Spigel and Olsson (eds): *Television After TV*, pp.193–112.

4   See Lotz: *The Television Will Be Revolutionized*.

5   See Richard Butsch (ed.), *Media and Public Spheres* (Basingstoke: Palgrave, 2007).

6   See Jurgen Habermas, *The Structural Transformation of the Public Sphere: An Inquiry into a Category of Bourgeois Society*, trans. T. Burger (Cambridge: Polity, 1989).

7   See, for instance, Timothy Havens, *Global Television Marketplace* (London: BFI, 2006); Toby Miller, Nitin Govil, John McMurria and Richard Maxwell, *Global Hollywood 2* (London: BFI, 2005); Lisa Parks and Shanti Kumar (eds), *Planet TV: A Global Television Reader* (New York: New York University Press, 2003); and Daya Kishan Thussu (ed.), *Media on the Move: Global Flow and Contra-Flow* (London: Routledge, 2007).

8   BBC, 'CSI show "Most popular in world"', available online at *http://news. bbc.co.uk/2/hi/entertainment/5231334.stm*, 31 July 2006.

9   Edward W. Said, *Orientalism* (New York: Vintage, 1978), pp.40, 57.

10 Ibid., pp.42, 66.

11 Ibid., p.123.

12 David Richards, *Masks of Difference: Cultural Representations in Literature, Anthropology, and Art* (Cambridge: CUP, 1995).

13 Catherine A. Lutz and Jane L. Collins, *Reading National Geographic* (Chicago: University of Chicago Press, 1993).

14 William M. O'Barr, *Culture and the Ad: Exploring Otherness in the World of Advertising* (Boulder, CO: Westview, 1994).

15 M. Shahid Alam, *Challenging the New Orientalism: Dissenting Essays on the 'War Against Islam'* (North Haledon, NJ: Islamic Publications International, 2006).

16 John Hutnyk, 'Magical mystical tourism', in Raminder Kaur and John Hutnyk (eds), *Travel Worlds: Journeys in Contemporary Cultural Politics* (London: Zed, 1999), p.99; Sunaina Maira, 'Trance-formations: Orientalism and cosmopolitanism in youth culture', in Shilpa Dave, Leilani Nishime and Tasha Oren (eds), *East Main Street: Asian American Popular Culture* (New York: New York University Press, 2005).

17 John Hutnyk, *The Rumour of Calcutta: Tourism, Charity, and the Poverty of Representation* (London: Zed, 1996).

18 David Morley, *Home Territories: Media, Mobility and Identity* (London: Routledge, 2000).

19 Chinua Achebe, 'An image of Africa: racism in Conrad's *Heart of Darkness*', in Bart Moore-Gilbert, Gareth Stanton and William Malley (eds), *Postcolonial Criticism* (London: Longman, 1997), p.118.

20 Julia Kristeva and Homi Bhabha, both quoted in Morley: *Home Territories*, pp.222, 265.

21 Horace Newcomb and Paul Hirsch, 'Television as a cultural forum: implications for research', in W. Rowland, Jr and B. Watkins (eds), *Interpreting Television: Current Research Perspectives* (Thousand Oaks, CA: Sage, 1984), pp.58–73.

22 Patricia Mellencamp, 'Situation comedy, feminism, and Freud: discourses of Gracie and Lucy', in Joanne Morreale (ed.), *Critiquing the Sitcom* (Syracuse: Syracuse University Press, 2003), p.49.

23 See Glen Creeber, *Serial Television: Big Drama on the Small Screen* (London: BFI, 2004).

24 Moreover, while I find the multi-season interrogation of Othering impressive, this interrogation could have been considerably more meaningful if the Others were at least multinational and multiracial, thereby requiring viewers to connect Othering to Orientalism and to age-old scripts of national and racial chauvinism.

25 See Morley: *Home Territories*.

26 Stuart Hall, 'Which public, whose service?', in Wilf Stevenson (ed.), *All Our Futures: The Changing Role and Purpose of the BBC* (London: BFI, 1993), p.32.

XIII. 'A Fabricated Africanist Persona':

Race, Representation and Narrative Experimentation in Lost

Celeste-Marie Bernier

In the early 1990s, the African American writer Toni Morrison vehemently opposed the view that 'traditional, canonical American literature is free of, uninformed, and unshaped by the four-hundred-year-old presence of, first, Africans and then African-Americans in the United States'.[1] She took this cultural, historical and literary erasure of a black presence to task in *Playing in the Dark: Whiteness and the Literary Imagination*. In her book-length essay, Morrison suggested that the

> fabrication of an Africanist persona is reflexive; an extraordinary meditation on the self; a powerful exploration of the fears and desires that reside in the writerly conscious ... It is an astonishing revelation of longing, of terror, of perplexity, of shame, of magnanimity ... It requires hard work *not* to see this.[2]

Morrison's examination of the ways in which European works of American literature are haunted by an African presence can be mapped onto the relationship between race and narrative structure in *Lost*. By drawing on her identification of the presence of a 'fabricated Africanist persona' in American literature in this essay, it becomes possible to investigate the ways in which Africa, slavery and race are thematically, metaphorically and structurally embedded in the psychological odysseys that constitute the drama, horror and tensions of this television series.

In her critical analysis, Morrison sheds light on the ways in which the creators of *Lost* subvert, at the same time as they frequently re-inscribe, artificial boundaries of racial, national, class and gender differences. Moreover, her emphasis upon the fact that white definitions of an 'Africanist persona' are always 'fabricated' introduces important issues surrounding myth, fantasy, projection and illusion when it comes to understanding the representation of African and African American characters in *Lost*. In this chapter, I examine the characters' discovery of a buried slave ship, *The Black Rock*, as well as a Nigerian drug runner's plane, to analyse the ways in which the island provides visceral reminders of African and African American histories of European colonization and slavery. By discovering these artefacts towards the end of the first series, the castaways experience the realities of buried African and African American histories. In the same way that distorted narratives of black suffering resurface in a guilt-ridden Western consciousness, the survivors suffer from psychological breakdowns caused by suppressed fragments of memory. They are compelled to relive their pasts to liberate themselves from the emotional fetters of their previous lives. In this chapter I also provide in-depth readings of the African gang-leader-turned-priest, Mr Eko (Adewale Akinnuoye-Agjabe) and his relationship with white American John Locke (Terry O'Quinn), to explore specific issues related to race, identity and stereotyping.

One of the main concerns of this chapter is to investigate the ambiguities and paradoxes presented by the inextricable relationship between race and narrative experimentation in this series. Toni Morrison's discussion of the ways in which 'a breakdown in the logic and machinery of plot construction implies the powerful impact race has on narrative – and on narrative strategy' is relevant for an investigation into *Lost*'s complex and unresolved storytelling structures.[3] By layering the present and the past, *Lost* effaces temporal differences to highlight emotional continuities. If the underlying themes of this series can be summarised, then they consist of a preoccupation with the inescapability of each characters' previous lives, which exist in a fraught continuum of past and present. As J.M. Berger argues, 'past and present are not distinctly separated – and *Lost*'s most compelling stories often stem from unusual transactions between the two timelines'.[4]

In this series, the hidden histories and 'lost' testimonies of shackled African slaves haunt the survivors' personal quests for self-discovery and freedom. Individuals remain socially and psychologically shackled within the moral schema of *Lost* as long as there are 'Others' suffering from injustice, prejudice and discrimination. Thus, as is the case for many canonical American writers, for the creators of this series the relationship between self and other is racially coded. Juxtapositions of African and African American with European identities throughout *Lost* accentuate, at the same time that they elide, hierarchies of race, nationhood, power and difference. The buried and resurfacing histories of African and African American slavery and colonialism play a fundamental role in the narrative structure of *Lost*. Toni Morrison's concept of a 'fabricated Africanist persona' operates as a self-reflexive touchstone for European and European American explorations of self-hood throughout the series.

Although initial readings of *Lost* may suggest that the series conforms to stereotypes of racial identities and national differences, this is far from the case. While the series plays with caricature and dramatises scenarios which exalt in fantasies of racial difference, these problematic aspects break down at the level of narrative. Just as histories of African and African American slavery have variously been torn apart, denied, erased, marginalised and fragmented, so too do the characters in *Lost* experience dislocation, denial and ellipses in tortured attempts to get to grips with the repressed dimensions of their own personal narratives. As the introduction of anachronistic slave ships and planes suggests, the creators of *Lost* rewrite colonialist and slave-owning histories by redefining Western binaries of civilisation versus savagery.

This series debates polemical issues concerning society and the individual, class hierarchies and power relationships, political freedom, violence, race, nationhood, religion and difference. These themes complicate the already ruptured and multi-directional narrative trajectories of *Lost*, which functions as a post-modern pastiche overflowing with literary allusions and literary, philosophical, and religious intertexts. Thus, these characters' quest for spiritual redemption, physical rescue and psychic renewal testify to similarities between the creators of this twenty-first-century television series and the conviction of nineteenth-century philosopher, Ralph Waldo Emerson that, 'No man at last believes that he can be lost.'[5]

'THE DARK TERRITORY':
SLAVERY, AFRICA AND BURIED ARTEFACTS

'Slaves', whispers John Locke in the concluding episode of the first season of *Lost*, which ends unexpectedly in the discovery of a nine-teenth-century slave ship buried deep in the island's wilderness. In the second part of the finale, 'Exodus' (1.24), characters and audiences are surprised to learn that *The Black Rock* is not a geological landmark but a marooned slave ship. As Jack Shepard (Matthew Fox), John Locke and Kate Austen (Evangeline Lilly) walk amidst shackled skeletons, box-manufacturer-turned-hunter-and-spiritual-leader, Locke, hits his head on hanging chains before explaining, 'This ship must have been en route to a mining colony – probably set off from the eastern coast of Africa – Mozambique.' The stage is set for the discovery of a slave ship even before they begin their journey towards *The Black Rock* when French castaway Danielle Rousseau (Mira Furlan) reveals that its loca-tion is 'in the dark territory'. In Part One of 'Exodus', they find a piece of black cloth hanging from a tree. As Rousseau explains, they have entered, 'Le Territoire Fonce', which Jack translates as, 'The Dark Ter-ritory'. She warns, 'The Black Rock is not far. This is where it all began – where my team got infected – where Montan lost his arm. We must move quickly.' Almost immediately, the creators of *Lost* establish this slave ship as a source of disease, death, mutilation and trauma in its associations with unknown racial 'others'.

By evoking racialised terms such as 'the dark territory', the slave ship resonates with European definitions of Africa as the 'Dark Conti-nent'. The fact that this vessel is the site at which Rousseau's 'Montan lost his arm' further accentuates the ship's and, by extension, slavery's significance as a threat to Western civilisation and humanity. This ar-tefact also symbolises the ways in which Africa exists in the French and American imagination as something unknown, fearful and de-structive. As such, the slave ship and the island on which it is found are implicated in histories of colonialism, slavery and brutal conflicts between so-called 'civilised' and 'savage' peoples. The seemingly im-possible appearance of a historical artefact on the island, a geographi-cal no-place, offers a tangible embodiment of the horrors of the 'Af-rican holocaust' or Middle Passage by which 13 million or more were captured and transported from Africa to the Americas. Moreover, the presence of a slave ship makes it impossible for either the characters or viewers of *Lost* to lose themselves in national fantasies of new beginnings unbesmirched by the sins of the past. Just as the Puritans' America of the seventeenth century was no *tabula rasa*, the island populated by the crash survivors is as fraught with issues of colonialism, nationhood, race, difference and military conflicts for power.

By relying on a fragmented, cyclical, and elliptical narrative framework, this series dramatises the ways in which hidden histories of racial difference and legacies of amnesia, as perpetuated by dominant groups, can impact upon the personal psychological journeys of individuals, regardless of historical period or national origins. In the same way that any attempts to remember slavery must negotiate the silences of buried testimonies in order to unearth elided traumas, characters in *Lost* similarly rely on disjointed fragments of memory to piece together their unfinished histories. For the fictional survivors of this series, the only way to heal is by a visceral and emotional return to sites of suffering and commemoration. Resurfacing memories and fragmented narratives which haunt individual characters' inner lives can be mapped directly onto theoretical discussions of the ways in which the history and memory of slavery haunts Western consciousness.

The tribal drums which accompany Jack's, Locke's, Kate's, Hurley's (Jorge Garcia's) and Arzt's (Daniel Roebuck's) first glimpse of the mysterious slave ship accentuate fears of difference and otherness for the all-white group. A dumbfounded and fearful Arzt refuses to step aboard, calling this wreck 'a ghost ship'. In so doing, he signals key themes concerning death, haunting and memory that surround not only the slave ship but also the series as a whole. Arzt's determination not to confront the ship fails to save him, however, as the dynamite excavated from its hold brutally ends his life. His death offers further proof that the characters in this series can only find redemption on the island – in this case, the dynamite that will unlock the 'hatch' – as a result of human sacrifice. His loss of life also communicates an underlying conviction of the series that a fear of difference is frequently punishable by death. Regardless of their national and racial origins or their identities as castaways, 'Hostiles' or 'Others', characters in *Lost* must traverse boundaries of difference to confront their pasts and prejudices and to achieve greater self-understanding.

Following Jack's lead, Locke and Kate enter the ship's dark hold accompanied by the sounds of screeching birds and clanking chains. Locke hits his head on chains suspended from above while Jack hears a crunch beneath his foot and shines his flashlight to reveal a fragment of bone. He then pans the torch upwards to illuminate a human skeleton fettered to the side of the ship with hands held to its mouth, as if in terror. His flashlight reveals a row of skeletons, shackled side by side in a gross parody of the castaways' own earlier experience as passengers seated in rows prior to the plane crash. This visual echo or thematic juxtaposition collapses not only racial and national boundaries but also temporal frames to invite parallels between those on the plane and those on the slave ship. Suggesting that the contemporary international community of crash survivors are in any way similar to rows of shackled Africans from the past draws attention to a key feature of the narrative structure in *Lost*. The physical and psychological enslavement of Africans who were forced into captivity during the 'African holocaust' of slavery can be mapped onto each characters' search for freedom on the island. The narrative structure of this series privileges flashbacks and an unsettling interweaving of past, present and future to communicate the ways in which hidden histories and fractured testimonies are structurally embedded in the construction of *Lost*. Just as a history of slavery and colonialism is repeatedly erased, denied, marginalised or distorted, the lives of the castaways and 'Others' are similarly fraught with omissions and repressions.

In 'Exodus' (1.24), Rousseau's telling words that 'This is where it all began' locates the slave ship in the island's imaginary as a point of origin or genesis as well as the locus of death and destruction. It is no coincidence that this ship houses the dynamite that explodes the doorway to the hatch, a symbol of individual and collective freedom, as well as coming moral struggles in an ongoing fight for survival. Towards the end of season three, Jack rejects attempts to negotiate with the 'Others' by relishing instead in military domination via a vengeful use of dynamite from the slave ship. As he proclaims in 'Greatest Hits' (3.21), it is time to 'stop living in fear of them. Because when they show up, we're gonna blow 'em all to hell.' Far from the Old Testament prophet Moses, or the Western man of reason, Jack becomes synonymous with acts of senseless savagery in the defence of one so-called civilisation against an 'Other'. By focusing on Jack's vengeful use of violence and superior assumption that the 'Others' are destined for damnation, the creators of *Lost* critique the moral superiority of the survivors' society. As Scottish monk-turned-visionary saviour of the world, Desmond (Henry Ian Cusick), observes to ex-heroin addict, Charlie (Dominic Monaghan), 'You know brother, by my count, you've killed more of them than they've killed of you' ('D.O.C.', 3.18). As a repository of fettered skeletons and dynamite, the slave ship testifies to guilt-ridden histories which expose the moral relativism of racial terrorism and war.

The discovery of the nineteenth-century slave ship, *The Black Rock*, at the end of the first season is not the only way in which issues of Africa and race haunt this island. In this first series, Locke and Boone (Ian Somerhalder), significantly dubbed 'Captain America' by his half-sister, Shannon (Maggie Grace), locate a Nigerian aeroplane. In contrast to the slave ship, this aircraft houses both skeletal remains and a drug-runner's cargo, which consists of heroin bags secreted in statues of the Virgin Mary. This wreck is not buried in the wilderness but hangs precariously above the hatch, initially a symbol of the survivors' promise of freedom but eventually a testing ground for the characters' belief in fate versus free will. In the discovery of a Nigerian plane, the creators of *Lost* juxtapose African economic, spiritual and physical enslavement to poverty, drugs and corruption with a 'hatch' that seems to hold the promise of Western freedom. On first viewing it seems that this plane operates problematically as a site not of black cultural exploration but of white sacrifice. A pacifist and all-round selfless figure, Boone as 'Captain America', a national symbol of US identity, dies in attempts to board the plane and send out a distress signal on its radio transmitter. In contrast to Arzt's anti-heroic demise, Boone's death is weighted with heavy symbolism to suggest his martyrdom. The fact that this plane had previously been unveiled to Locke in a vision compounds its initial significance as a springboard for European American explorations of self.

On the surface, discoveries of both the slave ship and the plane suggest *Lost*'s endorsement of popular representations of broken, black bodies only insofar as they act as catalysts for white redemption. Sites such as the slave ship and Nigerian plane appear to be rewritten in white European terms by operating as signifiers of Western colonialism and appropriation. Thus, just as the discovery of the slave ship privileges white struggles for freedom against the 'Others' in the search for dynamite with which to conquer a competing civilisation, the African plane similarly communicates stories of white Christian martyrdom rather than of black sacrifice. For example, the sacrificial death of the white American hero, Boone, is problematically juxtaposed with an unknown and unnamed African 'other' represented by the skeleton retrieved from the plane.

This is far from the whole story as it can be argued that the slave ship, which provides the dynamite by which one predominantly white group dominates another, and the plane, which supplies heroin concealed in statues of the Holy Virgin, both critique Western pretensions to civilisation. These artefacts offer physical proof that new nations emerge on the island, not as a result of civilised exchange and cultural cross-fertilisation, but because of imperial domination through war and myths of moral and religious superiority. Even more significantly, the extended serial narrative of *Lost* accentuates loss, mutilation, repression, memory and trauma to mitigate against oversimplified interpretations. The creators of this series open up rather than close down discussions of the impact of race on narrative structure by relying on open-ended and fragmented storytelling techniques that privilege ellipsis over and above explication. In the same way that the physical artefacts of slavery and colonialism operate as touchstones for untold histories, flashbacks reveal the internal lives of individuals to establish their need to exorcise repressed memories and come to terms with their respective pasts. As this series proves, it is the process of working through emotions that produces personal epiphanies, moral transformations and the ability to empathise with those of different national, racial, gender and class backgrounds.

While the slave ship and the plane operate as signifiers of both white death and destruction, they also carry the potential for the liberation of elided Western histories of African annihilation and destruction. The physical manifestation of a slave ship and an African drug-runners' plane offers the survivors the opportunity to learn from the lessons of colonialism and slavery. Both operate as altars of black sacrifice that whites can visit to atone for their sins. However, they can only gain redemption for their guilt if they know how to read these untold narratives. In the case of *The Black Rock*, countless skeletons bear witness to the horrors of Western civilised nations who sought to enslave Africans in dehumanising labour systems for their own aggrandisement. Similarly, Yemi's (Adetokumboh M'Cormack's) skeletal remains aboard the Nigerian plane testify to Western pillaging of African countries in the twentieth century. His ghostly presence on the island offers moral direction for his spiritually and morally 'lost' brother, Mr Eko. Ultimately, Boone's death sets the stage not for white redemption but for the recovery of hidden African legacies by excavating the plane which connects the histories of Yemi and Mr Eko.

The characters' discovery of a slave ship and Nigerian plane in the island's wilderness subscribes to Morrison's examination of the ways in which 'a breakdown in the logic and machinery of plot construction implies the powerful impact race has on narrative – and on narrative strategy'.[6] *Lost*'s overall structure betrays the impact of race by relying on fragmented narratives and an experimental storytelling structure which rupture linear teleologies of progress to reveal the savagery within so-called 'civilised' societies. The decision on the part of the producers to juxtapose John Locke's discovery of the hatch with Danielle Rousseau's unearthing of a slave ship, brimful of fettered skeletons, symbolises many of the conflicts and paradoxes of *Lost*.

By dramatising the lives of characters held captive in a fictional, mythic and imaginary place that is both real and unreal, this series examines themes of slavery and freedom, self and other, civilisation and savagery, society and anarchy, fate and faith, redemption and loss, belief and disbelief, sin and salvation. As J.M. Berger argues, 'they are caught in a strange nether place outside the realm of linear time where memory cannot be escaped – but neither can it be ignored'.[7] This series follows the characters' search for freedom from the sins and sorrows of their pasts as a result of which they have all experienced enslavement of some kind, whether it is to crime, terminal illness, physical disability, drug abuse, alcoholism, depression, murder, grief, unexpected pregnancy, work, marriage, family honour, war or government corruption. One of the key preoccupations of *Lost* concerns the ways in which characters simultaneously deny and confront their sense of psychological, moral or emotional enslavement in traumatic acts of remembering and forgetting.

'I AM A SLAVE TO NOTHING': SLAVERY, MEMORY AND IDENTITY

Toni Morrison's understanding that the 'fabrication of an Africanist persona is reflexive' is useful for understanding the ways in which mythologies of black and white identities and cultures are inextricably intertwined in this series. These relationships are far from straightforward as European, African and African American histories are characterised by slippage, distortion and confrontation. *Lost* blurs the boundaries between self and other, black and white, slave and free, lost and found to contest hierarchies of power and problematise racist biases in Western value systems. The creators counter tendencies towards eulogies of white martyrdom in the sacrificial death of 'Captain America' by introducing African drug-dealer and killer-turned-priest, Mr Eko, and his devout brother, Yemi, in the second series.

Both characters represent complex African religious belief systems which counter stereotyped representations of African American Christianity as represented by passive victim, Rose (L. Scott Caldwell). She encapsulates a history of suffering black womanhood in statements to Charlie such as, 'You think you're the only one on this island that's got something to be sad about? Baby, I got sob stories for you' ('Whatever the Case May Be', 1.12). When Charlie pleads with her, 'Help me,' Rose answers him with a prayer, 'I'm not the one that can help you. Heavenly father, we thank you.' These scenes privileging an African American woman's spirituality in the face of white British male scepticism support racist associations of black womanhood with a simplified black religiosity. In contrast, however, characterisations of Mr Eko as having the capacity for both vengeance and self-sacrifice mitigate against this portrayal. Thus, in comparison with Rose, who prays for redemption, Eko registers his temptations by etching the word 'hateth' onto a carved wooden stick on which he inscribes biblical verse and 'Things I need to remember' ('The 23rd Psalm', 2.10). As a way of reconciling the realities of his past, this object operates as a talisman of protest as well as a touchstone for memory.

Nonetheless, representations of Eko initially seem to subscribe to stereotypical notions of a passive, devout African male, particularly given his confession to Ben (Michael Emerson), the leader of the Others. As he explains:

I was dragged into the jungle by two men ... I killed these men – smashed in their head with a stone, felt their blood on my arms ... I regret my actions. I ask you for your forgiveness. ('Maternity Leave', 2.15)

On the surface, this scene provides a stereotypical vision of a murderous bestial black man seeking redemption from a civilised white man. However, this view is soon undermined, not only when we consider that Ben is an 'Other', but also when we examine Eko's confession in connection with his later refusal to ask the ghost of his dead brother, Yemi, for forgiveness. Eko asks Yemi's ghost:

Have you forgotten how you got that cross, brother, the day they took me? Is what I did that day a sin? Or is it forgiven because you were saved? ... I understand that you live in a world where righteousness and evil seem very far apart, but that is not the real world.' (2.10)

Remembering the day in which he shot another man to save his brother's soul, Eko's questioning of sin, salvation and forgiveness interrogates the absolute truths of the Old Testament in a fight for free will in the face of prescriptive religious dogmas. Eko addresses a major theme of *Lost* by questioning the reliability of absolute moral judgements and opening up a space for human fallibility in the justification of seemingly immoral acts for a greater moral good.

Eko's belief in the innocence of his actions establishes his internal ambiguities that counter racist polarisations of Africans and African Americans as either religious saints or vengeful barbarians. Moreover, his critique of authoritative religion and narrow definitions of good and evil provide an alternative way in which to recover the moral complexities of individuals and their personal narratives. Thus, Eko's murder of another man to save his brother helps to redeem African American artist and construction-worker Michael's (Harold Perrineau) killing of Ana-Lucia (Michelle Rodriguez) and Libby (Cynthia Watros) in the hopes of saving his son, Walt (Malcolm David Kelley). The ambiguous actions of African and African American characters such as Eko and Michael have implications for many of the larger issues surrounding individual agency and fate versus free will, which preoccupy *Lost* as a whole. The creators of this series overturn stereotypes of black savagery to examine inhumane systems of colonialism and slavery that create corrupt, lawless African societies at the same time as they tear apart African and African American families.

In a scene which takes place in the hatch in '?' (2.21) of the second series, Eko introduces a key concept of *Lost* concerning the fact that individuals must be 'tested' before earning their right to salvation. While John Locke suffers a crisis of faith as he despairs of his 'pathetic little life' and claims that their decision to push the button in the hatch means that they are 'rats in a maze with no cheese', Eko reassures him: 'It is work, John, we are being tested.' 'Yemi was a great man, a priest, a man of God. And because I betrayed him he was shot and died,' he insists:

> And somehow, here, I found my brother again. I found him in the same plane that took off from Nigeria. In the same plane that lies above us now – that has concealed this place. And I took this cross from around Yemi's neck and put it back on mine, just as it was on the day I first took another man's life. So let me ask you – how can you say this is meaningless?

Eko's recovery of his brother's body adorned by his own crucifix reconnects him to his past innocence and offers him a chance for spiritual, emotional and moral rebirth.

As Rose offers Charlie succour for his sorrows, Eko at first seems to play the stereotypical role of African spiritual foil to Western rationalism and scepticism. In 'Live Together, Die Alone' (2.23), Locke is paralysed by a crisis of faith and attempts to superimpose his own beliefs onto Eko:

Eko:	... I am going to push the button. Why wouldn't I?
Locke:	Because you don't want to be a slave.
Eko:	I am a slave to nothing.
Locke:	You're a slave to that, just like I was. So I'm going to tell you again – don't push it.
Eko:	Do not tell me what I can do.
Locke:	No, it's not real. We're only puppets – puppets on strings. As long as we push it, we'll never be free.

Eko's bold declaration of independence, 'I am a slave to nothing', undermines Locke's attempts to dismiss black spirituality and circumscribe free will by insisting 'you don't want to be a slave'. His steadfast rejection of the term 'slave' resurrects hundreds of years of African and African American history by evoking inequities of white and black power relationships during transatlantic slavery. However, traditional racist dynamics are divested of their power on this island as Eko resists rather than succumbs to Locke's white Western imperialism by appropriating his language to subvert the inequities of the master–slave relationships. As symbolised by the complex relationship between Eko and Locke, African manhood does not provide a platform for white redemption but instead offers a conduit to black liberation and agency.

By including Eko's unwitting repetition of Locke's mantra 'Do not tell me what I can do' in his declaration of independence from a white-imposed state of slavery, the writers of *Lost* collapse barriers of racial, national and religious difference. As Porter and Lavery argue, '*Lost*'s successful storytelling is its ability to layer meanings into simple dialogue; the words can take on different meanings for different members of its audience.'[8] Divisions generated by classist, racist, sexist or nationalist assumptions fall apart in the face of the empathy generated by shared human experience. The interrelated sufferings of Eko and Locke demonstrate the ways in which individual identities merge as they are reinvented and reconstructed on the island from their contact with one another. Eko's statement to Locke, 'Do not tell me what I can do', signifies Locke's fight for freedom from physical and emotional paralysis throughout the series. As early as 'Walkabout' (4.1), Locke tells the organiser of a 'walkabout' or 'journey of spiritual renewal', 'Don't ever tell me what I can't do. Ever. This was my Destiny. I was supposed to do this.' Similarly, in a much later conversation with Boone following their excavation of the 'hatch', Locke again refuses to heed any warnings by arguing, 'Don't tell me what I can and can't do ... We're supposed to find this' ('Deux Ex Machina', 1.19).

In a powerful *volte face*, Locke is forced into the position of the abject slave or victim. His disability is as physically and psychologically damaging in this instance as racist prejudice. This is no less the case in flashbacks that reveal his exploitation as a worker in a box company where he is bullied by his manager. It is Locke's sense of marginalisation and disempowerment that lies at the heart of his psychological paralysis and his need to embark on his 'own journey' at the end of season three ('The Brig', 3.19). Clearly, the relationship between

Eko and Locke in this scene is far more complex than it first appears. Locke's confession, 'You're a slave to that, just like I was', rejects racial hierarchies by appealing to Eko on the grounds of their shared slavery: 'As long as we push it, we'll never be free.' While Locke's sense that they are united in a common plight mitigates against histories of racialized slavery, his search for absolution for his sins adheres much more to conventional paradigms of racial difference. 'Sorry I gave up on my faith in the island,' Locke confesses to Eko. He admits, 'I messed up. Now our people are captured – if I'd just listened to you – if I'd just let you keep pushing the button, I could have gone with them, protected them. I could have saved them' ('Further Instructions', 3.3). As seemingly stereotypical black spiritual leader, Eko's absolution of the white man's sins constitutes a spiritual reprieve, 'You can still protect them.' It is not long after this scene that Eko dies, placing the emphasis on Locke to work out why the 'island killed him'. As he explains, 'Eko died for a reason. I just don't know what it is yet' ('I Do', 3.6).

Initial readings suggest that it is the black man's death and subsequent martyrdom that resuscitates the white man's faith. According to this view, Eko's death returns viewers to Boone's sacrificial death at the end of the first season to demonstrate how white lessons of Christian morality are still inscribed on the back of black suffering and sacrifice. However, if Porter and Lavery's sense that, 'these characters provide a mirror of international and interpersonal relationship in the larger world' holds true, then this series supports inequities of race and popular stereotyping only insofar as the creators dramatise ongoing injustices perpetuated within white mainstream racist discourse and dominant histories.[9] Set in a mythical space, but no less haunted by the inequalities and prejudices of the 'real world', the island examines the ways in which the characters must fight to liberate themselves from artificially created hierarchies of race, gender, class and nationality.

Contrary to these problematic associations, characterisations of Eko ultimately fail to adhere to racist stereotypes as he is neither the noble, heroic, self-sacrificing, black martyr nor the bestial, violent and murderous African savage of popular white racist mythology. Furthermore, his irreconciled internal contradictions, moral ambiguities and psychological complexities counter oversimplified constructions of what Morrison defines as a 'fabricated Africanist persona' in white mainstream culture. Eko's character is far from the fantasies of blackness popularly projected by ignorant whites in mainstream culture. Instead, he is an emotionally complex and psychologically profound individual whose actions are unpredictable and difficult to read. While he asks for forgiveness for the 'Others' he has slain, Eko refuses to acknowledge his murder of a man in Africa so that his brother may be saved, on the grounds that he willingly chose to sacrifice his own soul so that his 'brother's life' might be redeemed. In answer to Yemi's insistence that, 'It is time to confess. To be judged, brother', Eko states, 'I ask for no forgiveness, Father, for I have not sinned. I have only done what I need to do to survive ... I killed a man to save my brother's life' ('The Cost of Living', 3.5).

By showing the various ways in which Locke and many of the other characters experience states of emotional, psychological, sexual and even physical captivity, the writers of *Lost* displace associations of histories of racial terrorism and subjugation with spectacles of violated black bodies. Broken and physically mutilated in death Eko may be, but his spirit lives to challenge the religious schema of the island. The moral universe of *Lost*, according to which insubordinate African masculinity is punishable by death, provides a political commentary on wider historical and contemporary injustices. These and other racial tensions prove that socially ingrained cultural prejudices and racist assumptions survive on the island as unchallenged as with the characters' flawed and troubled lives before the crash. It is these terrible legacies with which they must contend in order to resist internal contradictions and obtain emotional closure.

In this context, the narration of the ambiguities and ambivalences embedded within Eko's character can be extended to consider the ways in which the writers rely on flashbacks and complex storytelling structures to examine the difficult relationships across other racial groups. Eko's earlier exchange with Locke sheds light on relationships between the white Southerner, Sawyer (Josh Holloway), and the Iraqi soldier, Sayid (Naveen Andrews), and between the Korean fisherman, Jin (Daniel Dae Kim), and the African American artist/construction worker, Michael. However mystical and fantastical it may be, the writers successfully establish that the island is as fettered in racial prejudice and power struggles as the 'real world'.

RESURFACING HISTORIES AND A
RETURN TO THE BLACK ROCK

In 'The Brig' (3.19), the slave ship assumes centre stage by bearing witness to the execution of one white Southern man by another before a
macabre audience of shackled skeletons. In contrast to earlier scenes
aboard this vessel, the flashlight reveals only one shackled skeleton as
Sawyer and Locke enter the dark hold of *The Black Rock*, while Locke
whispers the same explanation from before, 'It's an old slaving ship,
mid-nineteenth century.' This time the focus is not on the enslavement of African bodies but on the psychological captivity of the white
southern 'redneck', Sawyer, and box worker, Locke. By depicting both
characters through the vertical and horizontal bars of an overheard
grill, the camera dramatises their ongoing moral and psychological
enslavement. The writers go so far as to suggest that it is Locke and
Sawyer's inability to confront their troubled histories which led to the
visceral reincarnation of Locke's father, Cooper (Kevin Tighe) – also
responsible for the killings of Sawyer's parents – on the island. In this
episode, viewers and characters are confronted not only with artefacts
from the past but with the physical manifestation of a living relic from
their own personal biographies. It is significant that it is the white
southerner, Sawyer, the closest the island has to an emblem for an
American slaveholding tradition, who acts as the executioner of another white southerner and conman.

In a chilling moment aboard *The Black Rock*, Sawyer stands over an
unrepentant Cooper and strangles him with iron fetters while scream-
ing, 'You wanna got to hell, you wanna go to hell?' Cooper's murder
at Sawyer's hands reveals the heavy cost of repressed memories,
his inability to come to terms with his past ensuring his perpetual
slavery by participating in endless cycles of violence. As a site of black
suffering, it is fitting that *The Black Rock* bears witness to white ritu-
alised killings in the annihilation of both the physical body and the
spirituality of the soul. As is the case elsewhere in *Lost*, it is the series'
capacity for what Jason Mittel describes as 'storytelling spectacles'
that generates dramatic tension as characters negotiate their physical,
social and psychological shackles.[10]

It is no coincidence that at the moment in which Locke stands
guard and ignores Sawyer's pleas to be released from his imprison-

ment in the slave ship hold with Cooper, Rousseau enters the slave ship in search of dynamite. In this scene, the white southerner remains at the mercy of European Old World morality as symbolised by the two philosophers, Jean-Jacques Rousseau and John Locke, the characters' namesakes. Locke's warning that Rousseau should be 'careful' because 'it's unstable' not only reflects his own psychological instability, but also the morally problematic reasons for Rousseau's search for the dynamite. Whereas the hunt for explosives on *The Black Rock* in the first series was motivated by the desire to open up the 'hatch', a portal promising freedom, towards the end of the third season of *Lost*, the sticks of dynamite aboard the slave ship are wielded as weapons of destruction to exterminate the 'Others'.

As early as the 'Pilot' (1.2) of the first series, John Locke tells Walt that:

> Backgammon is the oldest game in the world … 5000 years old, that's older than Jesus Christ … Their dice weren't made of plastic, their dice were made of bones. Two players, two sides, one is light, one is dark.

Locke's emphasis upon a racially coded conflict between 'light' and 'dark' or, as the counters he holds to the camera show, between black and white, betrays the ways in which themes of race, representation and identity are thematically integral to this series. His grisly emphasis upon ancient dice 'made of bones' resonates with the later discovery of skeletal remains and dynamite aboard *The Black Rock* to accentuate visceral connections between racialised bodies and histories of violence. However, his faith in a dichotomous morality, as he describes 'Two players, two sides, one is light, one is dark', soon proves illusory as categories of black and white, good and evil, slave and free, blur, shift and are transformed throughout all three seasons of *Lost*.

Michael O'Shaughnessy's understanding that 'popular culture in general and television in particular are contradictory sites' which possess 'oppositional possibilities' provides a very apt summary of the racial complexities and narrative ambiguities of *Lost*.[11] As Boone insists, 'Everybody's got a story' ('Deus Ex Machina', 1.19). The advice of white medical doctor and fount of reason, Jack, that 'It doesn't matter … Who we were, what we did before this … Three days ago we all died. We should all be able to start over' is soon shown to be flawed. It is no

accident that Jack states this in an episode titled 'Tabula Rasa' (1.3), a
concept popular among Puritans who had fled religious persecution in
Europe and settled in the Americas in the seventeenth century. Desperate to see this 'new found land' as a blank slate, they erased thousands of years of Native American history in the interests of bloody
conquest and territorial expansion.

By highlighting the limitations of Western knowledge through
Jack, a symbol of white progress and science, the creators of *Lost* reveal their determination to insert denied testimonies into otherwise
dominant mythologies of Western civilisation. As the slippery charac-
terisation and ambiguous narrative structures of this series demonstrate, it is the illusory attempts by white men of reason such as Jack
to erase histories which leads to national amnesia, racial terrorism and
the resurfacing of trauma. As Locke warns chef-turned-murderer and
diamond stealer, Paulo, in the third season: 'Things don't stay buried
on this island' ('Exposé', 3.14). In the same way that the artefacts of
slavery cannot be 'buried', the characters will stay 'enslaved' to their
personal autobiographies if they refuse to unearth their pasts.

As Lynette Porter and David Lavery argue, '"Lost" as a descriptor
also can apply to the viewing audience', given that we live in a 'pre-
carious post-millennium, post-9/11 world' in which 'Dichotomies are
deepening, dividing one religion against another, one political party
against another, one country against another, one worldview against
another.'[12] The struggle of characters to reach across emotional, physical and racial divides in this series can indeed be mapped onto contemporary injustices, tensions and conflicts. Porter and Lavery's discussion of the relevance of a 'post-9/11 world' betrays the biases and
prejudices of a Western perspective that haunts the creators of this
series as they struggle to undermine problematic representations of
non-white cultures in the elided histories of racial 'others'.

In this context, Morrison's view that, 'the imagination and historical terrain upon which early American writers journeyed is in
large measure shaped by the presence of the racial other' is relevant
to *Lost*, in which tensions of otherness, discrimination and prejudice
play out with little promise of resolution or reconciliation.[13] This series thoughtfully examines the blurred boundaries between slavery
and freedom as expressed centuries before in the political treatises
of the eighteenth-century French philosopher and revolutionary,

Jean-Jacques Rousseau. *Lost*'s creators share Rousseau's conviction that, 'MAN was born free and he is everywhere in chains. Those who think themselves the masters of others are indeed greater slaves than they.'[14]

Notes

I would like to thank Roberta Pearson for her editorial vision. I would also like to acknowledge invaluable academic advice from Mark Gallagher, Paul Grainge, Andy Green, Lisa Rull and Julian Stringer.

1   Toni Morrison, *Playing in the Dark: Whiteness and the Literary Imagination* (Cambridge: Harvard University Press, 1993), pp.4–5.

2   Ibid., p.17.

3   Ibid., p.25.

4   J.M. Berger, 'Flashbacks, memory and non-linear time', *Lost Online Studies* i/2, available at *www.loststudies.com/1.2/index.html*.

5   Ralph Waldo Emerson, 'Experience', in Richard Poirier (ed.), *Ralph Waldo Emerson* (Oxford: OUP, 1990), p.231.

6   Morrison: *Playing in the Dark*, p.25.

7   Berger: 'Flashbacks, memory and non-linear time'.

8   Lynnette Porter and David Lavery: *Unlocking the Meaning of Lost: an Unauthorized Guide* (Naperville: Sourcebooks, 2006), p.101.

9   Porter and Lavery: *Unlocking the Meaning of Lost*, p.58.

10   Jason Mittel, 'The value of *Lost* part two', *Flow-TV* ii/10, available online at *www.mtv.com/movies/news/articles/1544350/story.jhtml*, 5 August 2005.

11   Michael O'Shaughnessy, 'Box pop: popular television and hegemony', in Andrew Goodwin and Garry Whannel (eds), *Understanding Television* (London: Routledge, 1990), pp.91, 93.

12   Porter and Lavery: *Unlocking the Meaning of Lost*, p.48.

13   Morrison: *Playing in the Dark*, p.46.

14   Jean-Jacques Rousseau, *The Social Contract or Principles of Political Right*, trans. Maurice Cranston (London: Penguin Books, 1968), available online at *www.amazon.com/gp/reader/0140442014/ref=sib_dp_pt/102-3063494-8120137#reader-link*, accessed 21 October 2007.

XIV. Queer(ying) Lost

Glyn Davis and Gary Needham

The absence of a queer castaway poses one of the biggest mysteries for *Lost*'s gay, lesbian, bisexual and transgender television viewers. *Lost*'s having one of the largest and most culturally diverse ensemble casts on network television makes this queer absence all the more obvious. Statistically, surely not every one of the 48 survivors of the crash of Oceanic Flight 815 can be straight. But even if they are all card-carrying heteros, wouldn't time to kill on a desert island and all those bushes to hide in at least make some of them want to indulge their bi-curious tendencies?

From a production standpoint, *Lost* is screened by ABC, which, despite being owned by Disney – a corporation commonly associated with conservative family values – is also the US network with the most queer-friendly programming. As 'Where we are on TV', a 2007 report by GLAAD (the Gay and Lesbian Alliance Against Defamation) pointed out, broadcast series in the 2007–8 American television season featured only seven regular gay characters, six of whom were on ABC shows: *Ugly Betty* (Touchstone Television, 2006–), *Brothers and Sisters* (After Portsmouth, 2006–), *Desperate Housewives* (Cherry Alley Productions, 2004–) and *Cashmere Mafia* (Darren Star Productions, 2007–). (The seventh was on NBC's *The Office* (Reveille Productions, 2005–).) Considerably more queer characters (40 in the same 2007–8 season) appeared on cable channels such as FX, HBO and Showtime; viewers paying to watch these channels may expect a more sexually varied menu than those merely tuning in to the major networks.[1]

As the GLAAD report highlights, the dearth of queer characters on mainstream networks marks a pressing concern, particularly for gay and lesbian viewers. For if public visibility through mass media forms can enhance or promote social tolerance (and this argument is a cornerstone for those who debate the politics of representation), then the paltry number of fictional queer people on US network television will have to work extremely hard to fill the void, to operate as 'positive images', to represent the diversity of queer lives, and so on. Although this chapter is not especially concerned with 'positive images' (a now rather exhausted topic of debate that frequently avoids confronting the varied ways in which embodied audiences may take up and engage with particular representations, however stereotypical or 'negative'), we take *Lost*'s representational gap – our lost figure of desire, if you will – as a jumping-off point for considering what this space, this neglect, this glaring omission can reveal about fictional US television series and, indeed, television per se.

We begin this chapter by examining the network context (and its complex protocols of depicting queer characters and lives) within which *Lost* was launched, before turning to a detailed search for sexual dissidence, however sketchy or marginalised, among *Lost*'s content. Here we focus on specific characters – Boone (Ian Somerhalder), Ana-Lucia (Michelle Rodriguez), Kate (Evangeline Lilly), Jack (Matthew Fox) and Sawyer (Josh Holloway) – and examine *Lost* within its generic boundaries and permutations, promotional discourses and intertextual manifestations. Queerness exists in *Lost* for its characters, we suggest, as a liminal trace, the merest of echoes or fleeting possibilities; seemingly eradicated from the spaces of the series, it nevertheless haunts the fringes of the programme as yet another elusive tease or suggestion, an enigma that invites audience speculation. Arguably, there is as much online fan chatter about the lack of gay characters in *Lost* (some of which will be reiterated and examined here) as there is about, for instance, the Hanso Foundation. In this sense, then, the lack of gay characters in *Lost* has become a vital extra-textual component of the series: the representational absence in itself promotes audience discussion.

In the absence of openly and overtly queer characters in the series, we then move to explore alternative aspects of *Lost*'s construction that may afford queer pleasures: specifically, we focus on the distinctive diegetic shape adopted by the programme, both within individual episodes and across seasonal arcs, and argue that *Lost* relies on a rather queer narrative strategy of secrecy and disclosure in its flashback and flash-forward structure. Ultimately, we will argue that the queer pleasures made possible by television, and the investments made by queer viewers in particular series, are not necessarily tied up with or restricted to questions of gay and lesbian visibility and representation. *Lost* evinces a sort of heuristic potential in that it allows us to frame a number of questions and speculations about contemporary US network television's relationship to queerness and form. In particular, *Lost* reveals how mainstream television can consistently employ queer narrative strategies while disavowing the very queerness that gives those narratives their shape. The queerness of television is often beyond the purview of visibility debates; *Lost* suggests ways in which queerness itself is built into the very fabric of the medium.

THE NETWORK CONTEXT IN 2004

Lost premiered in the fall season of 2004, a year in US television marked by controversy and conservatism, owing in large part to Janet Jackson's now infamous 'wardrobe malfunction'. At the finale of Janet Jackson and Justin Timberlake's raunchy half-time Super Bowl performance, broadcast live in February 2004, Timberlake pulled a piece of Jackson's costume away, revealing a naked breast adorned by nipple jewellery. Shock horror followed, and a record 200,000-plus complaints and several lawsuits were filed with the Federal Communications Commission (FCC). The fallout from this was a crackdown by the FCC primarily aimed at curtailing the chances of live broadcast television from ever repeating a similar moment of grandiose indecency.

The public reaction, arguably the most shocking aspect of the event, seemed to correspond to the markedly conservative climate of US culture post-9/11, in which the cultural industries (which remain largely staffed by liberals) attempted to handle carefully and sensitively any topic, narrative, star or product that could potentially offend or upset the perceived moral status quo. US daytime television was most affected by the fear of FCC charges of indecency and a number of shows such as the long-running CBS daytime soaps *Guiding Light* (CBS 1952–) and *As the World Turns* (CBS 1956–) removed, re-edited or toned down sexual material. One of the most notable changes in primetime network television was from the third season of *Star Trek: Enterprise*

(Paramount Television, 2001–5). In an episode rather appropriately called 'Harbinger' (3.15), a shot depicting a very brief flash of naked male buttock during the love-making scene between the Vulcan T'Pol and the human character Trip was removed. Other changes to broadcast television following the 'wardrobe malfunction' included time delays on live televised events such as that year's Grammys and a general content clean-up across US broadcast media, especially terrestrial radio. To say how particular television shows and networks responded in altering content for fear of reprisals, mostly by self-regulation, would be guesswork without testimonies and documentation. But the generally cautious approach of US network television at this time, driven by such hazily defined concepts as 'indecency' and 'obscenity', formed part of the cultural and ideological context in which *Lost* premiered on ABC in September 2004. It is worth asking, as an initial provocation, whether US broadcast media and ideological mainstream pressures were responsible for *Lost*'s lack of queer characters.

Highlighting 2004 as an especially conservative year for the US media is, of course, a somewhat sweeping and artificial argument to make: despite the pressures on programme-makers, fictional depictions of queer sexuality – on programmes as diverse as the sitcom *Will and Grace* (KoMut Entertainment, 1998–2006) and the Showtime version of *Queer as Folk* (Cowlip Productions, 2000–5) – continued to be aired. And 2004 was hardly 1974, a year in which, according to Steven Capsuto:

> in the fall ... TV season, six prime-time dramas portrayed lesbian, gay, bisexual, or transgender characters. *All* were rapists, child molesters, or murderers. On popular variety hours and game shows, the mere mention of homosexuality was treated as a cause for hysterical laughter.[2]

As histories of the treatment of lesbian, gay, bisexual and transgender individuals by television in the USA by scholars such as Capsuto, Ron Becker and Larry Gross demonstrate, the decades of broadcasting have fluctuated between more or less liberal and conservative phases – although all three authors identify the 1990s as an especially open and accepting period.[3]

Certainly, the US networks have often had a fraught and turbulent relationship with their queer audiences, as is clearly illustrated by the

Ellen (Black-Marlens Company, 1994–8) debacle. The slump in viewing figures and the lobbying of ABC and its advertisers by the religious right after Ellen Morgan (the character) and Ellen DeGeneres (the actor) both came out eventually resulted in the sitcom's cancellation. (In marked contrast, DeGeneres' current syndicated daytime chat show *The Ellen DeGeneres Show* (Time Telepictures Television, 2003–) maintains high ratings. Arguably, this is because of the show's lack of lesbian content, with DeGeneres conspicuously and consistently avoiding discussing her own sexual orientation.) Anna McCarthy suggests that the sitcom's cancellation can be understood as symbolic of the difficulties of accommodating queerness into the normative and quotidian flows of television: the liminality, the marginality, the sheer otherness of queerness struggles to find a place within television's ordinary and everyday rhythms.[4]

Despite ABC's problems with *Ellen*, as noted in the introduction to this chapter the network has of late exhibited a strong track record in catering for the pleasures of queer audiences. Indeed, throughout the history of the US networks ABC can boast a number of landmarks for gay and lesbian audiences in terms of character visibility and storylines dating back to the 1970s: relevant programmes here would include *Soap* (ABC, 1977–81), *Dynasty* (Aaron Spelling Productions, 1981–9) and *Roseanne* (Carsey-Werner Company, 1988–97). The recent line-up at ABC includes *Desperate Housewives*, *Ugly Betty* and *Brothers and Sisters*, all created by queer writer/producers who are extending the possibilities of what network television can offer its queer viewers – indeed, *Brothers and Sisters*' creator Jon Robin Baitz was honoured with a GLAAD Media Award in 2007 for 'Outstanding Drama Series'. Why then does *Lost* as an ABC flagship show not follow the trend set by other programmes on the network – if not in sensibility (it is, after all, a mystery/fantasy series, rather than a comedy or a family drama), at least in terms of inclusiveness?

Desperate Housewives and *Brothers and Sisters* are (at the time of writing) scheduled together on ABC's Sunday nights from 9pm to 11pm, implying a shared demographic carrying over from one show to the other: the address of both series seems to be predominantly towards women and gay men. This scheduling strategy is in broadcast industry jargon referred to as 'stacking', a common programming technique used to keep an audience tuned in by scheduling together shows with similar appeal.[5] *Lost*, which airs on ABC on Wednesday nights, was in its first season stacked with the reality television series *The Bachelor* (Bobby Weisman Caterers, 2002–). *The Bachelor* is a reality series presently in its eleventh season, in which the male title character is courted by 25 single women in an elimination contest that is both depressingly politically retrograde and bluntly heteronormative. Why was *Lost* stacked with this series? And who exactly was the demographic for this two-hour programming block of mystery, action, drama and competitive heterosexual dating?

The scheduling of *Lost* is also indicative of the broadcasting strategy known as counter-programming, in which series which appeal to different demographic sectors are scheduled against one another. *Lost* was initially counter-programmed against the super-gayness of *America's Next Top Model* (10 by 10 Entertainment, 2003–) in 2004 and subsequently, and more surprisingly given both series' cult credentials, *Veronica Mars* (Silver Pictures Television, 2005–7). It is debatable whether the listings can actually tell us anything about the assumptions network programme-makers and schedulers make about sexuality, as opposed to their more common assumptions about age and gender, but the stacking and counter-programming strategies used with *Lost* clearly conform to the logic of heteronormativity. That is, fans of *The Bachelor* might also watch *Lost*; many queer audience members will pass on *Lost* and instead tune into *America's Next Top Model* (a show which gets queerer with every passing season).

Lost's scheduling with *The Bachelor* and against *America's Next Top Model* suggests a connection of some sort between the fictional series and successful reality television formats. It is worth remembering that *Lost*'s own genesis was partly inspired by the reality TV series *Survivor* (Mark Burnett Productions, 2000–). The reality television connection is a key issue in terms of *Lost*'s queer character absences, as this genre of programming has afforded some of the medium's most viable spaces for queer representation. Key series here would include MTV's *The Real World* (Bunim-Murray Productions, 1992–), *Big Brother* (Evolution Film and Tape, 2000–), *Queer Eye for the Straight Guy* (Bravo, 2003–6) and *Project Runway* (Bravo, 2004–). Like many reality television series, *Lost* is somewhat self-conscious of its diverse and multicultural cast, ticking all the boxes (race, ethnicity, nationality, gender, age, class and body types) except sexual orientation.

Lost is also indebted to another form of generic television, that of fantasy/science fiction, which has attempted over the decades to provide its audiences with visions of alternative possibilities, other worlds and races, whether utopian or dystopian. Although the genre is traditionally associated with geeky fans, some of the most success-ful US television series and films of the last few years have belonged to the science fiction or fantasy stable. In an article in the *Guardian* on the popular and commercial success of *Lost*, *Heroes* (NBC Univer-sal Television, 2006–) and the re-launched *Battlestar Galactica* (NBC Universal Television, 2004–), Gareth McLean recognised the political salience and perspicacity of some science fiction, and claimed of these series that

> This is science fiction for the 21st century. What's more, it's sci-fi about the 21st century. Fans of the genre have long known that qual-ity sci-fi and its sister genre fantasy hold up a mirror to the times in which they were created, but never before have the TV shows in-volved seemed so resonant or indeed so influential. Science fiction has never been more now, fantasy never more real.[6]

But, as Lyle Masaki observed in a blog entry on the gay pop culture website *afterelton.com* entitled 'If sci-fi is a metaphor for society, then where are the gays?':

> McLean calls *Lost*'s multi-ethnic cast a 'metaphor-for-America' which might be an apt way to see the drama, except the metaphor apparently lacks any LGBT representatives. [...] While science fiction has matured in recent time and has done a better job talking with its audience about who we are as a society, LGBT people don't seem to be a full part of that dialog.[7]

While science fiction television series can successfully feature regularly recurring queer characters – and Russell T. Davies' polymor-phously perverse *Torchwood* (BBC/CBC, 2006–) is exemplary in this regard – *Lost* does not, just like the other successful US science fiction/ fantasy series discussed by McLean. Genre form (and the importance of such standardised forms of storytelling and production to the US networks) is crucial to understanding *Lost*, then, torn as it is between the reality television imperative of ancestors like *Survivor* and the mystery/science fiction format also adopted by *Heroes*.

LOST'S GAY CHARACTER(S)

J.J. Abrams does not have an especially strong track record for creating queer characters, in either his film or television work. Admittedly, in the 'Love and Marriage' (1.15) episode of *Felicity* (Touchstone Television, 1998–2002), the eponymous heroine (Keri Russell) did almost marry her gay boss Javier (Ian Gomez) so that he wouldn't be deported, and helped one of her boyfriends, Noel (Scott Foley), while his older brother Ryan (Eddie McClintock) came out of the closet. In the end, Javier served as a recurring character across the show's four seasons. However, *Alias* (Bad Robot, 2001–6) sorely lacked lesbian and gay characters – indeed, an article in a 2006 edition of *Out* magazine, published just before *Alias'* fifth and final series came to a close, identified both *Alias* and *Lost* as two of their 'six network TV shows that *really* need to get a gay character'.[8] And Abrams' *Six Degrees* (Bad Robot, 2006–7) was cancelled after only eight episodes had aired – perhaps a queer twist connecting two or more of the characters together was planned, but we may never know.

Lost, as we have already observed, does not have a regular and recurring queer character. Or does it? There is the possibility that one or more of the characters is bisexual, but that audiences are only being presented with opposite-sex attractions and stories in relation to them. Both Kate and Ana Lucia, for instance, are feisty and sometimes styled somewhat androgynously. Both characters are also violent. Kate, we discover in season one, was being transported in handcuffs on the Oceanic aeroplane to the USA, while former cop Ana Lucia is revealed in 'Collision' (2.8) to have killed the man who caused her to lose a baby. Michelle Rodriguez, the actress who played Ana Lucia, has a personal history of violence and bad behaviour: not only did she play the lead role in the film *Girlfight* (Karyn Kusama, 2000), as well as gun-wielding tough chicks in *Resident Evil* (Paul W.S. Anderson, 2002) and *S.W.A.T.* (Clark Johnson, 2003), but her driving-under-the-influence incident while filming *Lost* was widely reported by the press. On her own website, Rodriguez criticised lesbian magazine *Curve* for putting her on its cover: 'I don't know what the intent behind the *Curve* magazine cover was. I wasn't informed of it, I had no idea they were planning on using my image to sell magazines,' she wrote in May 2007.[9] And yet the Internet buzzes with rumours that Rodriguez is either bisexual or a lesbian – see, for instance, Perez Hilton's website, on which he scrawls the words 'I ♥ Pussy' over a picture of the actress.[10] Of course, we do not mean to imply here that lesbianism or sexual alterity is innately connected to a violent disposition. However, as Lynda Hart has pointed out in her book *Fatal Women*, mediated representations of aggressive women often carry an associated suggestion of lesbianism or queerness, a useful observation when considering the positioning of Kate and Ana Lucia in *Lost*'s narratives.[11]

There have been fleeting allusions in *Lost* to the possibility that one of the peripheral characters might be gay. On the whole, these have centred on Boone, who works in the 'marriage business' (perhaps a rather gay profession?). In 'Whatever the Case May Be' (1.12), Boone's step-sister Shannon (Maggie Grace), with whom he is infatuated, snaps at him, asking him whether Locke is his 'new boyfriend'. The 'new' in this phrase renders her comment ambiguous: has he had a boyfriend before, or is she merely making a catty remark that calls into question his masculinity? A podcast on 21 March 2007 by *Lost* executive producers Carlton Cuse and Damon Lindelof suggested that the upcoming season three episode 'Exposé' (3.14) might reveal a gay character. But the suggestion was rather muted. 'I wouldn't hold your breath looking for the gay character. It's not like the gay character comes out and says, "Hey, I'm gay",' said Cuse. The gay character, it seemed, was Boone; this despite the episode's primary focus being on the relationship between Nikki (Kiele Sanchez) and Paolo (Rodrigo Santoro). Boone's sexual orientation was allegedly disclosed in a split-second throwaway line from a flashback at the airport when Shannon chastised him for 'flirting with random guys'. Was this simply another of Shannon's putdowns, or actually a revelation about Boone's sexual orientation?

Politically, there are problems with Boone being *Lost*'s gay character (if indeed he is). Boone died in season one from injuries sustained from exploring an aircraft precariously balanced on a cliff edge; on the whole, he was established as being rather inept as a castaway, and driven by jealousy related to his quasi-incestuous relationship with Shannon. While it is not necessary for every queer fictional character on television to be a 'positive' one, aligning homosexuality with incest is a retrograde representational strategy that needs to be criticised as such. In addition, 'outing' a character who is already dead relieves the programme-makers from having to confront the implications of their character revelation (and reveals the 'outing' podcast as meretricious series promotion to a dissatisfied and disenfranchised audience niche). Boone, as already written out of *Lost*, is a character relegated to the margins of the programme's serialisation and flow, thus echoing Anna McCarthy's suggestion regarding queerness being incompatible with the normative, quotidian 'everydayness' of television.

The disclosure of Boone's sexuality as possibly gay, at least bisexual, or maybe neither, is further complicated by the hetero-centric framing of the 'Exposé' episode in the flashbacks of Nicki and Paolo's story. The episode begins as an instalment of the fictional television programme of the same name, starring Nicki Fernandez as an undercover agent. *Exposé* is clearly modelled on the ABC series *Charlie's Angels* (Spelling-Goldberg Productions, 1976–81), which Hurley refers to at one point in the episode as '*Baywatch* but better'. The allusions to *Charlie's Angels* and *Baywatch* (Pearson All American Television, 1989–2001), both programmes notorious for their objectification of women for the pleasures of a male audience, establish *Exposé* as the heir to a particular strand of sexist fantasy programming. 'Exposé's flashback begins in a strip club with an erotic pole-dancing number performed by Nicki. The opposition between *Lost* and *Exposé* may be clearly registered on an aesthetic level – one is 'tacky', the other 'quality' – yet the episode's construction legitimates the erotic display of the actress Kiele Sanchez. Queer audiences tuning in, anticipating the revelation about a character's sexuality that was touted a week earlier in the *Lost* podcast, would find themselves trapped in an episode with extended sequences clearly designed to appeal to the sexual fantasies of some male heterosexual viewers.

INTERTEXTS, EXTRATEXTS AND THE REGULATION OF SEXUALITY

The allusions to *Charlie's Angels* and *Baywatch* in the 'Exposé' episode, and the references to other aspects of Michelle Rodriguez's career mentioned above, point towards the centrality of both inter- and extra-textual strategies in making sense of *Lost*, especially in the context of discussing the programme's handling of queerness. Ian Somerhalder brings with him the baggage of being an ex-fashion model in addition to having played flamboyantly queer in the film *Rules of*

Attraction (Roger Avary, 2002). His lithe body and pretty face stand in opposition to the bodies of Matthew Fox and Josh Holloway, whose more rugged masculinities are expressed not only through the broad, muscular shapes of their torsos and the confident ways in which they carry themselves, but their overall agency in the *Lost* narrative, including their competitive sparring for Kate's attentions. Somerhalder, therefore, is not only 'queered' (however obliquely) by his previous acting roles and his associations with the fashion sphere, but by being contrasted with the more overtly masculine personae of Fox/Jack and Holloway/Sawyer.

As an example of the importance of inter-texts and extra-texts for making sense of *Lost*, both Fox and Holloway have recently featured in advertising campaigns – respectively, for a L'Oréal Men Expert moisturiser and for the Davidoff Cool Water aftershave. The L'Oréal campaign positions Fox within an urban milieu. The music is jazzy, the images convey activity and sport, showing him hanging out with friends and jogging alongside the Brooklyn Bridge; intercut are close-ups of Fox's face, and black and white images of him boxing in a style that evokes *Raging Bull* (Martin Scorsese, 1980). He talks to the viewer, saying that the L'Oréal product can be used to fight the signs of aging. In contrast, the Davidoff Cool Water advert is more concerned with natural raw sensation than urban sophistication, with Holloway walking through splashing water, then diving off a rocky cliff to the grinding sounds of rock music. There is a significant amount of rippling torso and of slow-motion, which styles Holloway in a manner close to the macho image of his *Lost* character, with the association reinforced by the setting of tropical blue water – albeit filtered through familiar homoerotic and narcissistic tropes associated with Bruce Weber-style advertising from the 1980s. Lest audiences forget this is really about heterosexuality, the gaze of an unspecified female onlooker filters the slow motion images of Holloway enjoying his own beauty and body in the cool water. The two adverts work around a set of binary oppositions which resonate with *Lost*'s contrasting handling of Jack and Sawyer, including the culture/nature divide, good boy/bad boy, and identification with Jack/desire for Sawyer.

Using Fox to sell male audiences moisturiser chimes neatly with the 'metrosexual' stylings of his star persona, an identity which bleeds into, and is reinforced by, the depiction of Jack in *Lost*. Certainly, the

soft version of masculinity that Jack represents would wholly conform
to the need for L'Oréal moisturiser (in fact, how long can Jack last
on the island without his beauty products?). It is also notable that
Jack, unlike Sawyer, cries a lot. Crying on television and because of
television is often assumed to be an expression of emotion specific to
women's genres (melodrama, talk shows, soap operas) and their female viewers. Jack's gender possibly can be conceptualised or 'read'
queerly through his command of a culturally gendered emotional
range and the provision of frequent close-up shots of his teary eyes, a
melodramatic trope. Yet, perversely, Matthew Fox's ability to produce
convincing tears – which he also regularly demonstrated on *Party of
Five* (Columbia Pictures Television, 1994–2000) – has been defended
as manly by *Lost*'s executive producer Damon Lindelof, who said in an
interview in *Time* magazine that

> Matthew has elevated crying to an art, where somehow it's a form
> of badassness. He never cries because he's sad. He cries because he
> wants to hit someone. I can't think of any other hero characters who
> have cried. If Patrick Dempsey cried on *Grey's Anatomy* people would
> be like, 'Meredith, don't waste your time with that crybaby.'[12]

Fox's relentless and spectacular blubbing – a potential sign of
sissyness, surely – is here rescued from the faggot taint and elevated
to a display of butch prowess.

Attempting to queer Jack and Sawyer – unlike Boone or Ana Lucia
– is hard work, and involves considerable disavowal. Certainly, Sawyer
regularly removes his shirt, and his body is framed and lit for viewer
pleasure; Jack has a 'soft' (perhaps suspiciously soft?) masculinity,
coupled with a muscular torso that is also regularly displayed as spectacle (see, for instance, the image of Fox in a wet, clinging t-shirt that
adorned the cover of *Entertainment Weekly* in September 2005). Nevertheless, there is a significant amount of queer chatter about both
characters, both online and in print. Richard Andreoli, for instance, in
gay magazine *The Advocate*, went so far as to ask Fox whether Jack and
Sawyer would 'hook up', to which Fox responded 'I don't think that'll
be happening.'[13] But despite the diffuse cultural presence both actors
have, and their dissemination across (and appearances within) a plethora of media spaces, the resolute heterosexuality of Fox and Holloway,
and of Jack and Sawyer, affords very little space for pliability.

LOST TALES, LOST TIME

Is there another way in which *Lost* can be understood queerly? Are there ways of reading, particular approaches to comprehending the series, specific strategies available for queer viewers that can open up a new take on the show? Here we want to suggest that the queerest thing about *Lost* is not its characters, but its diegetic construction. In particular, specific narrative devices employed by the series seem to chime with queer theoretical comprehensions and models of storytelling and time. We isolate three particular devices – the revelation, the flashback/flash-forward and the open-ended narrative – all of which may be used in a queer reading of *Lost*.

Almost every episode of *Lost* contains a revelation of some sort, whether about a place (the hatch's contents, the Other's village) or a person (Libby's appearance in the mental institution, Locke's former paralysis). When revelations occur, the audience is provided with another piece of the puzzle, but the wider cast of characters remain, intra-diegetically, largely in the dark. Sometimes a plot revelation remains localised information for a small number of the castaways, who keep it a secret from the rest of the troupe: the number-punching system, for instance, or Charlie's (Dominic Monaghan) drug problem. These 'secrets' are structured as closeted information: the revelations are often shocking, fundamentally altering audience knowledge or belief relating to the universe of the series. Like the axiomatic example of the closeted secret – homosexuality – the revelations in *Lost* are often very personal to one or more of the cast, with their unearthing or uncovering occurring as a traumatic or emotive peak experience. A useful example here from season one is Sun's (Yunjin Kim) revelation, first to Michael (Harold Perrineau) then later to Kate, that she can speak English and has been maintaining the pretence that she only speaks Korean; once the truth is known, the castaways privy to the revelation help Sun to keep her secret safe.

In *The Epistemology of the Closet*, Eve Sedgwick identifies the queer closet as a vital paradigm for understanding the dualistic structuring of knowledge in Western economies and cultures, operating as it does through a basic binary: inside/outside, homosexual/heterosexual, hidden/revealed.[14] Sedgwick proposes that other fundamental

structuring binaries – male/female, for instance – can be better understood through a comprehensive interrogation of the shape and origins
of the closet as a system both real and metaphorical. *Lost*'s narrative
construction prevents its audiences from ever knowing the full picture
(an argument to which we will return shortly), substituting instead a
piecemeal process of individual revelation. In this sense, the regular
viewer of *Lost* is actually afforded a position of some authority, if not
of omnipotence: through the process of slow accumulation of revelations, we know more than any of the cast of characters about the collective group and their island habitat.

The committed viewer of *Lost*, then, is not unlike the regular reader of gossip magazines and websites, forums that trade in the weekly
(if not daily) build-up of facts and trivia relating to a complex array of
personalities and people. This information (that is, gossip) can operate as useful social currency in communication with others similarly
invested (usually women and gay men), but also promotes continued
(addicted?) consumption of the very sources used to access the details. *Lost*'s revelations, like gossip, require audiences to keep up to
speed with developments – or to be adept at avoiding spoilers should
they come to particular episodes late. Like gossip, *Lost*'s revelations
quickly become old news, absorbed into the everyday textures of the
series. This necessary handling of information – crucial for the mechanics of fan formations, and a fascinating queer link between committed television viewers of this series and gossip hounds – makes the
Lost viewer particularly adept at handling and understanding closet
dynamics.

The second key narrative strategy we wish to highlight is the flash-
back/flash-forward structure. Every episode of *Lost* contains unfolding backstory about at least one character (and, in a new development
in the final episode of season three, a flash-forward of a story to come).
The passage between narrative segments in each episode – the island
to the past, the past back to the island – is accompanied by a building 'wumph' noise, which sounds like the sucking noise of the plane's
engines. The space of the aircraft, and the historically localised time
of its fated flight, acts as a pivot between 'now' and 'then', a hinge between disconnected moments, bringing those time periods together
such that both the present-day story and the historical anecdote are
given additional depth and resonance. The 'past' date is not usually

specified exactly, although set and costume design give significant hints (when did Locke have that much hair?).

Although many television series use flashbacks – all three of the *CSI* series, for instance, include reconstructions of crime scenes in every episode – *Lost*'s flashbacks are one of the programme's unique textures and pleasures. Incidental detail is accrued, revelations built up – and, in some episodes, flashbacks return us to places and scenes we already know, in order to provide a little more information or a slightly different perspective. Sometimes – as with the repeated visits to Sydney airport for the Oceanic 815 check-in – there is an almost psychoanalytic return to a moment of trauma, puzzling away at one crucial historical scene of decision and coincidence, as though persistent interrogation of that moment will finally reveal why these specific people have ended up stranded on this island. In other sequences, such as the replaying of moments in Korea from Sun's and Jin's (Daniel Dae Kim's) perspectives, audiences are presented with different versions of the same story, encouraging retrospective assessment of the content of previous episodes.

Lost is marked, then, by its complex non-linearity – by the lack of precise dates given to the flashbacks, which strands them in a hazy chronology, by the use of repetition, and the way the back-and-forth sucking shuttle is often prioritised over the forward motion of the 'life on the island' story. Further, fan discussion of the series during the first two seasons (at least until the revelation in the 'Live Together, Die Alone' finale that other people beyond the island are aware of its existence) often speculated on whether the cast of characters were lost somewhere in a different time period or out of time entirely, trapped in purgatory – possibilities which complicate further any reading of the flashbacks and flash-forwards as located in a comprehensible linear timeframe. But how can these aspects of the series be understood or read as 'queer'?

A number of queer theorists have, in recent years, attempted to identify and interrogate what 'queer time' might be, and how this may differ from 'straight' conceptions of temporality: key monographs in this area include Annamarie Jagose's *Inconsequence*, Lee Edelman's *No Future* and Judith Halberstam's *In a Queer Time and Place*.[15] Indeed, thinking beyond time and history as meta-concepts still largely and normatively conceived of as processes of linear development from one day to the next, or one epoch to the next, a diverse array of queer authors have considered the perverse potential of such disparate topics as pauses, asynchrony, coincidence, momentum, repetition, déjà vu, memory and archives, waiting, regression, apocalypse, and so on. Others have attended to particular periods of history – the early modern or medieval eras, for instance – in order to queerly interrogate those times and some of their defining (or sorely ignored) features. In the process, all of these authors have attempted to unsettle how history (as a discipline, as a known story, as a process) is understood and performed, as well as to draw attention to ignored, derided or sidelined aspects of time and their queer political potential.

What makes *Lost*'s flashbacks and flash-forwards queer is not merely their prevalence, with the structural and affective pleasures of the 'whoosh' arguably prioritised over narrative progression, but the location of these time-slips in a series that regularly and repeatedly undermines and complicates stable understandings of time and chronology – especially as audiences have come to understand the ways that time operates in other 'quality' US serial dramas. In *Lost*, backstory and contemporary events are folded together, layered, looped, repeated and revisited; although it has now been running for several years, the main events of the series take place, somewhat confusingly, over a fairly small number of days. For a long stretch of episodes, the time on the island becomes measured not according to watches or the movements of the sun, but by the ticking of a mechanical system in the hatch. Regular normative time halts with the plane crash in the pilot episode. Liminal, marginalised, potentially 'queer' aspects of time – alternative clocks, explosive unpredictable disruptions, the rhythms of life in the geographically isolated commune, the impressions and echoes of history within contemporary experience, even the time of death – are foregrounded in *Lost*, unsettling and potentially opening up audiences' understandings of chronology, narrative and character.

Linearity, as we have suggested, is arguably less important in *Lost*'s narrative structures than the intra-episodic temporality of the back-and-forth. However, looking at the show across seasonal arcs, the programme's creators have taken a daring approach to the unending, open serial form familiar to audiences of soap operas. Within soap operatic narrative, storylines may run for days, weeks or months, but most arcs come to fruition, sometimes quietly, at other times explosively. With *Lost*, the creators have been honest about their lack of direction for the programme, their reliance on fan forum chat for suggestions as to how to develop the direction of the programme, and so on. This is a series with almost no resolution of any form. Not only is there no great conclusion planned (although now that a likely end-date for the show has been announced, the remaining series may be more carefully thought out in advance), but 'answers' at the level of plot detail and mechanics, such as they are, are never concrete and satisfying, usually merely provoking more questions and queries.

Considering *Lost* at this meta-level could be disconcerting – the narrative seems to career from episode to episode, with twists and turns thrown in to heighten the dramatic rollercoaster nature of consuming the series, but with the track for the rollercoaster being laid only seconds before we rattle over them. And yet this thrust, this directionless meander – often a wander, sometimes a speedy thrill-ride – is only disconcerting if audiences hold on to the need for resolution, a standard narrative trope that theorists of storytelling (including Vladimir Propp) have suggested is a basic requirement of tales.[16] Abandoning closure and the desire for such would be a supremely queer move – one that *Lost* regularly holds out as a tease. What if the series just ends? What if, together, the producers and audiences reject any perceived need for an ending, and gave in to the flow? Is this perhaps why cancelled television programmes – ones that just stop with all of their separate narrative strands interrupted – often seem, formally and affectively, to be the queerest?

Conclusion

Searching for a queer character in *Lost* is an exhausting exercise, and ultimately fruitless. Although lesbian, gay and bisexual audiences can take pleasure in the spectacle of attractive men and women wearing little clothing in island heat, and various inter-texts and extra-texts connected to *Lost* open up star personae to potentially subversive appropriation (admittedly, with sustained work), and although there are fleeting connotative remarks and comments made related to Boone, these do not make up for the representational gap. Considering the generic positioning of the series as shaped by reality television (often queer-friendly) and science fiction (with its utopian possibilities), this omission is all the more frustrating. As we have identified, what may be queer about *Lost* is its narrative shape, which operates according to dynamics that fit with queer theoretical musings on time, temporality and storytelling. In the end, however, this is just as politically problematic as the lack of a lesbian or gay character: queer strategies or dynamics are being harnessed or appropriated by a mainstream network television company in order to enliven this tale of castaways. While it is useful to identify and consider the queer narrative dynamics of the series, who exactly benefits – economically, politically, culturally – from their employment?

Notes

1   Gay and Lesbian Alliance Against Defamation (GLAAD), 'Where we are on TV: 2007–2008 season', available online at *www.glaad.org/eye/ontv/index2007.php/*.

2   Steven Capsuto, *Alternate Channels: The Uncensored Story of Gay and Lesbian Images on Radio and Television* (New York: Ballantine Books, 2000), p.xii.

3   See Capsuto: *Alternate Channels*; Ron Becker, *Gay TV and Straight America* (New York: Rutgers University Press, 2006); and Larry Gross, *Up From Invisibility: Lesbians, Gay Men and the Media in America* (New York: Columbia University Press, 2002).

4   Anna McCarthy, '"Must see" queer TV: history and serial form in *Ellen*', in Mark Jancovich and James Lyons (eds), *Quality Popular Television: Cult TV, the Industry and Fans* (London: Routledge, 2003), p.91.

5   See Edwin T. Vane and Lynne S. Gross, *Programming for TV, Radio and Cable* (Boston: Focal Press, 1994), p.175.

6   Gareth McLean, 'The new sci-fi', *Guardian*, available online at *www.guardian.co.uk/media/2007/jun/27/broadcasting.comment*, 27 June 2007.

7   Lyle Masaki, 'If sci-fi is a metaphor for society, then where are all the gays?', available online at *www.afterelton.com/taxonomy/term/364*, 2 July 2007.

8   Anon, 'Six network TV shows that *really* need to get a gay character', *Out*, available online at *www.out.com/detail.asp?id=17350*.

9   Michelle Rodriguez, entry for 2 May 2007 at *www.michelle-rodriguez.com/frommichelle_05_07.htm*.

10 See Perez Hilton, 'The party machine', available at *http://perezhilton.com/?cat=97*.

11 See Lynda Hart, *Fatal Women: Lesbian Sexuality and the Mark of Aggression* (New York: Princeton University Press, 1994).

12 Joel Stein, '*Lost*'s sensitive action hero', *Time*, available online at *www.time.com/time/magazine/article/0,9171,1584784,00.html*, 1 February 2007.

13 Richard Andreoli, 'Matthew Fox', *The Advocate*, available online at *http://findarticles.com/p/articles/mi_m1589/is_2005_March_29/ai_n13595942*, 29 March 2005.

14 See Eve Kosofsky Sedgwick, *The Epistemology of the Closet* (New York: Prentice-Hall, 1990).

15 Annamarie Jagose, *Inconsequence: Lesbian Representation and the Logic of Sexual Sequence* (Ithaca and London: Cornell University Press, 2002); Lee Edelman, *No Future: Queer Theory and the Death Drive* (Durham, NC, and London: Duke University Press, 2004); Judith Halberstam, *In A Queer Time and Place: Transgender Bodies, Subcultural Lives* (New York: New York University Press, 2005).

16 See Vladimir Propp, *Morphology of the Folktale*, 2nd edn (Austin and London: University of Texas Press, 1968).

Contributors

Stacey Abbott is Senior Lecturer in Film and Television Studies at Roehampton University. She is the author of *Celluloid Vampires* (University of Texas Press, 2007), co-editor of *Investigating Alias: Secrets and Spies* (I.B.Tauris, 2007) and General Editor for the 'Investigating Cult TV' series (I.B.Tauris).

Ivan Askwith lives a dual life. By day, he is a creative strategist with Big Spaceship, the Brooklyn-based digital shop behind the original Oceanic Airlines website. By night, he is an advisor to MIT's Convergence Culture Consortium, an occasional writer for publications such as *Slate* and *Salon*, and (along with Jonathan Gray and Derek Johnson) one-third of *The Extratextuals* (*www.extratextual.tv*), a blogging trio dedicated to all things TV-related.

Celeste-Marie Bernier is Lecturer in American Literature in the School of American and Canadian Studies, University of Nottingham. She is the author of *African American Visual Arts* (Edinburgh University Press, 2008). She is currently writing a book for Routledge called *Slave Heroism in the Transatlantic Imagination*.

Will Brooker is Principal Lecturer and Director of Studies for Film and Television at Kingston University. He has published widely on popular culture and its audiences. His authored and edited books include *Batman Unmasked: Analyzing a Cultural Icon* (Continuum, 2001), *Using the Force: Creativity, Community and Star Wars Fans* (Continuum, 2002), *Audience Studies Reader* (Routledge, 2002), *Alice's Adventures: Lewis Carroll in Popular Culture* (Continuum, 2004) and *The Blade Runner Experience: The Legacy of a Science Fiction Classic* (Wallflower, 2005).

Glyn Davis is a lecturer at the Glasgow School of Art. He is the author of monographs on *Queer as Folk* (BFI, 2007) and *Superstar: The Karen Carpenter Story* (Wallflower, 2008), and is the co-editor of *Queer TV* (Routledge, 2008).

Paul Grainge is Associate Professor of Film and Television Studies at the University of Nottingham. He is the author of *Brand Hollywood: Selling Entertainment in a Global Media Age* (Routledge, 2008) and *Monochrome*

Memories: Nostalgia and Style in Retro America (Praeger, 2002). He is also co-author of *Film Histories: An Introduction and Reader* (Edinburgh University Press, 2007) and editor of *Memory and Popular Film* (Manchester University Press, 2003).

Jonathan Gray is Assistant Professor of Communication and Media Studies at Fordham University. He is author of *Watching with The Simpsons: Television, Parody, and Intertextuality* (Routledge, 2006) and *Television Entertainment* (Routledge, 2008) and co-editor of *Fandom: Identities and Communities in a Mediated World* (NYU, 2007), *Battleground: The Media* (Greenwood, 2008) and *Popular Communication: The International Journal of Media and Culture*.

Derek Johnson is a PhD candidate at the University of Wisconsin where his historical research considers the development of media franchises as creative, economic and cultural phenomena.

Jason Mittell teaches American Studies and Film and Media Culture at Middlebury College. He is the author of *Genre and Television: From Cop Shows to Cartoons in American Culture* (Routledge, 2004), numerous essays in a number of journals and anthologies, and the blog *JustTV*. He is currently writing a textbook on television and American culture and a book on narrative complexity in contemporary American television.

Angela Ndalianis is Head of Screen Studies at the University of Melbourne. Her book *Neo-Baroque Aesthetics and Contemporary Entertainment* (MIT Press, 2004) explores the parallels between seventeenth-century and contemporary baroque cultures, and she is currently completing a book about the history and cultural significance of the theme park.

Gary Needham teaches on television in the Media and Cultural Studies Department at Nottingham Trent University. He is the co-editor of *Queer TV* (Routledge, 2008).

Michael Newbury is Director of American Studies and Professor of English and American Literatures at Middlebury College. He is currently working on a book about nationalism and the American popular theatre in the first half of the twentieth century.

Roberta Pearson is Professor of Film and Television Studies and Director of the Institute of Film and Television Studies at the University of Nottingham. She has authored, co-authored and co-edited numerous books and articles, among which are the co-edited *Cult Television* (University of Minnesota Press, 2004) and several essays on *Star Trek*. She is currently editing *Blackwell Companion to Television Genres*.

Julian Stringer is Associate Professor of Film Studies at the University of Nottingham and co-ordinating editor of *Scope: An Online Journal of Film and Television Studies* (www.scope.nottingham.ac.uk). His latest book, co-edited with Alastair Phillips, is *Japanese Cinema: Texts and Contexts* (Routledge, 2007).